Settling the South Carolina Backcountry

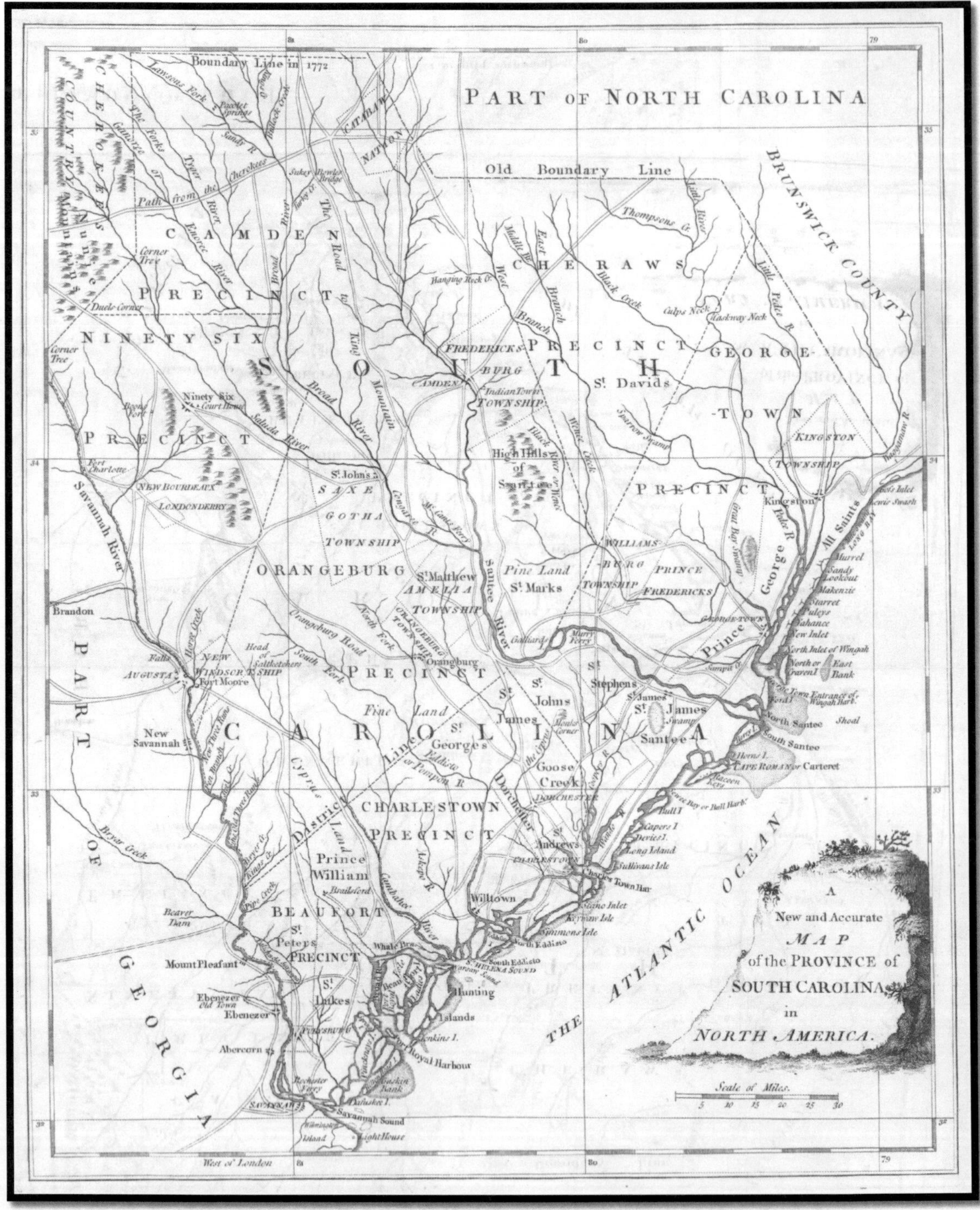

Frontispiece: Anon. "A New and Accurate Map of the Province of South Carolina in North America." *The Universal Magazine,* London: J. Hinton, 1779. From Library of Congress. *Map Collections.* Geography and Map Division.

Settling the South Carolina Backcountry

The Pressly Family and Life Along Hard Labor Creek, 1767–1850

Nancy L. Pressly

Alpharetta, GA

The author has made every effort to give credit to the source of any images, quotes, or other material contained within and obtain permissions when feasible.

ISBN: 978-1-61005-691-5

Library of Congress Control Number: 2016907917

10 9 8 7 6 5 4 3 2 1 0 2 5 1 6

Printed in the United States of America

∞This paper meets the requirements of ANSI/NISO Z39.48-1992 (Permanence of Paper)

Cover Image: Detail from *View of Charleston Harbor* by Thomas Leitch, 1774, oil on canvas. Courtesy of the Museum of Early Southern Decorative Arts (MESDA) at Old Salem, Winston-Salem, North Carolina.

For David, William, and Caitlin
and in honor of Dad,
William Laurens Pressly (1908–2001)

Contents

Your descendants shall gather your fruits.
Virgil [Publius Vergilius Maro], *Eclogues,* Book X

A map of the province of South Carolina, London 1773. Drawn by James Cook and engraved by Thomas Bowen. Courtesy of the John Carter Brown Library, Brown University.

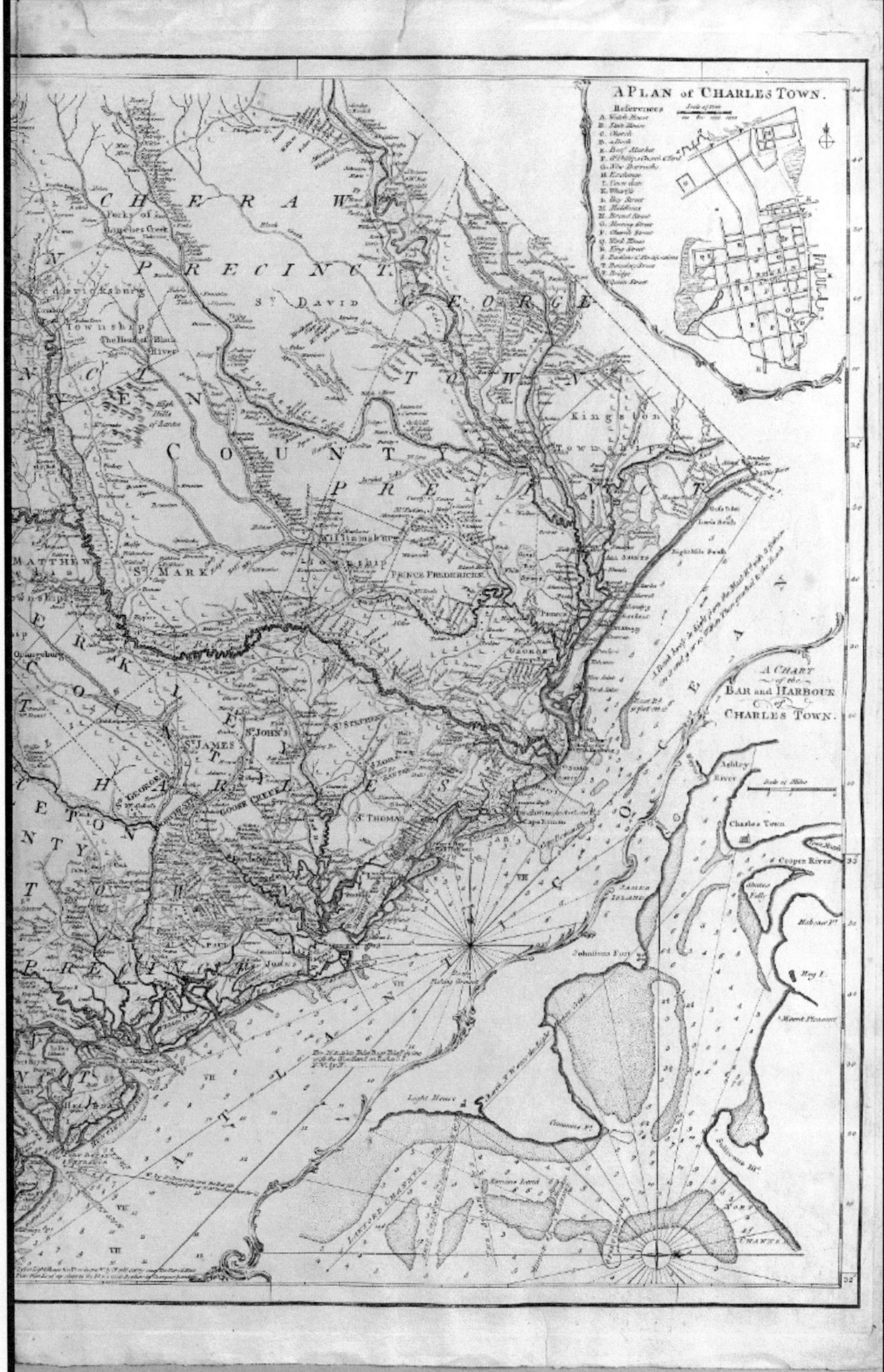

A PLAN of CHARLES TOWN.
References
C H E R A W
P R E C I N C T
S.T DAVID
G E O R G E
T O W N
Kingston
C O U N T
P R E C I N C T
Williamsburg
S.T MARK
PRINCE FREDERICKS
MATTHEW
Orangeburg
S.T JAMES
S.T JOHN'S
S.T STEPHEN
S.T THOMAS
GOOSE CREEK
S.T GEORGE
A CHART of the BAR and HARBOUR of CHARLES TOWN.
Ashley River
Charles Town
Cooper River
Johnsons Fort
Light House
A T L A N T I C
O C E A N

Preface

I have written this history of the first few generations of the Pressly family in America, beginning with David Pressly's arrival in Charleston in 1767 and that of his brother John, our direct ancestor, in 1772, for my son, David Blake Pressly, and his children, William Laurens Pressly and Caitlin Elizabeth Pressly. It is also written for my husband, Bill Pressly, my brother-in-law, Paul Pressly, his wife, Jane, and for the entire Pressly family with hopes that all of us will have a deeper understanding of the family's first century in America. It is dedicated to my much loved father-in-law, Dr. William Laurens Pressly of Atlanta, who embraced family history with a passion. It is indebted to his earlier endeavors and other research by family members.[1]

This project began as a simple quest to learn more about the first generations of Presslys who settled in the backcountry of South Carolina in the second half of the eighteenth century. My hope was to create a sense of the historical and social context of their lives during the family's first years in South Carolina and in the process bring them more vividly to life. It became clear as I submerged myself in this research that there was an important, larger story to be told about the vital rural farming community around Cedar Springs and Hard Labor Creek. The text that follows is somewhere between a family history and the larger contextual story. It focuses on the Hard Labor Section and how it evolved from a newly settled frontier in the 1760s to a center of wealth and power in the decades before the Civil War. It is very much a story about a physical place and the interconnectedness of neighbors over several generations. It is also the story of a small group of eighteenth-century Scotch-Irish Seceder and Covenanter immigrants who settled in the backcountry of South Carolina and formed the nucleus of so many of the ARP churches later established throughout the Midwest, Texas, and the South.

I am especially grateful to Dr. James Gettys, Professor Emeritus at Erskine College, for so generously sharing documentation, research, and information with me and for his careful reading of an early draft of the manuscript.[2] Jim, and occasionally his brother, Paul, were always delightful companions on treks through the area where our family lived. All of us have also benefited from the efforts of Professor William L. Pressly (1907–1993) of Due West, who prepared an undated *Pressly Family History* photocopied circa 1980,[3] and a nineteenth-century family historian, the Reverend John Samuel Pressly, who wrote an unpublished "Brief Memoir of the Pressly Family in the United States" sometime before 1863.[4] John S.

Pressly (going forward referred to as JSP) was the son of Samuel Pressly and grandson of David Pressly (imm 1767), and his account is the only one we have from someone who actually knew the children of John Pressly (imm 1772).

Researching the early history of the family has been more challenging than anything I could have imagined. The lands on which the family lived, along with the vital community they helped form, have been abandoned for over a century. They have literally retreated back into the woodlands of Sumter National Forest. Crumbled foundation stones and small abandoned cemeteries are hidden or barely visible, and the archaeological surveys undertaken so far provide only hints of eighteenth-century and early nineteenth-century life.[5] There is a very limited amount of primary documentation about our direct ancestor, John Pressly (imm 1772), and his brother, David Pressly (imm 1767), or their children. Despite the fact that so many of the first Presslys born here were well-educated and successful doctors, clergymen, and businessmen, almost no primary letters or records of family history survived, the important exception being JSP's account.

The large size of individual families, the astonishing longevity of many family members, and Scottish naming customs also added to the complexity. The fact, for example, that the first son was generally named after the father's father, the first daughter after the mother's mother, the second son after the father, and the second daughter after the mother, allows for the possibility that within one generation there could be several individuals named David, John, or William Pressly, sometimes even with the same middle name. Additionally, the surname, especially in the eighteenth century, was not consistently spelled, even in the same legal document, and it was variously recorded in South Carolina as Plessley, Pressly, Presly, Pressley, Presley, Preslie, Prestly, and Presslie.[6] Analyzing eighteenth- and early nineteenth-century documents is further complicated by the use of "Senior" and "Junior," which did not necessarily imply a father and son relationship because it could refer to older and younger first cousins or even a grandfather and a grandchild living together as a way to keep track of who-was-who in records. Adding to the challenge of analyzing South Carolina records, there were also several families, probably unrelated, with some variation of the Pressly surname living in the backcountry of South Carolina in the late eighteenth and early nineteenth centuries in Abbeville, Edgefield, and nearby Chester, Union, Kershaw, and York districts (see Appendix A).

In terms of methodology, I was able to gather important new factual and contextual information from census records, wills, church, and land records and also from family accounts of several families with whom the Presslys were either connected by marriage or closely associated as neighbors, including the Hearst, Patterson, McCord, Weed, Perrin, Chiles, Cothran, Harrison, Crozier, Foster, Devlin, Wideman, Thompson, and McClinton families. Pressly family members are named as witnesses, executors, administrators, or as neighboring land owners in various legal records, providing additional information about their lives. In the course of my research I have also been in touch with some of David's (imm 1767) and John Pressly's (imm 1772) descendants who have researched their direct family lines. I would like particularly to acknowledge Linda McCartney, who has gathered extensive information on her family which descends from John's (imm 1772) grandson, Dr. Samuel Pressly, and who made this available online in her Young-Vassar and Allied Families Tree on Ancestry.com (tree 34074085). Yvonne Di Francesco and Milton Presley, both descendants of David Pressly's son, David Pressly, also kindly shared information with me, as did Scott Pressly from Atlanta who is a direct descendant of Reverend John E. Pressly, a great-grandson of immigrant John. I am especially grateful to Frank and Lisa Wideman, who graciously showed my husband and me their beautiful home, Sylvania, and shared important records and information about the Hearst and Wideman families and the history of Sylvania. Likewise, I would like particularly to thank Wade C. Harrison, who has generously shared family papers and information about his family and the Hard Labor Section where his ancestors, the Chiles, Perrins, Cothrans, and Harrisons first settled, and was a wonderful guide to the area. I would also like to thank his cousin, John N. Harrison, who shared information about Millway Plantation and Chiles Crossroads.

I am especially grateful to Jim Bates, archaeologist for the USDA Forest Service, Marion and Sumter National Forest, for generously sharing information with me related to maps and archaeological surveys and also about his own ancestors who settled in the area around the same time as the Pressly family. I have also benefited from the research of earlier historians of Abbeville and Greenwood County, in particular H. C. Cook's *Hard Labor Section*, published in 1923, and Margaret Watson's *Greenwood County Sketches*, published in 1970, and the more recent work of Bobby Edmunds on McCormick County. The South Carolina Department of Archives and History were an invaluable resource for state land grants and recorded wills, as was the Probate Record Office and Abbeville County Courthouse for estate-related material. Additionally, the South Carolina Library at the University of South Carolina, the Wilson Library at the University of North Carolina, the Abbeville County Public Library, the Greenwood County Public Library, and the Atlanta History Center's James G. Kenan Research Center were also immensely helpful repositories. I am grateful to their accommodating staff. "The Presley/Presslar/Pressly Newsletter," which was particularly active in the 1980s and early 1990s, was also an extremely helpful guide, although one that needed to be vetted carefully for accuracy. The internet was always a surprising and wonderful resource, providing access to a vast array of historical records, family websites, ancestral trees, and other worldwide vital records and genealogical resources. However, there was also an overwhelming amount of misinformation perpetuated on these sites, especially the Family Tree search available on Ancestry.com and FamilySearch which is linked to the Latter Day Saints records in Utah, and its related Wiki site. While immensely helpful, they are mostly undocumented resources, and it is here that one has to proceed with great caution to extract accurate information. Many available archival sites are constantly being updated, so it remains a challenge to stay apprised of the changing information. I also searched for families with some variation of the Pressly surname who could have been part of the large migration of Virginia families, mainly from Augusta and Rockbridge Counties (which later became Russell County and Buchannan County) who settled in the Ninety Six District and nearby districts in South Carolina in the second half of the eighteenth century.

This history contains substantial new information and provides a more accurate and fully textured account of early family history than has previously existed, especially about all of the children of our direct ancestor, John Pressly (imm 1772). It frames new hypotheses, which change significantly what we know about our early ancestors. It introduces the presence of a third Pressly family, Jane and William Pressly, living adjacent to our relatives, probably by the mid-1770s. This family, who has not been discussed previously, was almost certainly closely related to John and David Pressly. It also introduces important new information related to recent DNA testing results that provided an exact thirty-seven marker DNA match for my husband, Bill Pressly, with descendants of James Presley, born in Rockbridge County, Virginia, in 1783. This indicates that a close relative of our family, possibly a cousin, uncle, or brother of the immigrant brothers, was living in Virginia in the 1780s. However, despite my extensive research (and that of my predecessors) and the wealth of detail I have collected, many important questions remain unanswered or are not fully resolved. This was immensely frustrating to me, and it took some time to accept that genealogical research results in many dead ends and that the document trail may never definitively lead us back to our late seventeenth-century and early eighteenth-century Pressly ancestors in Great Britain or even to unraveling all the connections between the Presslys living in Abbeville County in the late eighteenth century. Other families with the Pressly surname searching for European ancestors have had a similar lack of success. Additional research still needs to be done in eighteenth-century parish and civil archives in Northern Ireland, Glasgow, and Yorkshire.

I have tried to correct errors in earlier research efforts, but undoubtedly there will still be mistakes and gaps of information that hopefully will be amended by others in the future. I apologize for the amount of detail that may encumber this text, but I believe it was necessary for tracking connections which could prove helpful to others who pursue this further at a later date. The year 1850 may seem like an arbitrary stopping point, but it was chosen because by that date all of John and David's children, with the possible exception of Martha and Joseph, were dead, and only George Pressly and his family and possibly a few of Alexander

Pressly's children still lived in the area where the family first settled. I will leave it to others to undertake the next phase of history that includes the later years of E. E. Pressly, John Taylor Pressly, Dr. George Pressly, the Civil War and its aftermath, and the development of Erskine Seminary and College in the second half of the nineteenth century as well as the enormous changes that took place in the Associate Reformed Presbyterian Church during this period. I have also prepared a more traditional Family Ancestry Tree which is by no means complete and remains a work in progress. It provides a more extensive, although by no means complete, genealogy of the family than has previously existed (Appendix B).

For the purposes of this document, the family name is spelled Pressly unless quoted from a specific document. The tombstones of both David Pressly (died 1818, son of John (imm 1772)) and David Pressly (died 1834, son of David (imm 1767)) use the spelling "Pressly."[7] At some point in the early to mid-nineteenth century, most of David's (imm 1767) descendants, with the exception of David Pressly Jr.'s son, Alexander Edmiston Pressly and his family, began using "Pressley" with relative consistency.

I would like especially to thank my husband for his enthusiasm and support and for his careful reading of the manuscript and always helpful insights. He was a wonderful companion on our many trips to South Carolina, and his love of history and new discoveries made this an all the more rewarding effort. Lastly, I realize I am not a blood relation, but I hope I can be forgiven for using the term "our family."

Nancy L. Pressly, Atlanta, Georgia, September 2015

The First Generation and Their Children

Children of David Pressly (Immigrated 1767) Married to Esther Brown

1) **Samuel** (1756–before 1810)
m. Elizabeth Thompson

2) **David, Jr.** (1760–1834)
m. Ann Edmiston

3) **William** (1774/78–1820)
m. Elizabeth Elinor Adams

4) **John** (1774/78–)
m. Isabelle Brown

5) **Mary Ann** (??)
m. Stephen Thomas

6) **Agnes** (1762–??)
m. Henry Wyly

7) **Esther** (1767/8–1848)
never married

Children of John Pressly (Immigrated 1772) Married to Elizabeth

1) **David** (1756–1818)
m. Jane Patterson

2) **William** (1758/62–1809/10)
m. Elizabeth Knox Hearst

3) **John** (ca. 1775–ca. 1836)
m. (1) Margaret Patterson
(2) Elizabeth Weed

4) **Joseph** (1775/76–1840/50)
m. (1) Rebecca (?)
(2) Mary Ann Stuart

5) **Mary Patterson** (before 1756–before 1810)
m. Robert Martin

6) **Martha** (1773–after 1840)
m. Archibald Hamilton

Chapter 1

Ancestral Roots: Searching for Connections

Of English origin, the derivation of the Pressly surname is thought to have come from Priest Leigh or Priest lands, referring to people who lived in wooded areas or meadows cleared by and near the church. The surname base is extensive, including a wide range of spellings with patriarchal branches coming from Great Britain and from Germany, where the surname Bresslar, Presslar, and Preslar became Presley and Pursley in America. The earliest records for the surname are said to date back to Richard de Presteley in 1292 in Yorkshire and John de Presle in 1311 in London. By the late seventeenth and eighteenth centuries, there were large clusters of baptism and marriage records with variations of the spelling in England, including London, Wiltshire, Dorset, Nottinghamshire, and the border counties of Yorkshire and Northumberland. We know from late seventeenth- and eighteenth-century marriage and baptismal records that there were numerous clusters of families with the surname Preiesly, Preesely, Preestley, Presley, Priestly, Pressly, Pressley, Preistly, Presly, Prestly, and Priestley in Yorkshire in the areas around Elland, Rippondon, Snaith, and in the parishes of Brodsworth, Kirkheaton, and Kirkburton.

Our family line in America descends from John Pressly (going forward he will be referred to as imm 1772), our direct ancestor, and his brother, David (going forward he will be referred to as imm 1767). John sailed with his family from Newry, County Down, Ulster, on the *Free Mason,* arriving in Charleston, South Carolina, on December 22, 1772, with at least three children and probably his wife. David (imm 1767) sailed with his wife and children from Belfast, County Antrim, Ulster, on Christmas Eve, 1766, on the *Earl of Hillsborough,* arriving in Charleston on February 18, 1767. John and David settled in the old Ninety Six District, later Abbeville District, in the backcountry of South Carolina, at a time when it was still very much the frontier. We know little about their history or origins except for the dates they sailed from Ulster, and important parish records from villages near Glasgow that document where four of David Pressly's (imm 1767) children were christened: Samuel, in Ayr, in 1756, and his next three children in nearby Lochwinnock, between 1757 and 1762.[1] For the first time, these records give us a definitive date and geographical location for where at least one member of our family was living before migrating to the American Colonies by way of Charleston. They do not tell us, however, where the family came from or even if David was the only member who lived there. John was probably the older of the two brothers because his eldest son, David Pressly, who died in 1818, is said to have had the family Bible that recorded eighteenth-century family births.[2] The family Bible, the proximity of John's and David's land to one another, the fact that David took care of John's youngest children after his death, the frequent references to their children as first cousins and dear friends in family documents, especially in John S. Pressly's (JSP) writings, and the close intimacy of John and David's children and grandchildren in the decades after their death, all help to support the conclusion that John and David were brothers.

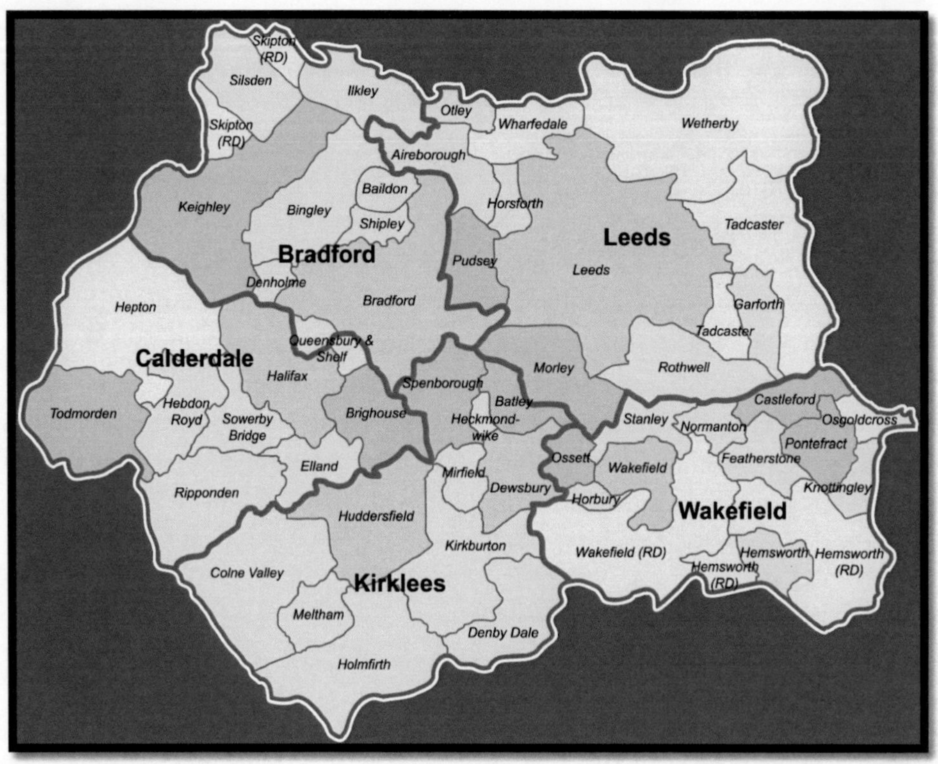

Figure 1-1. A map of the metropolitan county of West Yorkshire.

One of the hopes for this project was to be able to trace our family lineage back to the parents and grandparents of John and David Pressly before they immigrated to America. However, beyond the Scottish baptism records related to David Pressly (imm 1767) in the 1750s and early 1760s, preliminary research failed to uncover any definitive links with any other family with variations of the Pressly surname in English, Scottish, and Irish parish records.[3] It did, however, reveal several substantive leads. By focusing on given names used in our family over several generations, which include Samuel, William, John, David, Martha, and, to a lesser degree, Joseph, Mary, and Agnes, and by narrowing the lens further to the names David, Samuel, and Martha, which are less common within the larger Pressly surname group, I was able to uncover some intriguing, possible early eighteenth-century connections in several Yorkshire parishes (Figure 1-1). Particularly interesting are baptism listings in the parishes of Elland, Rippon(don), and Snaith.[4] A David "Priestley" was baptized in Elland on April 6, 1681 (father listed as Samuel), and in July 18, 1717, a child "Pressley" with no given name, father's name given as "Samuel Pressley." The name Samuel "Priestley" appears again on May 12, 1723, with a marriage to Mary Ramsden. Turning to Rippon(don), a Samuel "Preestley" is baptized May 6, 1714, (father given as George), and a Martha "Prestley" is baptized April 6, 1708 (father given as David). A few decades later, also in Rippondon, a David "Priestley" was baptized on December 26, 1728; a Martha "Priestley" on November 12, 1729; and a Martha "Prestly" on July 19, 1730, father John "Prestly." Also of interest are records in the parish of Snaith, York, where, on October 27, 1730, a William "Preistly" was baptized with father's given name as Samuel. On June 11, 1753, in the nearby town of Throapham in the parish of Dinnington, "John Presley" (b. 1731) and Elizabeth Gilberthorp (b. 1733) were married. This is intriguing because our ancestor John was also born circa 1731, and Elizabeth is the given name of his wife in his 1778 will.

Yorkshire is also of particular interest because of its possible connection with an eighteenth-century Virginia family with a variation of the Pressly surname. One of the more interesting findings during the course of this research was the uncovering of a close DNA connection between my husband, Bill Pressly, and Dale A. Presley, whose earliest known ancestor is James Presley, who was born in 1783 in Rockbridge County, Virginia. My husband submitted DNA samples to Family Tree DNA, one of the largest worldwide DNA testing groups, whose data is also linked through YSearch to a much larger sample pool. Within Family Tree DNA, we also joined a Presley/Pressly surname project, which currently has ninety-three members.[5] Bill's DNA test results shared an exact thirty-seven-marker match with Dale Presley and a close match with two other individuals in this group who also claim James Presley as their most distant known ancestor.[6] This is an extremely important finding, because in DNA testing an exact thirty seven match means there is a 97.28 percent probability of sharing a common ancestor within eight generations and a 99.55 percent within ten to twelve generations. Eight to ten generations take us back to John Pressly's generation (imm 1772) or that of his father or grandfather. The testing results strongly suggest that a close and heretofore unknown relative of our ancestor, John Pressly, possibly a brother, uncle, or first cousin, was living in the Virginia area by the second half of the eighteenth century. James Presley's parents were almost certainly the "William Presley" and "Esther Cowan," whose marriage bonds were listed in Virginia on September 18, 1780.[7] Some of James's descendants believe his father came from Yorkshire, although they have no solid documentary evidence to substantiate this claim.[8] Although James's descendants are well documented, we know nothing more about his presumed father, William Pressly, except that in addition to his marriage in 1780, he is probably the William "Presley" who appeared in the Russell County tax lists of 1783, where he is charged "for self." He is listed as a weaver, not a farmer, suggesting that he may have been a recent Irish or Scottish immigrant.[9] There were two other individuals with the given name of William and a variation of the Pressly surname in Rockbridge and Augusta counties in the late eighteenth century who could be considered possible, although less likely candidates for being James's father. See Appendix A for a fuller accounting of them and other Presslys in Virginia in the late eighteenth century as well as additional families with the Pressly surname in eighteenth-century America and South Carolina.

In terms of Scotland, the Pressly surname is found in parish records beginning in the late seventeenth century, mainly in the high country around Aberdeen, with only a few families living in the low country near Glasgow until the nineteenth century. The earliest known records in Scotland date to 1678, with the marriage of "John Presley" in Aberdeen; and 1680, when "Elizabeth Presley" married James Alexander in nearby Peterhead Parish.[10] The next reference, also in Peterhead, is in 1686, when Andrew "Presley's" son Andrew is baptized, followed by James (1695) and John (1699). Early recorded variants of the surname in the Glasgow area appear as early as 1714 with the death of "William Parsley" in the parish of Glasgow. In 1734 "William Parsley" is baptized in the Parish of Beit, Ayr, with his father's given name as "Nanina." It is possible that our ancestors moved at some point from Aberdeen to Glasgow, but our DNA line is significantly different from that of known Aberdeen area Presslys. It is more likely our ancestors moved through northern England, settling there for a time, before traveling to the Glasgow area with some eventually moving to Northern Ireland. In his book, *Albion's Seed,* David H. Fischer identified the "Borderlands" of northern England and the southern lowlands of Scotland as one of the four major British "Folkways" settling in the United States. Our family almost certainly belonged to this group of immigrants who moved through the Borderlands to Ulster and then to the southern Colonies, where they helped shape the agrarian culture of the South Carolina backcountry.[11]

In terms of Northern Ireland, where large communities of Scottish Presbyterians settled in the seventeenth and first half of the eighteenth centuries, the Pressly surname has been much more difficult to trace because so many eighteenth-century church and local records have been destroyed. By the 1750s, Ulster was home to a large number of Seceder Presbyterians, to which our family belonged. The Public Record Office of Northern Ireland (PROVO) archives recently made available online indexes for previously inaccessible records, and they reveal several families of interest with the Pressly surname in Ulster in the eighteenth century. One interesting discovery was the baptism of James Prisly in 1751 and William Prisly in 1753 at the Rosemary Street Second Presbyterian Church, a Seceder Church in Belfast. Their father's given name, William, does not appear in any other Rosemary Street Church records.[12]

Figure 1-2. Map of Northern Ireland.

Several "Presly" baptisms in Drumbo, County Down, Ulster (Figure 1-2), probably relate to another family, who were thought to have been living in the lowlands near Glasgow in the seventeenth century and who had settled in County Down by 1700. They were among some fifty thousand Scots who migrated across the North Channel to Ulster between 1690 and 1700. These baptisms include John Presly on February 1, 1701, whose father was John; Margaret on July 9, 1707, whose father was Thomas; William Presly on July 17, 1707, a Presbyterian, whose father was John; and Mary on May 24, 1719, whose father was also John. Members of this family were among the group of Presbyterians who migrated to South Carolina in the 1730s as land leases expired in Ulster and settled in the nine new townships the Crown created in South Carolina, among which was Williamsburg Township where they settled. Two brothers, William and David, sailed on the *Good Intent,* which left Belfast on September 14, 1734, and landed in Charleston after a very rough journey in early December. They are referred to here as the "Williamsburg Pressleys." A third brother, John, is documented as in South Carolina by 1737 but probably arrived earlier. After landing in Charleston, William and David Pressley took a boat up the Black River and settled in the vicinity of Kingstree in Williamsburg Township which was part of Craven County. They sailed with John (1670–1737) and Janet

Witherspoon, who traveled with several of their children.[13] The Witherspoons are thought to have lived at Begardie, near Glasgow, before they moved to Knockbracken in the Parish of Drumbo, County Down, probably around the same time as the Pressleys. Other members of the Witherspoon family lived in nearby Ayrshire and Renfrewshire and near Glasgow, and there were several marriages between the "Pressley" and Witherspoon families both in Scotland and Ulster.

The "Williamsburg Pressleys" are of particular interest because for some 125 years their history has been confused with that of our family. In the early 1850s, John Gotea Pressley, a Williamsburg Pressley, studied law in Charleston under Judge Benjamin C. "Pressley," immigrant David Pressly's (1767) grandson. Around the same time, John S. Pressly (JSP), another of David's grandsons, was also in Charleston doing family research in the Charleston Record Office, where he discovered eighteenth-century colonial wills related to both families. They most likely all came in contact with one another and probably concluded that they shared common ancestors, in part because their families shared the same given names and surnames and each had the same history of coming from Scotland, through County Down, to South Carolina. At this point, the two family histories became conflated into one, and our family began, erroneously, to trace its patriarchal line to the Williamsburg Pressleys. The story first appeared in print in J. T. Bonner's "Biographical Sketch of Dr. E. E. Pressly" (immigrant John Pressly's grandson), which was published in *The Due West Telescope,* December 20, 1861. (It had not appeared in his earlier biography of E. E. from 1852.) John S. Pressly was probably the source of this information, which he subsequently recorded in detail in his *Brief Memoir,* written before 1863. It was still accepted over a century later in William A. Pressly's *Pressly Family History* (ca. 1980) and continues to appear in widely diverse and unrelated family trees on various genealogical sites, despite the fact that there are several accounts disproving this story—a reminder of just how easily misinformation can rewrite history. The distinctions between the two families was first discussed in depth in "The Presley/Preslar/Pressly Newsletter," and John Renning Phillips (who is linked by a nineteenth-century marriage to both families) also concludes in his 2007 book, *The Good Intent,* which provides a lengthy account of the Williamsburg family and their voyage on the ship *Good Intent,* that our family and the Williamsburg brothers were two separate families.[14] Additionally, South Carolina probate records, easily available today, document all three Williamsburg Pressley brothers as dead by 1751: David died March 31, 1749; John died October 17, 1750; and William died in 1751.[15] This connection is important, however, and may eventually lead us to yet to be uncovered records in the lowlands near Glasgow that provide further information on our ancestors and to a possible common seventeenth-century ancestors for these two distinct eighteenth-century families.

PART I

From Ulster to Charleston:
The First Generation in South Carolina, 1767–1785

Whole neighbourhoods formed parties for removal; so that departure from their native country is no longer exile. He that goes thus accompanied carries with him all that makes life pleasant. He sits down in a better climate, surrounded by his kindred and his friends: they carry with them their language, their opinions, their popular songs, and hereditary merriment: they change nothing but the place of their abode.

Dr. Samuel Johnson on Scottish Immigration to America, 1773.[1]

Chapter 2

Historical Overview:

Settling the South Carolina Backcountry, 1750–1770

John and David Pressly and their families were part of the Scotch-Irish "Great Migration" that lasted fifty-eight years, beginning in 1718 and ending at the start of the American Revolution. This was mainly a migration of families who were predominantly Presbyterian farmers and craftsmen searching for a better quality of life. Religious marginalization and oppression and rising rents were significant motivating factors. Many immigrants, referred to as Scotch-Irish, never lived in Ireland but rather sailed to America from an Irish port, generally in Northern Ireland. Up until the South Carolina Bounty Act of 1761, when Charleston became an important arrival port, the majority entered through Philadelphia as well as Chester, which is just south of Philadelphia, and Newcastle, in Delaware, and moved westward to the "great valley" in Pennsylvania and then southward through the Shenandoah Valley. They moved along what became known as the Great Philadelphia Wagon Trail (or Great Wagon Road), which was one of the most important "highways" of the Colonial Period (Figure 2-1). They settled first on available valley land, and then moved further south with each new migration, eventually reaching the piedmonts of North Carolina and then South Carolina. The western fork of the Great Wagon Road went to Knoxville, Tennessee. By the time the eastern fork reached South Carolina, it formed two branches with one going to Augusta, Georgia, ending near the Savannah River, and the other going on to Savannah, eventually extending its length to nearly seven hundred miles.

By 1750, small clusters of families moved south along the Great Wagon Road and began to settle in the backcountry of South Carolina along the Pacolet River, near Rocky Creek. They also settled around the Fairforest and Tyger Rivers, and in the fertile Catawba River Valley, which the Great Wagon Road traversed and included the Waxhaws and Camden. Already a major stopping-off point on the Great Wagon Road, the Waxhaws, after the defeat of the Cherokees in 1761, rapidly grew as a central distribution center for northern, mainly Scotch-Irish families, who began to settle in what became part of the upper Ninety Six District.[1] By 1755, Scotch-Irish immigrants, mainly Covenanters, also began to settle near Chester, South Carolina. They eventually formed a "Catholic" church made up of several different Presbyterian denominations on Rocky Mount Road, fifteen miles southeast of Chester. Land speculators also began to come into the area. In 1749, John Hamilton,

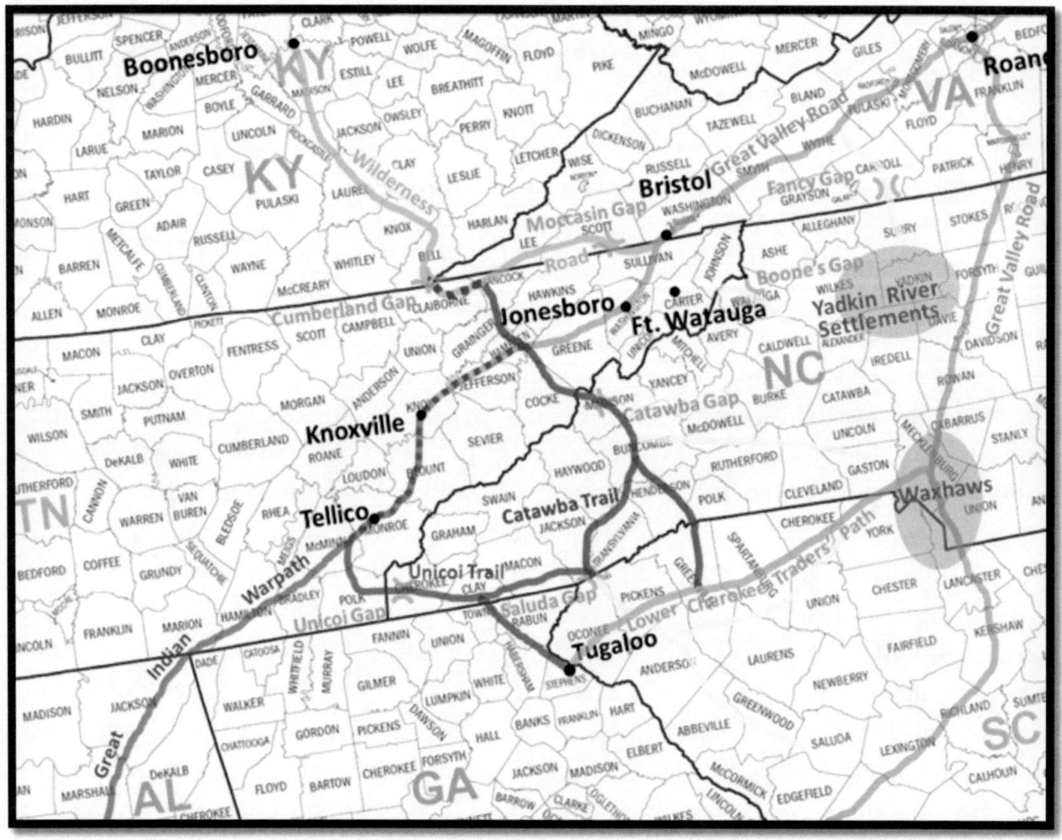

Figure 2-1. The Great Philadelphia Wagon Trail or Great Valley Road, one of the most important "highways" of the Colonial Period. The Philadelphia Wagon Road split at Roanoke, Virginia, with the western fork going to Knoxville and the eastern fork going through Waxhaws to Augusta, Georgia.

a Charleston speculator and merchant, received a grant for two hundred thousand acres further south on the headwaters of Stevens and Long Cane Creeks. His Great Survey of 1751 set out this property, and by circa 1751–1753, Robert Gouedy had opened his trading post in what became the village of Ninety Six along the Cherokee trade route to Charleston.[2] A few years later, in 1755, Hamilton sold the lower section of his land, a parcel of fifty thousand acres, to William Simpson and Dr. John Murray, who subsequently divided it, with Murray owning the southern portion in what became part of the lower Ninety Six District. Murray's land was near the area now known as Whitehall and was not far from where the Pressly family would begin their new lives little more than a decade later. In the same year, Hamilton also sold one hundred thousand acres to the Jewish merchant, Joseph Salvador.

In 1756, after stopping first at the Waxhaws to scout for new land, Patrick Calhoun, from Augusta County, Virginia, and several friends and their families from Virginia and Pennsylvania settled along lower Long Cane Creek. This fertile area was filled with pea-vine grass and dense canebrake, some as high as twenty feet. The region, according to John H. Logan in his fascinating 1859 *History of the Upper Country of South Carolina,* was stocked with deer and other game, and rivers and creeks supported abundant fish.[3] Most of the buffalo, which had been plentiful earlier in the eighteenth century, were gone by the 1750s. Land records from 1758 indicate that Patrick Calhoun, who became a surveyor, and his brother, William, acquired land on the northwest fork of Long Cane Creek, probably Little River. Another early settler in this area was Andrew Williamson, who was a cow driver and, by 1758, a supplier of horses, hogs, and pelts to the frontier forts. Williamson, later known as General Williamson, soon became very wealthy and by the mid-1760s owned a fortified plantation, which he purchased from Dr. John Murray and later named White Hall. Arthur Patton was another important early settler, buying land in the Long Cane Creek area in 1758.

In January 1760, the Cherokee conflict intensified, and on February 1, 1760, about 150 Long Cane Creek settlers in wagons, who were fleeing to Augusta, were attacked and twenty-three were killed, including Patrick Calhoun's mother, temporarily halting the influx of settlers. Patrick, the father of John C. Calhoun, later erected a marker denoting the burial site of those killed in the Long Cane Massacre. A memorial can be found on a dirt road west of Troy in McCormick County. By 1762, the Cherokee Uprising (1759–1761) had been quelled, but things were still far from stable. The Calhouns returned to their homes in 1763, and William Calhoun is said to have opened a store in March 1763; but late that year, the Creek Indians killed fourteen people on the Savannah River.[4] A letter from Patrick Calhoun, which was published in the *South Carolina Gazette* at the time, said there were twenty-seven men and 103 women and children at Fort Boone (located on Patrick Calhoun's property), thirty-four men and 105 women and children at Arthur Patton's home on Lee Creek near Long Cane Creek, which was surrounded by a stout palisade structure to guard it against Indian attack.[5] About the same number were at Dr. John Murray's at Hard Labor Creek. Both Patton and Murray had fortified home sites that were further strengthened as forts to provide refuge for settlers. Another stockade fort, Fort Long Cane, located on the east side of Long Cane Creek, was built after the Long Cane Massacre. These settler forts, probably little more than fortified log structures, soon became church meeting houses where basic schooling also took place.

During this same period, in an effort to settle the backcountry, the General Assembly of the Colony of South Carolina passed the Bounty Act on July 25, 1761. It provided the generous "head right" of one hundred acres for the head of household and for single individuals over the age of sixteen and fifty acres for each woman and child, which was to be owned by the head of the household. It encouraged significant emigrations to South Carolina, with Charleston becoming a major point of entry from Ulster. In 1762, the Colony of South Carolina created two square-shaped townships, Boonesborough and Belfast, which were respectively north and west

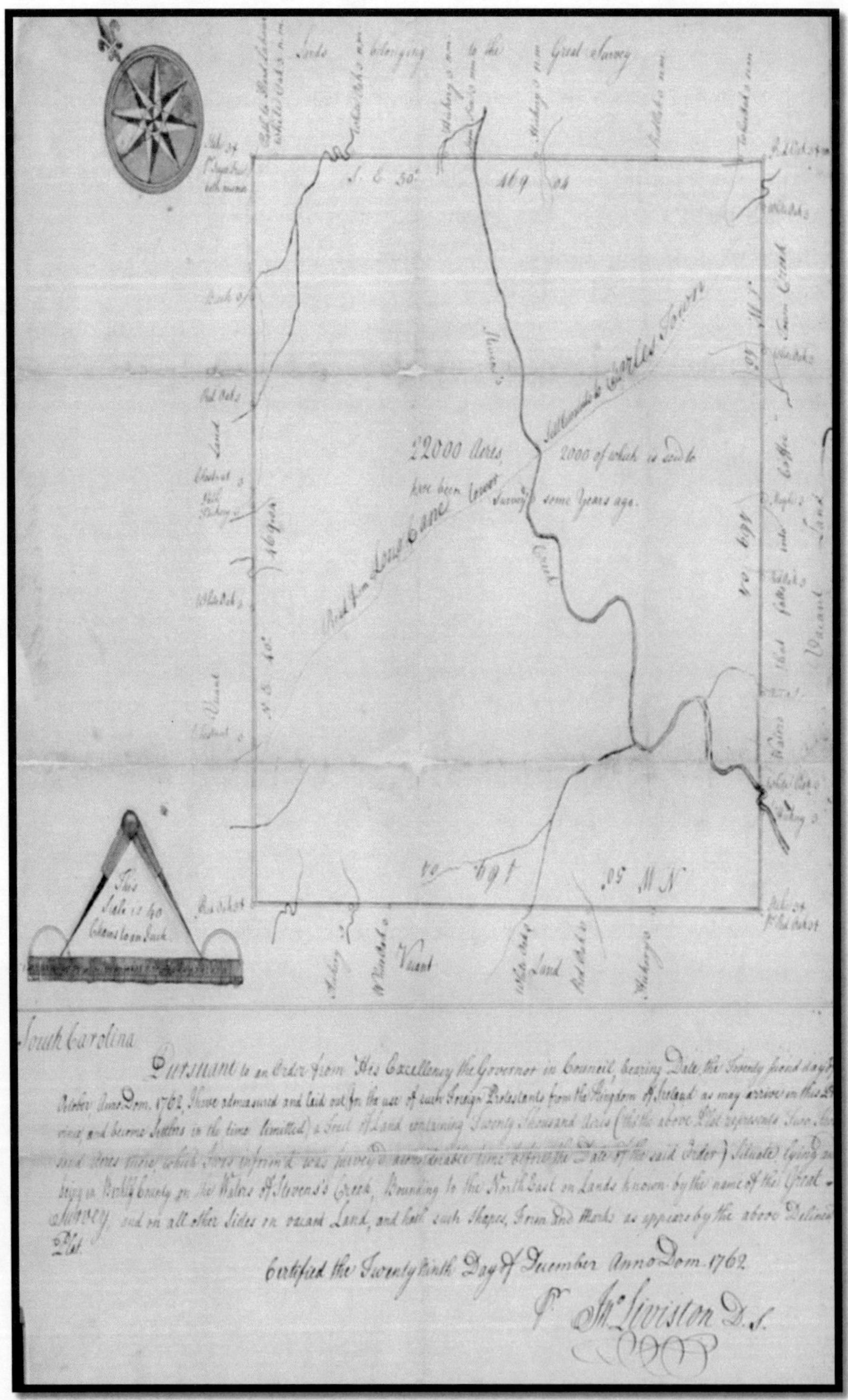

Figure 2-2. Survey for the Belfast Township, backcountry South Carolina, 1762, showing the road from "long Cane lower Settlement to Charles Town" crossing over Steven's Creek, an early name for Hard Labor Creek. South Carolina Department of Archives and History, Columbia, South Carolina.

of the village of Ninety Six, to accommodate the immigrants that were expected as a result of the bounty encouragement. These townships, created for "such foreign Protestants from the Kingdom of Ireland," helped create a buffer zone between the Indian Territory and the low country. The Cherokee Boundary was close to these townships. Boonesborough consisted of 20,500 acres near the headwaters of Long Cane Creek, two miles east of the present Due West. Belfast Township (Figure 2-2) comprised twenty-two thousand acres, including the fertile valleys on both sides of Hard Labor Creek above its junction with Cuffeetown Creek, where the Pressly family was to settle. The third township, Hillsborough, created in 1764, consisted of twenty-eight thousand acres near where Long Cane Creek enters Little River. It included the town of New Bordeaux, a Huguenot settlement led by Reverend John Louis Gibert, who came with his congregation of 212 French Huguenots in 1764. The township of Londonborough (for which no township map exists) was created in 1765 for a group of German Lutherans stranded in London in 1764. It is shown on a 1779 map of South Carolina as Londonderry (Figure 2-3). It overlapped with a portion Belfast Township and included land east of Hard Labor Creek with most Palatines settling near Cuffeetown, located twelve miles south of Ninety Six.

Figure 2-3. Detail showing Camden and Ninety Six "Precincts" and the Cherokee Boundary Line. Anon. "A New and Accurate Map of the Province of South Carolina in North America." *The Universal Magazine*, London: J. Hinton, 1779. From Library of Congress. *Map Collections*, Geography and Map Division.

After the easing of the Creek Indian crisis, an increasing number of Scotch-Irish settlers, many from Virginia and Augusta County, were attracted to the promise of more fertile land and headed south along the Great Wagon Road, settling in what became the old Ninety Six District of South Carolina. There was also a significant and ongoing influx of Scotch-Irish settlers from Ulster responding to the Bounty Act. Some sixty-two ships, sailing from Ulster ports, arrived in Charleston between 1760 and 1775. Several migrations included almost entire Presbyterian congregations from Ulster, many accompanied by their pastor. Two are particularly relevant to the history of the Ninety Six District and the Pressly family. The first occurred in 1764, when a group of three hundred Seceder (Associate Church) Presbyterian families from Ballybay, County Monaghan, Ulster, under the leadership of their pastor, Reverend Thomas Clark, departed Newry, County Down, on May 10 on the ship *John* and arrived in New York on July 28, 1764.[6] The Associate Church had its beginnings in Scotland in 1733, when Ebenezer Erskine and two other reverends carried out the Secession from the Church of Scotland, forming the Seceders, who later took the name of Associate Presbyterians. Within a decade, the Associates had quarreled and divided into two rival factions: Burghers, who accepted the Burgher Oath, which required holders of public offices to approve the true religion, professed within the realm but, in so doing, believed the Secession was the true Church; and Anti-Burghers, who did not accept the Oath, opposing any form of civil compulsion in religious affairs. Associate Presbyterians brought an orthodox theology and an evangelical zeal to Scottish Presbyterians in Ulster; and in 1750, the first Seceder Presbytery was organized there. The Seceders were concentrated in County Antrim and County Derry and also South Armagh, Monaghan, and West Down. Reverend Clark, a student of Ebenezer Erskine, was licensed to preach in 1748, and in 1749, the Associate Presbytery sent him to preach at Ballybay, County Monaghan, and elsewhere. On July 23, 1751, he was ordained at the Seceder Congregation of Ballybay, which was made up almost exclusively of Scotch emigrants (Figure 2-4).

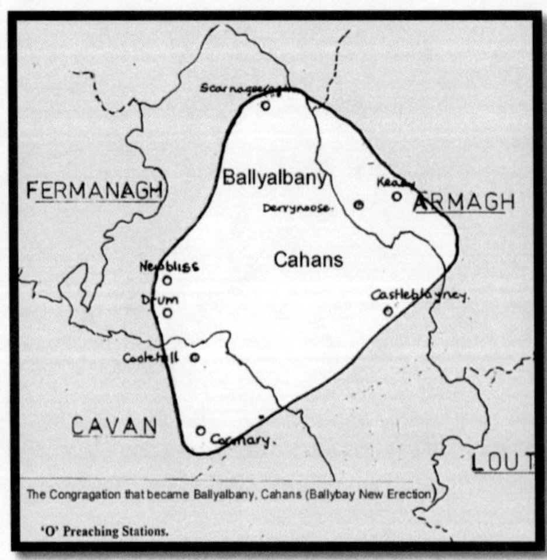

Figure 2-4. Ballyalbany, Cahans (Ballybay New Erection), Ulster. The Os represent the preaching stations.

Reverend Clark's departure on the ship *John,* from Ballybay, became known as The Cahans Exodus. Half of his congregation settled with him in New Perth, New York (after 1788, Salem), whereas the rest moved south, probably along the Great Wagon Road or by ship, eventually settling in the lower Long Cane area of the South Carolina backcountry where presumably they were able to take advantage of the South Carolina Bounty Act. Members of this core group eventually helped form three Associate Presbyterian congregations in the area: Little Run (later Little River, located near present day Mt. Carmel), Long Cane, and Cedar Creek (later Cedar Spring and sometime later still changed to Cedar Springs). Reverend Clark was to return twice to the area to visit his parishioners, in 1770 and again in 1779, before settling permanently among them in the early 1780s.

The second important emigration of a large congregation from Ulster to the South Carolina backcountry occurred in 1772, when members of Reverend William Martin's congregation of Covenanters, (Reformed) Presbyterians from the area of Kellswater and Ballymena in central County, Antrim, sailed to Charleston between August 25 and October 27, 1772.[7] The Covenanters date back to the seventeenth century, when they proclaimed the "Crown Rights" of Jesus as king over the Church and State. When Charles II rejected this covenant, they left the Church of Scotland and were severely persecuted both in Scotland and Ireland. Martin's group sailed from three ports on five different ships: from Belfast (*Hopewell* and *Pennsylvania Farmer*), from Larne (*James and Mary* and *Lord Dunlace*—the Ship Reverend Martin was on), and from Newry (*Free Mason*). John Pressly, our ancestor, and his family came on the last of these ships to leave Ireland, the *Free Mason,* which sailed from Newry on October 27, 1772, and arrived in Charlestown on December 22, 1772. Passengers on these ships mainly secured plats in the Ninety Six District, with a core group of Martin's congregation settling in the area of Rocky Creek, where Reverend Martin had accepted a call from the Catholic Presbyterian Church (founded 1759) near Rocky Mount Road, fifteen miles southeast of Chester. In 1773, Rev. Martin's congregation of Covenanters separated from this congregation, which consisted of various denominations and erected their own Covenanter meeting-house. Several smaller migrations from individual church communities, mainly Seceder, also settled in the backcountry, most notably King's Creek and Cannon's Creek in Newberry County, which were founded by Reverend John Renwick. Three groups followed him from County Atrium to the area in 1767, 1770, and 1772.

The settling of the backcountry generally involved a closely intertwined network of friends and extended kin who had a shared history. Bounty plats were usually between 100 and 350 acres in size, so families did not live far from one another, allowing communities to form quickly. This helped settlers develop small, self-sustaining, interdependent communities on what was for the most part very fertile land. One of the first things settlers did was designate a place of worship, even if it was only an altar under trees. As noted earlier, many early meeting houses were also settler forts where people could find refuge, and they frequently also served as a basic schoolhouse. Loosely affiliated, many without pastors, churches became an organizing factor of community life. The settlers from Virginia tended to be Presbyterian, whereas the Ulster immigrants were more likely dissenting Seceders and Covenanters. In the early years, supplies (a term for ministers) were in great demand with many positions needing to be filled. It was common for several small churches to be served by one minister. As a result, visiting preachers, traveling through the countryside, would sometimes baptize children. In 1764, the Reverend William Richardson visited the congregation that later became Hopewell Presbyterian Church in the Long Cane community and is said to have baptized some 260 children. Elders of the Church played an important leadership role. Even in the unstructured social landscape of the first decades in South Carolina, communities followed old country traditions by generally choosing men from "good families" to serve as elders.

The backcountry grew rapidly, but it was still very much the frontier. Backcountry settlers did not enjoy adequate representation in their colonial assemblies, and their legal systems were not sufficient for maintaining law and order. Roving bands of bandits and groups of settlers known as Schofielites, who sided with them, many of whom later became Tories, took advantage of the chaos in the wake of the Cherokee War to stage their own raids on law-abiding citizens on the frontier. In spite of repeated appeals from backcountry settlers, the Charleston government and low country planters failed to intervene, prompting prominent backcountry settlers to organize the South Carolina Regulators, a vigilante group formed to restore order. In 1767, the year David Pressly arrived, the Regulator movement, headed by leading planters and supported by small farmers, most of whom were later active Whigs, became an organized effort to restore law and order and regulate backcountry affairs. They brought criminals to justice and set up courts to resolve legal disputes. The colony's officials were forced to rein them in with the help of a countervigilante movement known as the Moderators or Scouties, who helped neutralize the conflict. By 1768, order was restored, and the Circuit Court Act of November 1769 provided seven judicial districts for the state—Georgetown, Charleston, Beaufort, Cheraws, Camden, Orangeburg, and Ninety Six—and for the construction of a courthouse in each, after which the Regulators disbanded (Figure 2-5). The village of Ninety Six, where Robert Gouedy operated his successful trading post, became prosperous after the courthouse and jail opened in 1772. The Regulator/Moderator conflict, however, sowed the seeds of bitter enmity among backcountry settlers and between backcountry and low country settlers. During the Revolutionary War, these old animosities were reignited, setting the stage for very personal and often vicious skirmishes between neighboring Tories and Whigs.

Beginning in 1767, it was into this unsettling frontier world, which was at least a ten-day trip by wagon over increasingly treacherous roads leading away from the comparatively sophisticated port city of Charleston, that the Pressly family began their new life.

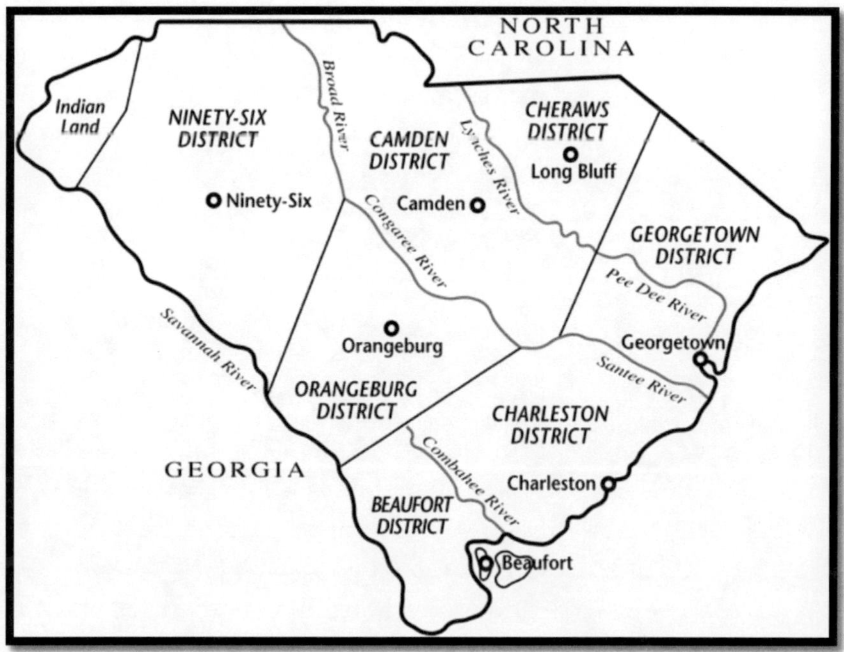

Figure 2-5. Seven judicial districts for the colony of South Carolina created by the Circuit Court Act of November 1769.

Chapter 3

Glasgow and the Ulster Migrations: John and David Pressly, Emigrating to America, 1767–1772

The earliest known verifiable records about the Pressly family, prior to their arrival in South Carolina, are the previously mentioned parish christening records from two villages near Glasgow for the children of David Pressly (imm 1767) and his wife Easter/Esther Brown. David's eldest son, "Samuel Presly," was christened January 15, 1756, in Ayr, near the coast of Scotland and the southwest border of Renfrewshire, by Reverend Hugh Hamilton (1707–1788), minister of the Gospel at Girvan, a nearby village (Figure 3-1).[1] His next three children were baptized further inland in Lochwinnock, Renfrewshire: William "Preslie" on April 23, 1758; David "Preslie" on September 21, 1760, and Agnes "Presly" on October 31, 1762. The Lochwinnock parish records list David as a weaver living in "Kirktown," and in 1757, David "Pressly" is listed in census-like records in the town of "Lochuinnoch, Glasgow"—occupation as a weaver and as a subscriber to *A Discourse of the Work of the Holy Spirit in Prayer,* by John Owen (1757). Although these records give us, for the first time, a geographical location for where at least one member of the family lived in Scotland before sailing to Charleston, we have no idea how long David had been there.

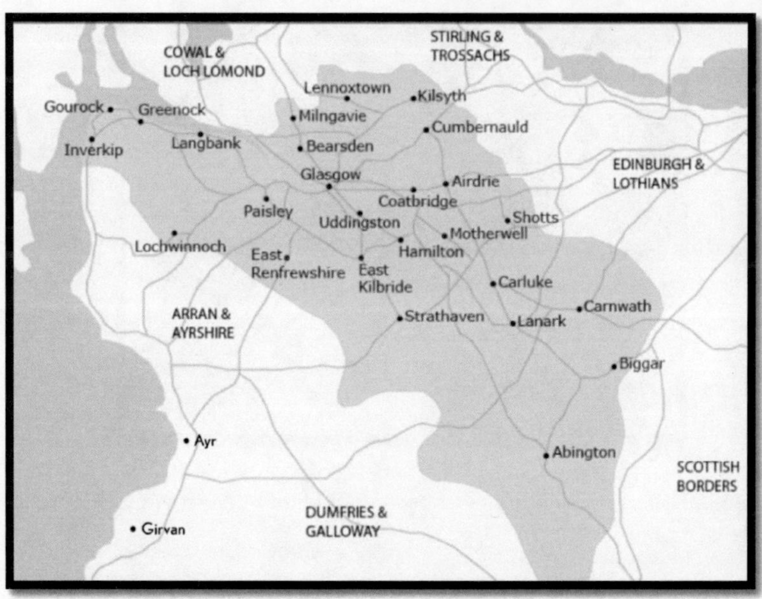

Figure 3-1. Towns and counties near Glasgow, including where David Pressly (imm 1767) lived.

Lochwinnock was a well-known eighteenth-century weaving center near the Ayrshire border on the River Calder. It is just west of Paisley, where Reverend Thomas Clark was born on November 5, 1720. The Kirktown of Lochwinnock, where David lived, was small and centered at the gates of a new church, which was built in 1729/1732, on Johnshill, the site of the Chapel of Lochwinnock, which had been owned by the monks of Paisley Abbey. Today, little more than a clock tower remains from this eighteenth-century church, known as Old Simon, which was part of the Church of Scotland (Figure 3-2). The Kirktown ran approximately one hundred yards along where the three roads, Eastend, High Street, and the Johnshill, met with the rows of houses coming close to the church gates. A typical weaver cottage from the period consisted of two rooms for living and a third room where the loom was placed. We do not know if David was one, but master weavers were regarded as men of some social standing. Lochwinnock was presumably similar to other nearby towns, such as Kilmarnock, described in contemporary travel diaries as having "a tolerable square but the streets are narrow and the houses thatched. Though adorned with stone cornices as in many other parts . . ."[2]

Figure 3-2. Eighteenth-century clock tower, Old Simon, Lochwinnoch, Scotland.

David and his family left Scotland for Ulster sometime after October 1762, when their daughter Agnes was baptized, and Christmas Eve 1766, when they departed Belfast on the ship *Earl of Hillsborough* for Charleston, South Carolina. Shipping agents advertised in local newspapers, such as *The Belfast Newsletter,* informing people of dates, fares, and provisions to bring. Because the South Carolina Bounty Act was meant to attract new immigrants, requirements for sailing were minimal apart from a certificate of recommendation from the passenger's minister and two church elders stating he/she was a Protestant of good character. Given how close much of Ulster was to the sea, traveling to the various ports of departure was, for many, relatively easy (Figure 3-3). For a period of time, people were allowed to bring one trunk free. Conditions on ships varied considerably, depending on the experience and benevolence of the captain, and the amount of cargo, but most passengers suffered long, cramped voyages in poorly ventilated surroundings. An advertisement for the ship, *Prince of Wales,* that left Belfast on December 19, 1766, noted that the commander was known for his "very humane Treatment and Care of the Passengers," and that "Plenty of Provisions shall be laid in, and as large an Allowance given as was ever done on the like Passage."[3] The sea voyage lasted seven to nine weeks, and many families forged friendships during the journey that helped build communities after they arrived.

Figure 3-3. Map of Northern Ireland showing counties and major towns.

There were a small number of agents in Ulster who negotiated transfer of commodities to and from the Colonies as well as people. Prior to the sailing of the *Earl of Hillsborough,* William Beatty, as agent, advertised that he would be in three market towns, Lurgan, Ballynahinch, and Dromore, each a few miles from the other in County Down, every week to meet with potential passengers. The *Earl of Hillsborough* arrived in Charleston on February 18, 1767, carrying "two hundred and thirty Protestant settlers encouraged by the large bounty given by this province, and the success their countrymen have met with in their several settlements here"[4] (Figure 3-4). David's family is described in South Carolina Council meeting records as "among poor Irish Protestants who did not have the means to pay for their bounty." A total of eight ships from Ulster ports arrived in Charleston in 1767, six from Belfast carrying together over 1,400 passengers. On at least one of these ships, the *Nancy,* immigrants arrived in very poor condition due to disease and overcrowding.[5] The Church wardens of St. Phillips asked for subscriptions that year to help care for desperately needy Scotch-Irish Protestants who had arrived from Belfast.

Figure 3-4. View of Charleston, South Carolina, that would have greeted new arrivals in the 1760s. *An Exact Prospect of Charlestown, the Metropolis of the Province of South Carolina,* engraved for the London Magazine (1762). Charleston's quayside seen from across the Cooper River.

According to South Carolina Council Records, David was accompanied by "Ester Plessly, 36," "Samuel Plessly, 11," "David Pressley, 6," and "Agnes Pressley, 4."[6] Their son, William, baptized in Lochwinnock in 1758, is not mentioned. On February 27, 1767, David "Pressley" petitioned for 350 acres of land on a branch of the western fork of "Stephenson's [*sic*] Creek, Belfast Township" (Figures 3-5a and 5b). This western fork is almost certainly Calabash Branch. Stephenson's or Steven's Creek was an early name for Hard Labor Creek. David and his family probably stayed in Charleston until at least May 5, 1767, when he would have appeared in person, as was required, to have his survey certified under the Bounty Act. His plat was formally

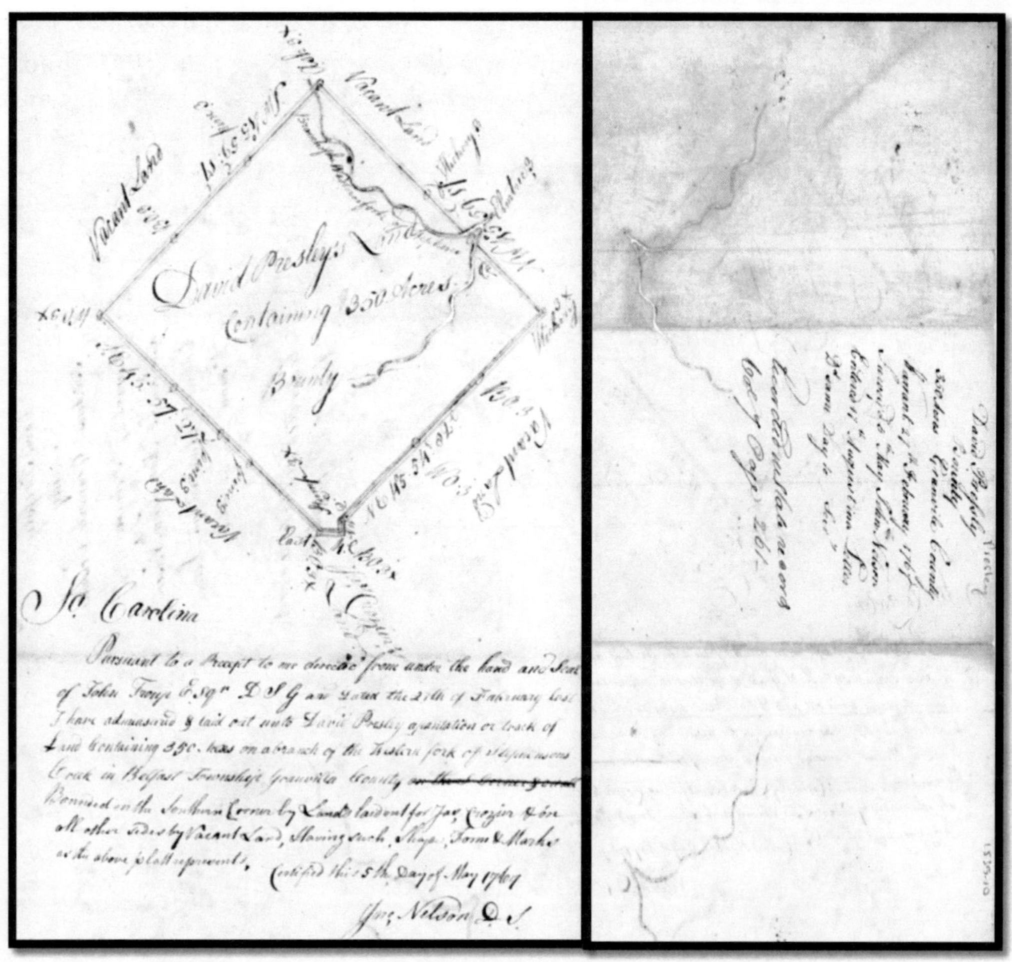
David Pressly's Land &c.
Containing 350 Acres
Bounty
Vacant Land

So. Carolina

Pursuant to a Precept to me directed from under the hand and Seal of John Troupe Esqr D S G and dated the 21th of February last I have admeasured & laid out unto David Pressly a plantation or tract of Land Containing 350 acres on a branch of the Western fork of Stephens Creek in Belfast Township Granville County Bounded on the Southern Corner by Land laid out for Jas. Crozier & on all other sides by Vacant Land, Having such Shape, Form & Marks as the above platt represents. Certified this 5th Day of May 1767

Jno. Nelson D. S.

Figures 3-5a and 3-5b. Recto and verso of David Pressly's 350 plantation track on the western fork of Stephens Creek Belfast Township, certified May 5, 1767. 5213182 Box 13 Folder 1539 Plat 10, Records of the SC Secretary of State, Loose Colonial Plats, 1731–1775, South Carolina Department of Archives and History.

granted on September 22, 1767.[7] The family would have been given basic supplies to begin farming and probably a twenty-shilling bounty and would have then traveled into the backcountry probably on the newly opened Charles Town to Fort Charlotte Road, which connected with the Old Cherokee or Keowee Path (Figure 3-6). During this period, a trip from Charleston to the Long Cane area would have taken at least ten days. The fact that David received 350 acres (one hundred for head of household and fifty for spouse and dependents under sixteen) suggests there was another child with them, possibly a yet to be named/baptized child born on the journey[8] or a child under the age of sixteen in their care. It is also possible that a child, perhaps the aforementioned William, born in 1758, died during the voyage. We know a second son named William was born after they arrived, probably circa 1775, and who, at the time of his father's death in 1785, was not old enough to be designated a specific parcel of land in his will. David had seven children living at the time of his death. In addition to Samuel, David, and Agnes, there were Mary Ann, William, John, and Esther.

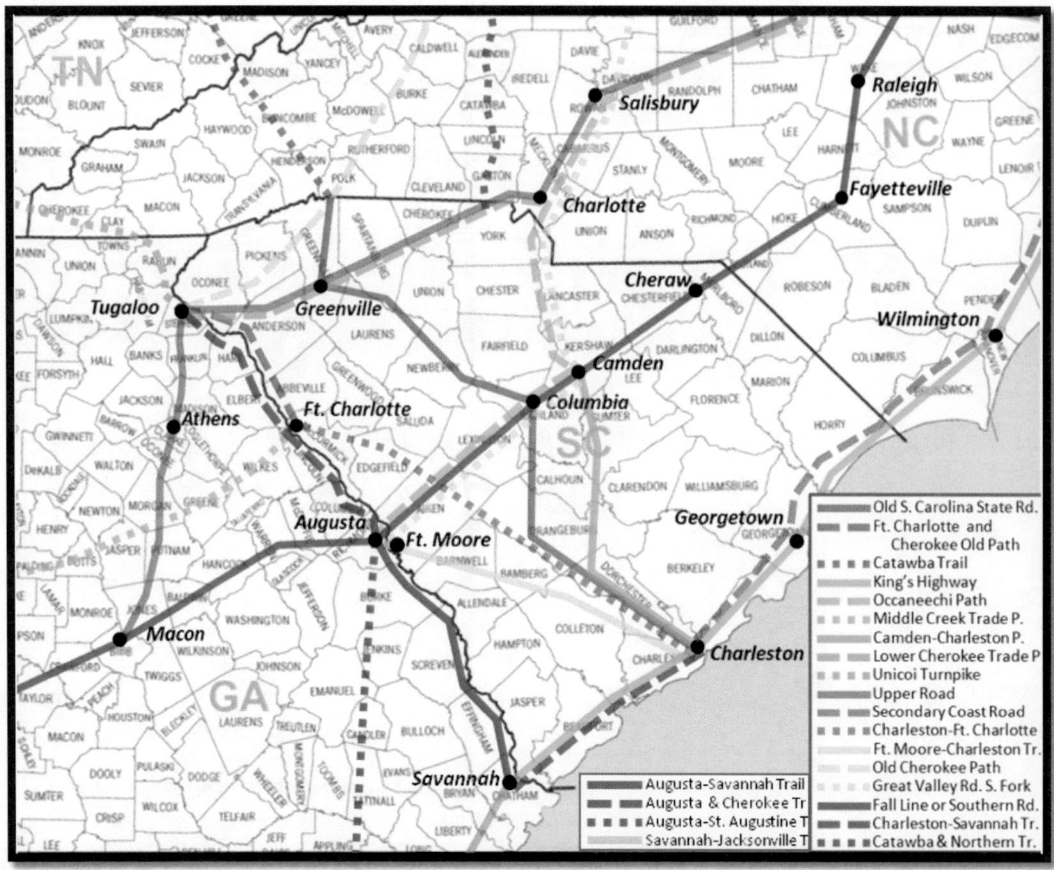

Figure 3-6. Map showing the Charleston to Fort Charlotte Road, which connected with the Old Cherokee Path.

The Colony allowed passengers arriving on ships some freedom of choice in terms of where their bounty plats were located, and many chose plats near relatives who had arrived earlier. Small groups of passengers from one ship were frequently awarded land adjacent to or near one another, although the Colony was careful not to allow all passengers from one ship to settle in the same place. Those who had means sometimes bought already cultivated land from old settlers, especially if they desired a particular location. This type of transaction was not recorded as part of ship manifests or in the South Carolina Council records. David's immediate neighbors included two other passengers on the *Earl of Hillsborough,* James Crozier (Crosier) and James Major, while George McCombe, Elizabeth Kirkwood, John Wright, and the Miscambles, who also came on the *Earl of Hillsborough,* lived close by. After his arrival, David Pressly was entrepreneurial enough to continue to acquire land, petitioning on March 3, 1772, for an additional 150 acres, possibly for his son, Samuel, who would have been sixteen years of age.[9] Then, on September 1, 1772, he petitioned for 135 acres, based on an April 15, 1772, survey, which was immediately adjacent to and north of his bounty plat and also adjacent to Thomas Cannon, Fallon, Patrick Gibson, and Samuel McClinton. David later bequeathed this land to his son, David Pressly, Jr. Additionally, a "David Pressley" is also listed among a group of thirty Protestants in the South Carolina Council meeting records of December 1, 1772, who were included with a group who "had arrived from Germany without warrant." He received a warrant for one hundred acres on Stevenson Creek.[10] This was almost certainly David (imm 1767) as the land was adjacent to and essentially shared the same coordinates as his bounty plat. This conclusion is supported by the fact that also receiving land on December 1, 1772, was "William Dourris," who also already owned land immediately adjacent to David.

David's older brother, John, sailed for Charleston from Ulster in October 1772, some five years after him. We know almost nothing about John Pressly prior to his arrival in South Carolina. There are no surviving baptismal or marriage records in Scotland, Ireland, or South Carolina related to him. There are, however, a few pieces of circumstantial evidence that suggest he spent some time in Northern Ireland, where a large number of Scottish lowland Seceders had settled by the mid-eighteenth century. There is an intriguing reference to a "John Presslie" in baptism records from the Scottish Village of Girvan. In 1758, Hugh Hamilton, Minister of the Gospel in Girvan, the same minister who baptized David Pressly's first child, Samuel, in the nearby Village of Ayr in 1756, baptized a child who was said to be the daughter of "one John Presslie in Ireland." The handwritten baptismal record from 1758 reads as follows: "Jean McQueen. Nayrural daughter to Margaret McQueen for one John Presslie in Ireland who she says is the father, has not yet owned his being so as bap. In the Bellman's Dec 25, 1758."[11] If this was our John Pressly, it could mean that he was already living in Ireland by 1758, which could explain why we have no baptismal records for his children in Scotland. It is possible that other members of the family were already in Ireland and may have had some connection to the previously mentioned 1751 and 1753 baptisms at Rosemary Street Church in Belfast.

Additionally, there is another piece of circumstantial evidence that could also link John to Ireland. His eldest daughter, born circa 1756, was named Mary Patterson Pressly, which suggests his wife's maiden name may have been Patterson.[12] Samuel Patterson, who is thought to have come from the parish of Dysart, Newry, County Down, emigrated to South Carolina on the same boat, the *Free Mason,* as John Pressly. Whether the Presslys and Pattersons knew one another in Ireland cannot be confirmed. However, given the close relationship that existed between the two families after they arrived in the Colonies, it is possible that John's wife could have been a sister or close relation to Samuel Patterson. Later, at least two marriages took place between John's and Samuel's children—John's son, David, marrying Jane Patterson, circa 1788–1789, and his son, John, marrying Margaret Patterson in 1798.

As noted earlier, John sailed on the brigantine, *Free Mason*, the last of five ships that included members of Reverend William Martin's Covenanter congregation.[13] The owners of these ships advertised in the *Belfast Newsletter*, and the passengers on all five ships included many Presbyterians from other Ulster congregations, among them a large group of Seceders. The *Free Mason* was advertised as "remarkably lofty between decks." It was apparently hard to fill these ships and records show that ships frequently did not leave on schedule. The *Lord Dunlace*, on which the Reverend William Martin sailed, left Larne on October 4, having been delayed twice from its original sailing date of August 15. Advertisements for the *Lord Dunlace*, as late as September 15, stated that many people had dropped out for lack of funds and 200 more passengers could be accommodated. Ships generally held between 180 and 300 passengers, depending on the amount of cargo that they were carrying and the type of vessel. The *Free Mason* was originally scheduled to sail on August 20 but it was delayed several times and it did not depart Newry, County Down, until October 27, 1772, arriving in Charleston on December 22, 1772.

Figure 3-7. *View of Charleston Harbor*, by Thomas Leitch, 1774, oil on canvas. Courtesy of the Museum of Early Southern Decorative Arts (MESDA) at Old Salem. Winston-Salem, North Carolina.

The view before John, when he arrived in Charleston Harbor after more than an eight-week journey at sea, would have been impressive. The New World would have looked very civilized, and the recently built New Exchange would have dominated the harbor, making what Josiah Quincy described in his diary on February 28, 1773, as "a most noble appearance." Thomas Leitch's painting, *View of Charleston Harbor*, depicts the impressive New Exchange with the church spire of St. Michaels at the left (Figure 3-7). Charleston, by that time, was a prosperous port with a diverse and growing population and close trade contacts with the Caribbean-British colonies. It was one of the four wealthiest cities in the colonies, along with New York, Philadelphia, and Boston. Numerous grand town homes had just been completed, including the Heyward Washington House (1772), William Gibbes House (ca. 1772) on South Battery, and Colonel John Stuarts's town home (1772). It was also a cultural center. Aware of its importance and legacy, the Charleston Museum, the first of its kind in the country, was founded in 1773, and the city was home to superb craftsmen and furniture makers. Most wealthy, low-country planters had town homes here, and because Charleston at this time was the seat of all legal proceedings, it was also where wealthy lawyers lived. The comparative elegance and sophistication of Charleston would have been in stark contrast to the frontier community, where John and his family were to settle. John, however, would also have been exposed to the plight of African slaves, arriving in destitute condition and sold off in a strange land. Contemporary accounts described the putrid port with bodies of slaves floating in the water.

We can deduce that John Pressly was not a poor Scotch-Irish immigrant like his brother, because he was one of the seven passengers, along with Samuel Patterson, who were able to pay for their families' passages. He may also have been a man of some education or status within the church because his son, William, our direct ancestor, was well educated prior to his arrival. Most of William's formal schooling would have had to take place before he emigrated, because there would have been few opportunities after he arrived.

Shortly after his arrival in Charleston, "John Presley" received a warrant for survey for three hundred acres near his brother on "Rocky Branch, waters of Long Cane Creek"[14] (Figure 3-8). The land bordered Robert Neiles (Neeland), who was also on one of Martin's ships, the *James and Mary,* and was adjacent to John's nephew, Samuel Pressly. His daughter, Mary, received a warrant for one hundred acres on January 21, 1773, next to him on "Stephenson Creek," which means she was at least sixteen and born no later than 1756.[15] Her land also bordered Samuel Pressly and John "Harser" (Hearst) as well as Margaret Daniel, who was also on the *Free Mason.* John would have gone through the laborious process of securing the warrant, paying for the surveys, getting the warrant endorsed, and then applying for a grant for the land. The fact John received three hundred acres indicates that he arrived with three minor children and his wife. By that date, the names of minor children are no longer mentioned in the Council records. This would mean that in addition to Mary, John had three other children with him on the voyage, David, William, and Martha, and that his two youngest sons, John and Joseph, were born after he arrived. Nineteenth-century census data indicates they were born between 1774 and 1776.

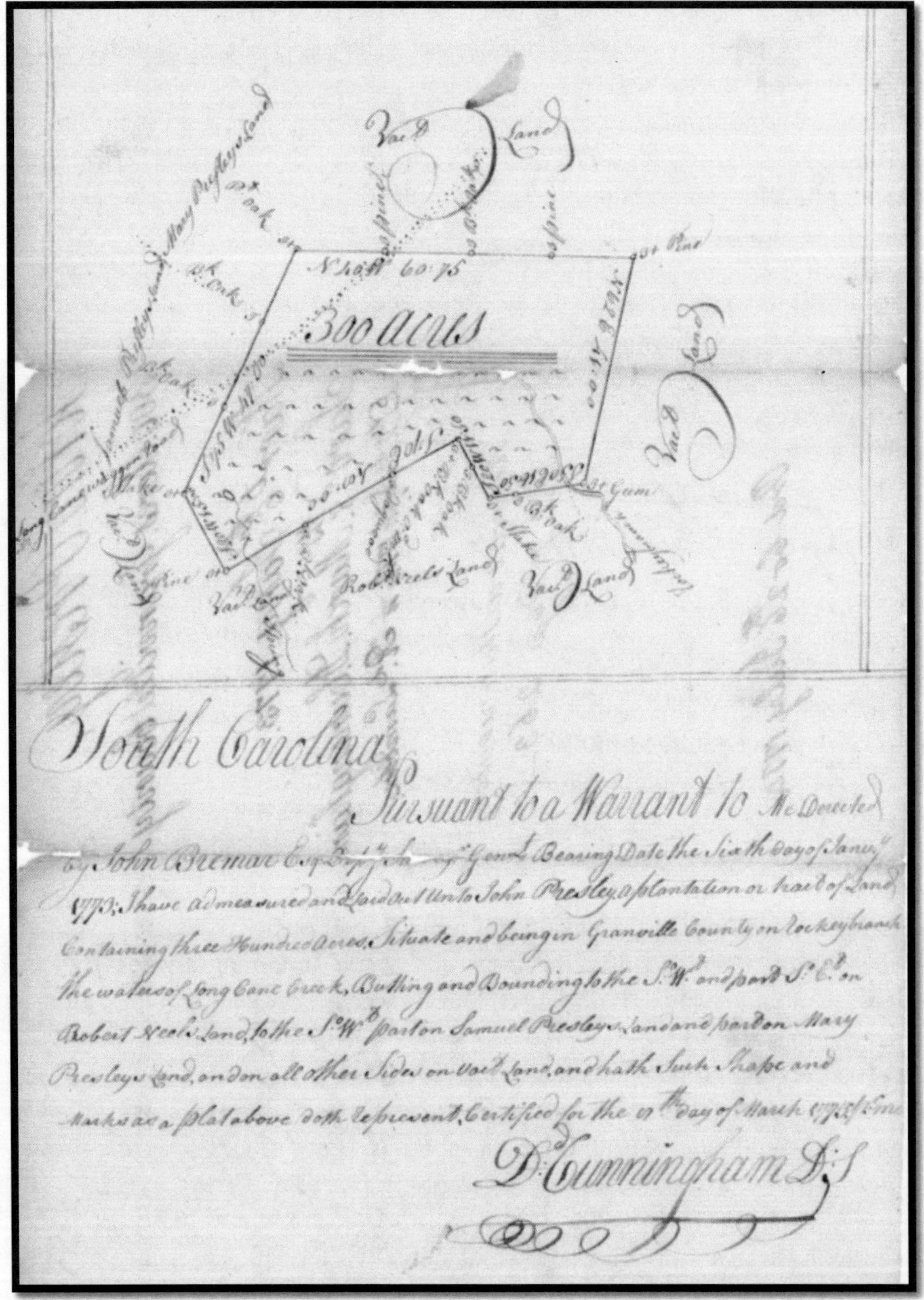

South Carolina

Pursuant to a Warrant to me Directed by John Bremar Esq. Dep. Sur. Gen. Bearing Date the Sixth day of Jany 1773: I have admeasured and laid out unto John Presley a plantation or tract of Land Containing three Hundred Acres, Situate and being in Granville County on lockey branch the waters of Long Cane Creek, Butting and Bounding to the S.W. and part S.E. on Robert Neel's Land, to the S.W. part on Samuel Presley's Land and part on Mary Presley's Land, and on all other Sides on Vac.t Land, and hath such Shape and Marks as a plat above doth represent. Certified for the 8th day of March 1773

D. Cunningham D.S.

Figure 3-8. Survey of plantation track for John Pressly for three hundred acres, certified March 8, 1773, showing "Long Cane Waggon Road" passing through his property and the adjacent plats of his daughter, Mary Pressly, and nephew, Samuel Pressly. 5213182 Box 13 Folder 1539 Plat 12, Records of the SC Secretary of State, Loose Colonial Plats, 1731–1775, South Carolina Department of Archives and History.

John and his family probably took the Charles Town Road, also known as the Old Cherokee Path, to the village of Ninety Six. From there they would have traveled on the Hard "Labour" Road that led from Ninety Six to where his plat was located within Belfast Township (Figure 3-9). Hard "Labour" Road crossed through Samuel McClinton's plat, whose land was adjacent to David Pressly. The area had changed since David's arrival. By 1773, some farmers were able to grow more than subsistence crops, including tobacco, indigo, and wheat and would travel to Charleston and possibly also to Camden and Augusta to sell their crops. They could bring back news so that communities were not as isolated as they had been earlier, and, given the number of ships arriving in Charleston from Ulster, settlers were able to maintain some contact with friends and family left behind. In terms of grants in the Long Cane area, there were a total of 147 grants in 1767—as compared to fifty-eight in 1766, fifty-five in 1768, and forty-three in 1772. With the opening of the new courthouse in 1772, Ninety Six, the seat of the Ninety Six Judicial District, was now a thriving village. At a store like Robert Gouedy's trading post, John and other new arrivals could have acquired basic supplies, cloth, and tools. The area was developed enough that, in addition to Robert Gouedy, there were other small trading posts and stores in place, as well as mills to grind wheat. In addition, court days at Ninety Six quickly became major social events, forerunners of country fairs and reminders of holy fairs that took place in Scotland. People camped out for two or three days at a time, selling livestock and trading homemade goods.

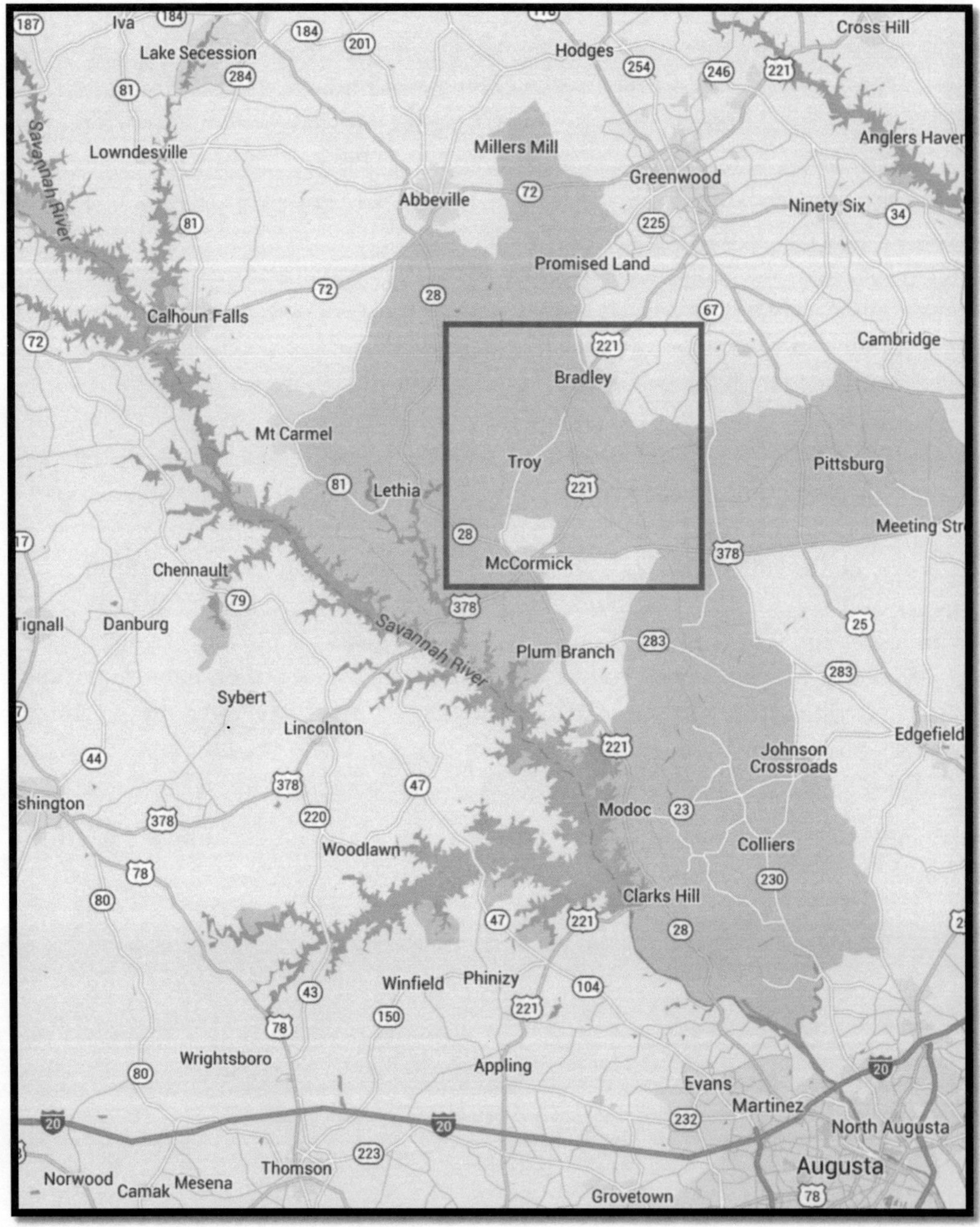

Figure 3-9. ACME Mapper-2 map with square showing a portion of the old lower Ninety Six District between Long Cane Creek and Hard Labor Creek in what is today part of Abbeville, McCormick, Edgefield, and Greenwood counties.

Chapter 4

Building a Community in the Ninety Six District

Arriving at Hard Labor Creek

David and John owned well-situated land, conveniently located near waterways; and by 1773, the infrastructure of basic roads, mainly well-established Indian trading paths, was already in place. Additionally, footpaths connected various home sites which occasionally are also shown on survey plats. As previously noted the Long Cane Wagon Road crossed over Long Cane Creek at Patterson's Bridge and went through the lower portion of John's property, and the Hard "Labour" Road from Ninety Six passed near David Pressly's plat. A spring branch of Rocky Creek ran through John's property and is still visible today. Several years ago, Bob Thompson, whose ancestors were also from this area, prepared a detailed, digitally reconstructed map of Colonial land grants in the Ninety Six District prior to the Revolutionary War.[1] It is an important document listing owner names and sizes of plats as well as major waterways. Accompanied by an index of plat owners with map location, it also provides access to images of recorded plats where available. This map reveals the surprisingly large number of settlers already living in the area before the Revolutionary War and how closely the bounty lots, which on average were between one hundred and four hundred acres, were spaced. It also indicates that some settlers owned multiple pieces of land (Figure 4-1). A close-up detail (Figure 4-2) shows the Long Cane and the Hard Labor Section where the Presslys lived and indicates that immediately to the east of David (imm 1767) and several of his Scotch-Irish neighbors were members of the first group of three hundred German Lutheran immigrants stranded in London in 1763 for whom the King eventually offered free passage to South Carolina. They arrived in the area in December 1764 and included George Frederick Erlbeck, Balsar and Conrad Merk, Christian Zang, John Adams Baurer, Philip Keiss, Johannes Zwilling, Johannes and Abraham Flick, Johann Anderson, Johann Clem, and Phillip Zimmerman. The later ships arrived between December 1764 and February 1765 and most arrivals on the later ships settled further east near Cuffee Creek, also known as Cuffetown Creek. Lt. Governor William Bull offered the German Lutherans bounty plats in the township of Londonborough (no map of this township exists), a portion of which overlapped the already existing twenty-thousand-acre Belfast Township for Irish Protestants created in 1762. Bull also ordered Patrick Calhoun to erect a large log cabin to shield the new settlers from inclement weather when they first arrived. It was probably located at the northwest corner of the intersection of today's Eden Hall and Millway Road, less than two miles away from David and John Pressly. It later became the Lutheran community meeting house and the Lutheran Church of St. George.[2]

Contemporary descriptions of this community provide a helpful insight into what David's world may have been like during these first years. According to Thomas Griffiths, an English agent of the potter Josiah Wedgewood who passed through the area in 1767, the German community was still struggling: "Coffee Creek (Cuffytown), a New Neighbourhood . . . here the people were all sick and Lay about the Room like Dogs, and only one bed amongst, em . . . So I bot some corn for my horse and

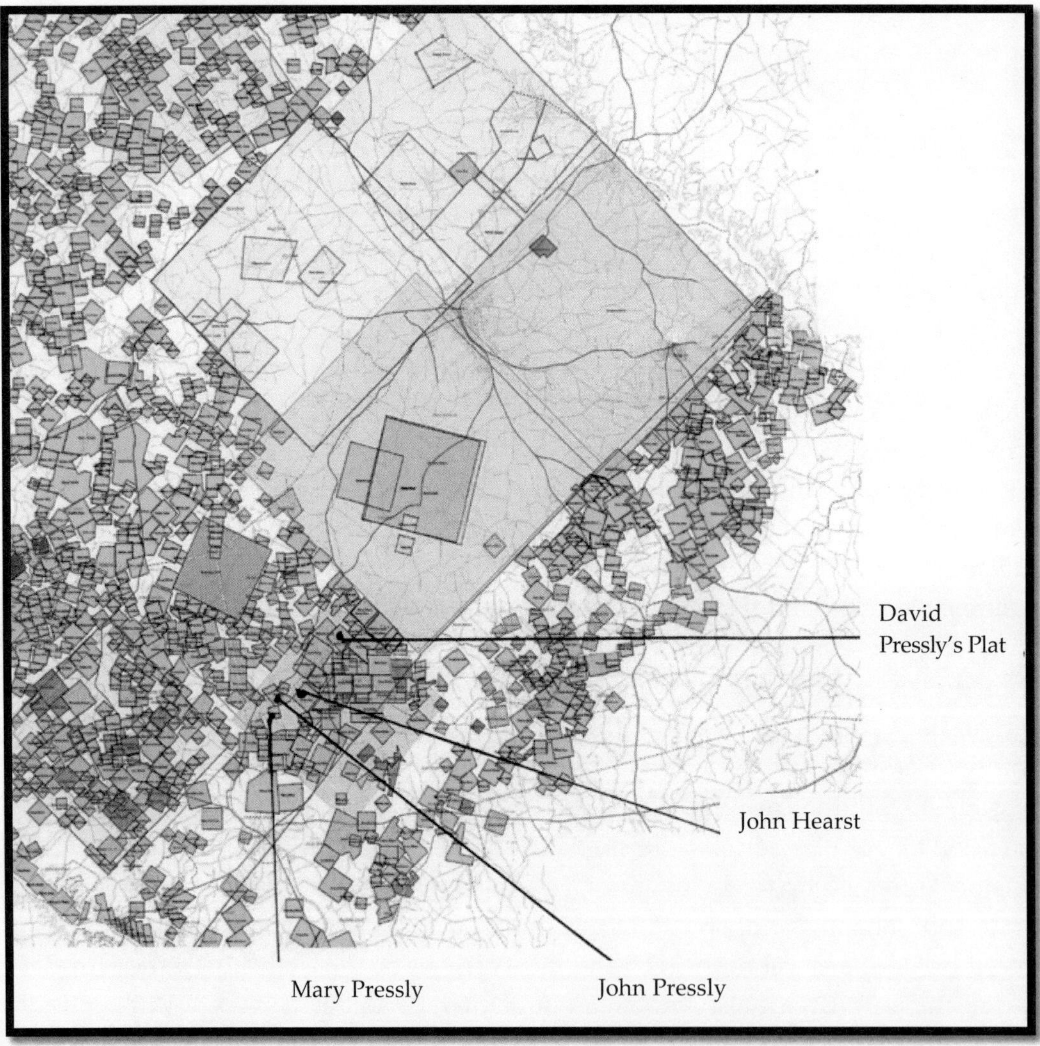

Figure 4-1. Digitally reconstructed Abbeville District Colonial Plats Map showing parcels of land granted by the British Crown prior to the Revolutionary War in the portion of the Ninety Six District later comprising Abbeville District. Arrows indicate location of the Pressly and Hearst plats. Courtesy of Bob Thompson.

Figure 4-2. Detail from Bob Thompson's digitally reconstructed "Abbeville District Colonial Plats Map" of a portion of the Ninety Six District (later comprising Abbeville District) showing a portion of the lower Abbeville District between Long Cane Creek and Hard Labor Creek. Numbers identify contemporary roads, land belonging to David and John Pressly, and German Lutheran settlers to the east.

1. John Pressly
2. Mary Pressly
3. John Hearst
4. David Pressly
5. Barksdale Ferry Road
6. Route 10
7. Route 221
8. Route 112 – Millway Road
9. Bradley
10. Troy

- ● German Lutheran settlers

potatoe bread and a fowl for my Self."[3] Two years later, in 1769, Lt. Governor Bull wrote a much more positive assessment in a letter to the London Board of Trade: "By their industry they (the Germans) now enjoy all such conveniences as are to be found with the humble state of life- comfortable houses, orchards, plenty of provisions, stock of cattle, hogs, poultry, horses for labor. They now raise more than they can consume and consequently add to their capital. Some raise flour and some raise hemp."[4] During this period there was the occasional large plantation, generally located near a major crossroads which would also serve as an inn. During Griffiths's trip he stayed at General Andrew Williamson's home, White Hall Plantation. He wrote that it was "near a place call'd Hard Labour" and that "This is one of the finest plantations in South Carolina; abounding with fine Rich Red Loamy Land, famous for Raising Corn, hemp, flax, Cotton, Rice. Cattle, Hogs, Fruits of all sorts." providing a helpful description of the possibilities of farming at this early date.[5] Williamson told Griffiths that in 1766 his plantation yielded close to three thousand bushel baskets of peaches.

Figure 4-3. Scene at the Cowpens by Benson J. Lossing, *Pictorial Field book of the Revolution in the Carolinas and Georgia*, vol. II, New York: Harper & Brothers, 1851–52.

Like most settlers the first task for David and John would have been to cut down trees, build their homes, and cultivate their fields with sustenance crops. They would have received help from their older sons. A typical home would have been a one or one-and-one-half story single pen log structure sometimes elevated off of the ground on pieces of stone or built on gravel. Clay and straw chinking placed between the logs would have sealed the cabin. Trees would have been cut down to build the house with stumps left in place as seen in Benson J. Lossing's sketch of Cowpens (Figure 4-3). Children would have probably slept on straw mattresses in the half story upstairs, and the bed on the ground level would have been the central piece of furniture in the house. Houses generally had front and back doors, sometimes a partition divided the downstairs, and many early cabins did not have windows. Later extensions to the basic structure were generally horizontal.

Remarkably several late eighteenth-century log cabins survive in the area. The well-preserved Templeton-Drake cabin circa 1764 (Figure 4-4), gives us a good idea of what a 1760s cabin might have looked like. It remained in family hands until the 1990s, when it was given to the Boonsborough Historical Society and subsequently reconstructed near its original site in Donalds, South Carolina, with

Fiure 4-4. The Templeton-Drake cabin (ca. 1764) near Donalds, South Carolina. Photo courtesy of author.

its original doors still intact. Another well-preserved log cabin is the Robert Morris home in east central McCormick County.[6] A less well preserved example is the Wideman-Hanvey house built by Adam Wideman, which still has the original logs supporting the porch. Particularly interesting is a late eighteenth-century log cabin built next to John's (imm 1772) land that survived into the late twentieth century (Figure 4-5). It may have belonged to the Russell family; the 1894 Grier survey shows M. M. Russell in this location.[7] We know from old photographs and descriptions of the structure that planed logs were slotted into corner posts and the cabin had two front doors leading to large paneled rooms that were wainscoted (presumably later additions when the cabin may also been an inn). A half flight of stairs outside led to a loft above. An early nineteenth-century conservation cabin (circa 1825) from Cedar Springs can now been seen in Abbeville (Figure 4-6).

Figure 4-5. Photograph of a late eighteenth-century log cabin, probably belonging to the Russell Family, near John Pressly's land on the old Long Cane to Charleston Road (present-day Eden Hall Road). Courtesy of Jim Bates, Greenwood, South Carolina.

Figure 4-6. Conservation cabin (ca. 1815) from Cedar Springs and now in Abbeville, South Carolina. Photograph courtesy of author.

Seceders and Covenanters in the New World

Early settlers would have almost immediately started the nucleus of a church and a communal Sabbath service, even if it was only outdoors. Nearby forts often served the dual purpose of safety and as places for community worship and basic schooling. The church, whether it was Presbyterian, Associate, Reformed, or Lutheran, was a central meeting place allowing for the exchange of information, assistance, and fostering of new friendships. Probably the most important activity in David and John's lives, apart from the consuming task of farming, was their worship both at home and in a communal setting. The Ninety Six District, apart from the New Bordeaux and Londonborough settlements, was mainly a Scotch-Irish community with settlers from Virginia and Ulster who were bound together by ethnic and religious ties and soon by extended family relationships. Congregations would have met even without a minister or stated supply, relying on previously ordained elders when possible. David and John would have held family worship every weekday morning and evening in their homes, consisting of Psalm singing, reading from the Bible, and reciting from the Westminster Confessions of Faith. On Saturdays, families prepared for the Sabbath, cleaning and cooking food. Sabbath services would have consisted of a morning and afternoon session, and even in the early years some type of Communion service would have taken place in the spring and fall.

John and David probably first worshipped at the Lower Long Cane Meeting House, which was organized as an Associate Presbyterian Church in 1771, probably with the assistance of Reverend Thomas Clark during his visit to the Waxhaws. This young congregation of new settlers would have been worshipping together for a period of time prior to being organized. Some were among Reverend Clark's parishioners who sailed with him from Ulster in 1764 and then went on to South

Carolina. Among them were John and Thomas Foster, James McBride, John Hawthorn, John McComb, John and Thomas Gibson, and James Young. In her history of the Lower Long Cane ARP Church, Nora Davis describes the first meeting house as located at Fort Long Cane, a settler fort about a mile from the current church on the east side of Long Cane Creek.[8] This site, later known as Laurel Hill, would have been, as the crow flies, no more than three or four miles from the Pressly brothers' land. This was a strategic location not only because of the pre-existing fort but also because a core group of Seceder settlers (several of whom or their sons would later become elders in the congregation) lived nearby, including, John Foster Jr., John Patterson, and Mathew Shanks. Reverend William Ronaldson, a Seceder minister at Loughaghery, County Down, from 1762 to 1773, became the church's first stated supply in 1774; and sometime in the 1770s, the church moved to the west side of Long Cane Creek, where a simple log meeting house was erected on or near where the present-day church and cemetery stand on the Long Cane Road to Troy (SC 33–36). This land, thought to have originally belonged to James Hutchinson, closely corresponds to where Hutchinson's plat is located on Thompson's map. The earliest marked grave in the Lower Long Cane Cemetery dates from 1790, and there are some 150 early unmarked graves.

This move across Long Cane Creek may have been one of the reasons a second Associate meeting house, Cedar Creek, was organized nearby circa 1779 to 1780, but it was probably functioning as a small congregation before that date and possibly while John Pressly was still alive. Given the fact John's son, William, was well educated prior to coming to the Colonies and that he became an Elder early on in the history of the congregation, it is possible that John, himself, had some leadership role in the Seceder Church in Ulster and was a leader among the Seceder settlers in the 1770s. It is also possible that there was a sufficiently large enough core group to form a new congregation. It is interesting to speculate that William, given his education, may have been preparing to enter the ministry before he sailed. As noted earlier, it was the custom in the backcountry (as it was in Scotland and Ireland) for members of good families to be Ruling Elders of the Church, a distinction William later held at Cedar Spring Church, probably as early as 1790. Clark may have helped organize Cedar Creek when he came to the area in 1779 as part of an order from the Associate Presbytery to visit "that part of his organization that settled in Abbeville, South Carolina." The new congregation may have been organized because of minor doctrinaire disagreements over worship, which was a not uncommon occurrence among Seceders, and frequently led to new splinter congregations.

Robert Latham describes Cedar Creek's first log building as follows: "The first house erected by the congregation was built of logs about two miles southeast of the present site. The name of the church was derived from a Cedar tree near the spring where the first church was built."[9] Nora Davis additionally noted that the church was a little more than half a mile from the Kerr House, which was near the

Figure 4-7. Map of a portion of Long Cane area and Hard Labor section, showing key early churches and cemeteries and other important early landmarks. Google map of a section of Abbeville, Greenwood, Edgefield, and McCormick Counties in South Carolina.

A. Little Run (Little River) Congregation (1770s)
B. Little River
C. Lower Long Cane, later Hopewell Presbyterian Church
D. Gray-Reid-Weed Cemetery
E. Indian Massacre (1760)
F. Tittle Cemetery
G. Lower Long Cane ARP Church (1771)
H. Long Cane Creek
I. John Pressly plat
J. John Hearst plat
K. Barksdale Ferry Road
L. Possible location of Cedar Creek Meeting House (ca. 1779)
M. Cedar Spring ARP Church
N. Whitehall Plantation (General Williamson)
O. Scotch Cross
P. Village of Ninety Six
Q. Upper Long Cane Presbyterian Cemetery
R. Abbeville
S. David Pressly plat
T. Hard Labor Creek
U. Lutheran Church later known as Swamp Meeting House
V. Reedy Creek

junction of Cedar Springs and Sumter Forest Roads. This would place it near a tributary of Reedy Branch, which at one point could have been called Cedar Creek.[10] The Cedar Creek Congregation, whose initial membership was predominantly Seceders, was the most important church in terms of the Pressly family. It was renamed Cedar Spring Associate Reformed Church in 1790; and in 1791, while Reverend Clark was still alive, it moved to its current site in Cedar Springs. Sometime in the late nineteenth or early twentieth century, it began to be referred to as the Cedar Springs (not Spring) ARP church.

The third Associate Reformed Church, which was also said to have been formed by some of Clark's original Ulster congregation, was Little Run (later Little River). Its exact location is uncertain, but it may have been some four miles west of the Old Hopewell Presbyterian Church near Little River and Calhoun Falls, close to Arthur Patton's fort (Figure 4-7). Two other important early Associate churches located in the lower Ninety Six District were the Kings' Creek and Cannon's Creek Meeting Houses in current day Newberry County, which were founded by Reverend John Renwick, circa 1767 to 1772.

There were also several early Presbyterian and other Protestant denominational churches of significance established in the Ninety Six District during this early period. Patrick Calhoun helped organize a meeting house at Fort Boone in 1760 to serve the Calhoun Settlement, and in an Act dated February 7, 1780, it was incorporated "as the Presbyterian Church called Fort Boone congregation at Long Cane Settlement." In 1788, the church was renamed the Hopewell Presbyterian Church; two cemeteries are connected with this church. Another Presbyterian Church, the Upper Long Cane in Abbeville, which was started in 1756, had a sufficient number of families to be organized, in 1763, as the Upper Long Cane Presbyterian Church. Reverend John Harris, an ardent Patriot, was its first stated supply, starting in 1772.[11] He also became pastor of the Fort Boone congregation and of a third Presbyterian Church called Bull Town Church, organized in 1772. Bull Town later moved to the site of the present graveyard originally known as the Bull Town Cemetery, and renamed Rocky River Presbyterian Church.[12] A fourth Presbyterian Church was located at Saluda, near Greenville.

Much closer to the Presslys (at the junction of Eden Hall Road and Millway) was the German Lutheran settlement. In 1770, the Church of England's Society for the Propagation of the Gospel in Foreign parts sent Reverend Samuel Frederick Lucius from Charleston to the settlement where he performed numerous baptisms. The group eventually organized here, the German Lutheran Church of St. George. It was later acquired by the Tranquil Methodist Church in 1805 and became more commonly known as the Swamp Meeting House (as it appears on Robert Mills's 1820 map, (Figure 9-1). A large, flat field stone said to be the step to the community log house is now in the Greenwood Historical Society in Greenwood, South Carolina. Unmarked graves once at the site are no longer visible.

Kinship and Enduring Friendships and the Death of John Pressly, 1778

Living next to David Pressly (imm 1767) in the Hard Labor Creek community in the last quarter of the eighteenth century was a third Pressly family, almost certainly closely related. It is not known when Jane Pressly and her husband settled there because no surviving immigration records or pre-Revolutionary War land deeds refer to them. They could have purchased already developed land from an early settler and therefore not be recorded in these pre-Revolutionary War plats. Circumstantial and related documentary evidence, including 1820s survey plats executed for Col. John Hearst that refers to the estate of William Pressly, strongly suggest that the given name of Jane's husband was William.[13] The family most likely arrived in the 1770s, either from Virginia or Ireland, and could have purchased improved land from an earlier settler (possibly even David Pressly) and therefore would not have been recorded on passenger lists or in bounty grants before the South Carolina Council. In his 1785 will, David leaves his son, David Jr., a parcel of land that is "next land laid out to me, William Pressly and William Drise [*sic*] [for Dorris] survey," indicating William Pressly owned land next to him before he fled to Charleston in 1781.[14] The South Carolina Land Office closed in 1775 and did not reopen until 1784, so there are no land records from the intervening years. In 1786, a William "Presly" acquired seventy-nine acres next to James Crosier, David Pressly, and land he already owned. He was dead by 1790, when his wife, Jane, appears in the 1790 Abbeville census as head of household. In 1791 she acquired an additional sixty-eight acres adjoining her land (see p. 65). What is indisputable is that Jane Pressly and her husband were living adjacent to David Pressly (imm 1767), and it is unlikely this was a coincidence. They were almost certainly close relatives. He could have been a brother of John and David, hence the confusion with the three Williamsburg brothers who shared the same given names or a cousin or an uncle related through their father's or grandfather's generation. It is interesting to speculate as to whether this Pressly family could have come from Virginia and therefore linked with James Presley, with whom the family shares a close DNA match. Their presence in this small rural community by the late 1770s or early 1780s certainly adds a new dimension to our understanding of our family's first decade in South Carolina. It is also a reminder of the extent to which familial connections bound settlers together.

Many early settlers formed close friendships that were to endure over several generations, and two families, in particular, were to play an important role in the lives of John's and David's children, the Pattersons and the Hearsts. They merit a brief diversion here. Samuel Patterson (1725–1791) and his family came over on the *Free Mason* with John Pressly (imm 1772). Although Samuel himself did not fight in the Revolutionary War, his son, John, substituted for him and many of his sons were staunch patriots. He may have been a man of some education in that he designates in his will specific books to be distributed to various family members.

Many of his children, like John's, were deeply involved in the Associate and later the Associate Reformed Presbyterian Church. His son, Samuel Patterson Jr., was an elder at the combined Lower Long Cane Church and Cedar Spring Associate Reformed Presbyterian Church which shared elders (Samuel Sr. may have briefly served as an elder as well) and was later elected a ruling elder in the Hopewell Congregation in Preble County, Ohio. As noted earlier, John's son, David, married Samuel's daughter, Jane (ca. 1789); and his son, John, married Margaret Patterson, another daughter, in 1798. Members of the Pressly and Patterson families witnessed each other's legal documents, served as occasional executors of each other's estates well into the 1820s, and remained sufficiently close enough that between 1807 and 1813 many members of both families traveled to Preble County, Ohio (see Chapter 8) and helped form a new community there. The Patterson family name was frequently used as the middle name for Pressly children over several generations, including for four of Jane Patterson's and David Pressly's children.

The other family that was to be central in the lives of many of John's and David Pressly's descendants was that of John Hearst (imm 1766). This was a notably close and intimate connection, and numerous marriages occurred over several generations as these two families became increasingly intertwined; the Hearsts and Presslys were neighbors, friends, and kin, and these bonds continued well into the 1850s. They attended the same church and served as executors, administrators, and witnesses in each other's wills. John Hearst (imm 1766), married first to Elizabeth Knox, possibly to a second wife, and lastly to Mary O'Bryan, arrived in Charleston probably in 1766, when he received a bounty grant for four hundred acres in Belfast Township.[15] His son, John Jr. (ca. 1754–1808), received one hundred acres nearby. John Hearst Sr. and his sons, John Jr. and Joseph (1760–1814), were Patriots and served as privates in the Revolutionary War. These families lived near one another and forged close, interdependent relationships as they survived the Revolutionary War and transformed the frontier, where they lived, into a prosperous backcountry farming community. See Part III for further discussion about the Hearsts and their relationship with the Presslys.

A little less than three years after John Pressly settled in the Hard Labor Creek area, the first land battle of the Revolutionary War, south of New England, was fought in the nearby village of Ninety Six. Tensions had been building between Whigs and Loyalists for several months, both sides having raised sizeable militias; in November 1775, some 1,900 Loyalist militiamen laid siege to Fort Ninety Six, which was defended by 600 Whig recruits. Loyalists and Patriots negotiated a truce and the siege ended effectively as a stalemate. The backcountry experienced further disruptions in 1776, when a British led attack pitted the Cherokees, Tories, and bandits against the Whigs in a conflict sometimes called the Second Cherokee War. For the most part, however, during the early years of the war, most backcountry settlers preferred to stay out of the political fray.

We do not know with certainty John's loyalties during the early years of the War. By 1778, less than six years after he arrived, he was dead. The only thing we know about his death is what JSP tells us in his *Brief Memoir of the Pressly Family*. He found John's will in the Office of the Ordinary in Charleston and wrote: "Fourth. There is also found the will of John Pressly of Ninety Six District. The testator deceased in 1778." He goes on to say that John's executors were David Pressly (either his son or brother) and John Livingstone and that the will named "his widow, Elizabeth, and four sons, David, William, John, and Joseph, and two daughters, Mary Patterson and Martha. It bequeathed land on Rocky Creek to his daughter, Mary Patterson . . . . and a tract of three hundred acres (300) to be equally divided between his sons David and William. This last named tract was probably situated on or near Hard Labor Creek." JSP also notes that John's daughter, Mary Patterson, "who[m] he did not know personally," was married to Robert Martin of Rocky Creek near Vernon's Ford.[16] The sequence of names, presumably as they appeared in the will, most likely follows the birth order making Joseph the youngest son. It is possible that John served the Loyalist cause during the first years of the Revolutionary War as he was listed as deceased in several Loyalist records and pay abstracts dating from 1781 and 1782. It is also possible that his brother, David, listed him as a Loyalist in order to receive money for his orphans.

We do not know where John is buried. In 2005, a "memorial," number 10371239, was posted on the Find A Grave website, listing John Pressly as buried in what was said to be the Old Cedar Spring Cemetery with coordinates N34 1 56 and W82 19 21.[17] On-site explorations of these coordinates did not reveal any graves. However, they turn out to be very near the so-called Tittle Cemetery located in Sumter National Forest. This cemetery is near Laurel Hill (although on the other side of Sumter Forest Road S24-177) where the first Lower Long Cane Meeting House was organized in 1771. It is off an unmarked dirt road that branches off from Sumter Forest Road before it crosses over Reedy Branch and closely follows a late eighteenth-century road that crossed Long Cane Creek at Bradley bridge and passed near the present location of Lower Long Cane Church. Portions of the old road bed are still visible. There are numerous head and foot fieldstones and the shallow indentations of some additional forty more graves scattered across the site.[18] A recent archaeological survey executed for the US Forest Service indicates Tittle cemetery (Site #38MC2571) was a communal cemetery and may have contained as many as one hundred graves. There are no references to John Pressly's headstone in any survey records, although this does not preclude that one had been identified near the site and subsequently lost, removed, or destroyed, because this area is subject to logging and controlled burns.

Today only three engraved headstones, dating from 1789 to 1844, survive in Tittle Cemetery. One is for Jane McBride, who died August 8, 1789, age eighteen, carved by a local carver, Andrew McComb[s], a millwright and owner of McComb's Mill on nearby Long Cane Creek. Jane may have been the daughter of the previously mentioned James McBride, an original grantor of the land, who came over with Reverend Thomas Clark and was later a Ruling Elder for the Church. The second stone is for John Patterson, who died January 5, 1824 (Figure 4-8); and the third for

Figure 4-8. Gravestone of John Patterson, died 1824, at Tittle Cemetery, Abbeville County, South Carolina. Photograph courtesy of author.

Rachael Shanks who died September 30, 1842, and was the wife of James J. Shanks, a grandson of Matthew Shanks. Both John Patterson and Mathew Shanks were also original grantees for nearby land. Alexander McBride and Mathew Shanks came over on the same ship as David Pressly, the *Earl of Hillsborough,* in 1767; while John Patterson came over on one of Reverend Martin's ships in 1772. What is significant is that James McBride, Hugh McBride, Mathew Shanks, and John Patterson were later elders of the combined Cedar Spring and Lower Long Cane congregations and that this communal cemetery had a close relationship with the early Associate Reformed Presbyterian Church and the first settlers in the area. As such, it would have been an appropriate place for John to have been buried.

Tittle Cemetery is one of several important late eighteenth-century and early nineteenth-century burial sites in the area. Another cemetery from the period, much better preserved, is the so-called Gray-Reid-Weed Cemetery inventoried as 38AB365 in the US Forest Service records and notable for its beautiful soapstone graves (Figure 4-9). The earliest surviving gravestone is the beautifully carved soapstone for Rebecca Gray, who died on September 15, 1778, at the age of five months followed by that of Arthur Gray Senior, who died in 1779 at the age of thirty-six. Several other members of the Gray family are buried here (on land granted to Gray in 1771) with engraved soapstone headstones, including the son of Reverend Daniel Gray, who was a pastor at the Hopewell Presbyterian Church, about a quarter of a mile away, as well as other families associated with the church. The cemetery is located off Mulberry Road in Calhoun Falls, South Carolina and was almost certainly associated with the Hopewell Presbyterian Church. Remnants of small family burial sites and larger "communal" or extended kin cemeteries are scattered across the Long Cane District of the Sumter National Forest. Family sites were generally adjacent or near dwellings, and often there are traces of an abandoned road leading to them. Many communal burial sites, marked only by rough "fieldstones," have been identified by the US Forest Service or by individuals looking to identify and preserve these sites.[19]

Figure 4-9. Gray-Reid-Weed Cemetery, Calhoun Falls, South Carolina. Courtesy of Jim Bates.

Chapter 5

The Revolutionary War: Chaos and Upheaval

The Revolutionary War had an enormous impact on the backcountry. Tensions among settlers reflected animosities simmering from the earlier Regulator movement; many Whigs were more closely identified with the earlier Regulators. During the early years of the war, most backcountry settlers tried to stay neutral and focus on protecting their land and own economic advancement, sometimes switching back and forth in their sympathies. Although battles were fought in other areas of the state, relative calm prevailed in the lower Ninety Six District, even though there were organized militias and occasional local skirmishes (Figure 5-1).

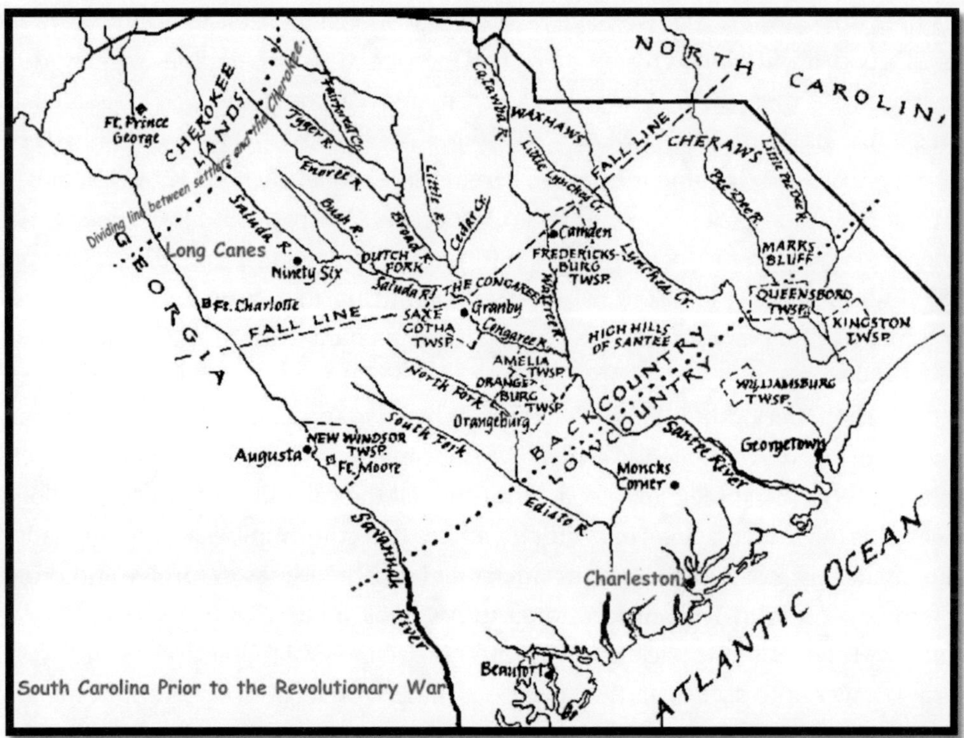

Figure 5-1. Map showing South Carolina prior to the Revolutionary War.

However, after the fall of Charleston in 1780 and the massacre of Patriot troops at the Battle of Waxhaws on May 29, 1780, previously neutral backcountry settlers, pressured by Patriot and Tory militia, were forced to take sides as the renewal of hostilities began. In the summer of 1780, the ranks of Patriot militia units grew, and these irregular troops, adopting the tactics of guerrilla warfare, inflicted heavy military and psychological damage on the British cause. Many of the Patriot militia leaders, including Andrew Pickens from Virginia, had been seasoned in their earlier skirmishes with the Cherokee Indians. The Long Cane Creek and Hard Labor Creek areas and the upper Long Cane Church, where Pickens was a parishioner, tended primarily to be Patriot supporters, although there were still numerous Loyalists. Ninety Six became a Loyalist stronghold early in the war, and there was a high concentration of Loyalists living between the Broad and Saluda Rivers. Patrick Calhoun, also a Patriot, was an important political figure during this period. He was a member of the Common House of Assembly from 1769 to 1772 and a member of the First Provincial Congress in 1775 and Second Provincial Congress from 1775 to 1776. By the war's end, he was a major planter with a spacious eight-room, two-story dwelling. By 1790, he had thirty-one slaves.

David Pressly (imm 1767) may have tried to remain neutral in the early stages of the war. In 1779, he is listed as "David Pressley" on the Grand Jury List and as "David Presley" on "the Petit Jury List for 96-District Long Canes & Places Adjacent."[1] Although not every resident was included on these lists, they are the closest thing to a household census of South Carolina that we have before the 1790 Federal Census. Only free white males of good reputation who owned "real" property were eligible for jury duty. Ostensibly, these men were Whigs; however, many became active Loyalists after the British capture of Charleston in May 1780. By June 1780, David, who would have been nearly fifty years old, became a Loyalist, serving in Colonel Richard King's Regiment, Long Cane Militia, as part of Captain Jesse Campbell's Company and the Upper Ninety Six brigade. He served for six months from June 12 to December 13, 1780, and was paid for 183 days of service. His son, Samuel, served during this same period in Captain George Neals' Company, which was also part of Richard King's Regiment. Another "David Presley," who was probably John's (imm 1772) son, served for three months during the same period in John Sloan's Company, also under Col. King's command.

One cannot underestimate the chaos and upheaval that took place in the Ninety Six District. This area, like others in the backcountry, felt the calamitous impact of a bloody civil war. The devastating effect of splitting families and communities and congregations was not made any easier by the fact that men often switched sides to survive and protect their families. As John W. Gordon noted in his book *South Carolina and the America Revolution:* "The war in the backcountry would prove integral to the larger struggle, but it was also a war unto itself—fratricidal, vicious, fought on its own terms and sometimes for its own reasons."[2] This was especially true in the Ninety Six District from 1780 to 1782. Writing from Camden in 1781, Nathaniel Greene, commander of the Revolutionary armies, wrote despairingly that "The Whigs and Tories are butchering one another hourly." He later wrote that the backcountry was "full of little armed parties who follow their resentments with little less than savage fury" (Greene to Reed, May 14, 1781).

Divided loyalties split neighbors and families. If we look at the small microcosm of David's neighborhood and family, we see these divisions. David and his eldest son,

Samuel, and his brother's son, David, are fighting as Loyalists by June 1780. However, his own son, also named David, was a Patriot, having entered service in 1776, fighting the Cherokees. He fought again in September 1780 as a private in Captain McCauley's company under General Francis Marion, two months after his father and older brother, Samuel, enlisted as Tories in July 1780. He served a total of twelve and a half months. Samuel Patterson's sons were active Patriots. The Neil family, who lived next to John Pressly (imm 1772), represents another family with divided loyalties: Andrew, George, Thomas, and John Neil were Patriots, whereas George and Henry Neil were Tories. The same was true of the Lindsey family who came over with John Pressly (imm 1772). In terms of neighbors, those who were Whigs included the Hearsts, McClintons, Croziers, Weeds, McCulloughs, Henry Foster, Charles and Samuel Hammond, William Gaston, Benjamin and Richard Tutt, John Cannon, John Gray, Benjamin and Samuel Lindsay, Abner Perrin, Jr. (Quarter Master), Adam Wideman, and the Thompsons. Other nearby neighbors who were Loyalists included John Hamilton, John Long, William Dorris, George McCombe, Thomas and James Lindsay, the McBrides, and many of the German Lutheran settlers who, in gratitude to the King's earlier support, were Loyalists. They included Arthur Reid, John Gamble, and Conrad Marks.

It would be interesting to research more deeply the role churches played during the Revolutionary War, especially in congregations with divided loyalties. We know that William Ronaldson was the minister or stated supply at Lower Long Cane from 1774 to 1781, which was when he was relieved of his duties because of his strong Tory sentiment. Clearly the Lower Long Cane congregation had, at least by 1780, strong Whig sympathies. We also know that Reverend Thomas Clark, who most likely helped organize the Cedar Creek congregation in 1779 and returned to the area in 1782, was a staunch Patriot. When the war broke out, Reverend Martin also supported the Patriot cause and openly urged others to do so. His Meeting House burned down in 1780, and he was imprisoned but eventually took refuge in Mecklenburg County, North Carolina, returning to Rocky Creek after the war. He was one of the few Covenanter preachers who later refused to join the newly formed Associate Reformed Presbyterian Church in 1782.

As we have seen, the first battle of the war in the South was fought in the nearby village of Ninety Six in 1775. Beginning in 1780, several battles were fought near where the Pressly family lived, including the battle at Long Cane (December 12, 1780) just a few miles from John Pressly's bounty plat between Patterson Bridge over Long Cane Creek on what is today State Secondary Road S-33-117 and Greenwood County line (Figures 5-2). British encampments were very close to where David lived, in the area today between where Barksdale Ferry Road and Cedar Springs Road intersect Route 10. Battles also took place at Hammond Store on December 30, 1780; the ongoing battle around Abbeville, which lasted from May 12 to June 19, 1781; Beatttie's Mill on March 21 or 24, 1781,[3] the Battle of Stevens Creek on October 5, 1781, and White Hall in December 1781).

From May 22 to June 18, 1781, Major General Nathanael Greene led one thousand troops in an unsuccessful twenty-eight-day siege against the 550 Loyalists at Ninety Six. The siege,

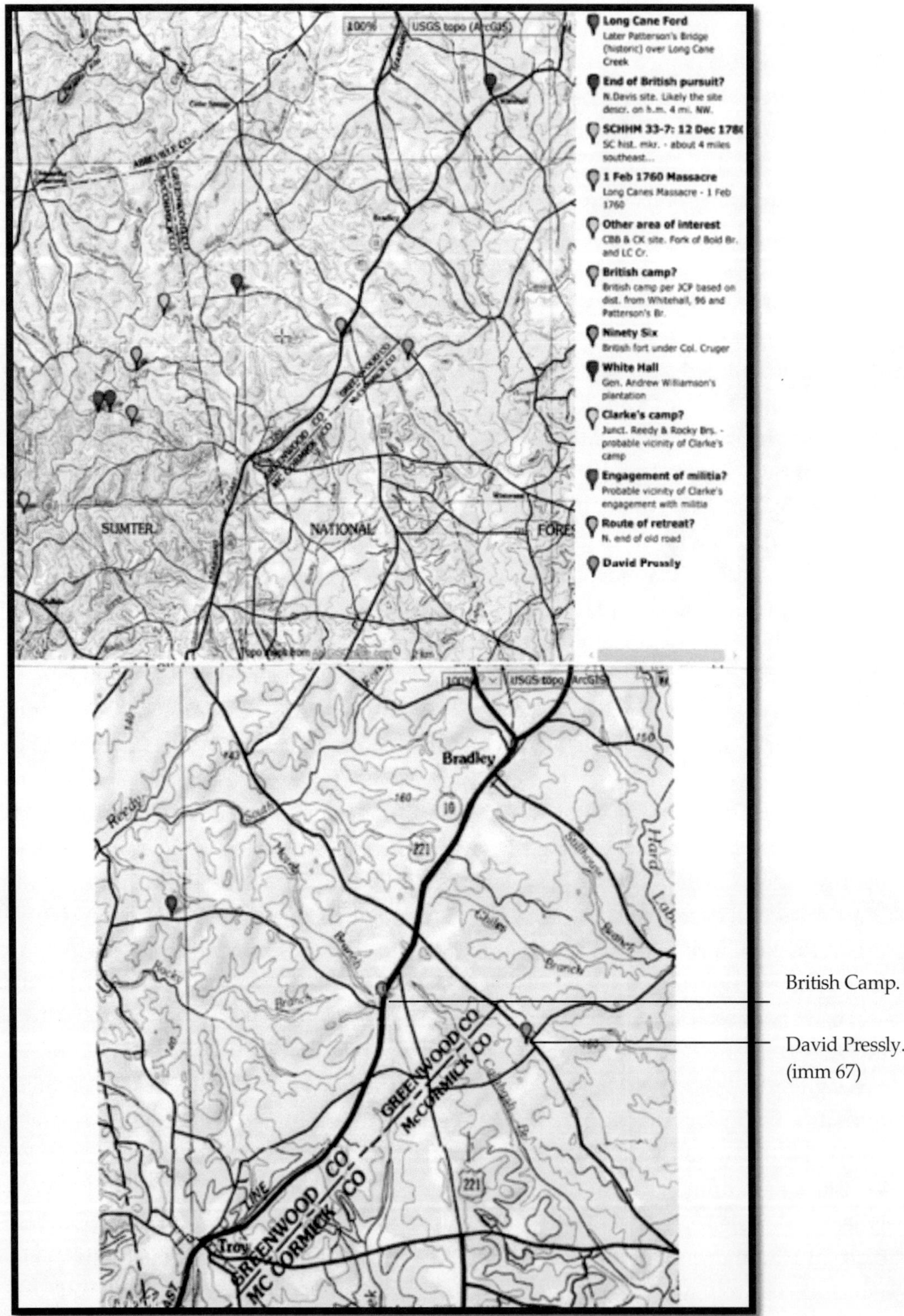

Figure 5-2. Sites related to encampments and Battle of Long Cane Creek indicating close proximity to where David Pressly lived and John Pressly's children lived. Artifacts related to Revolutionary War have been found near the proposed site of the British camp.

the longest of the entire war, centered on a recently built earthen fortification known as Star Fort. Despite having more troops, Greene's patriots were eventually unsuccessful in taking the town. During the siege, many women and children sought refuge within the village. By the end of the war, however, the village of Ninety Six was in ruins.

In June 1781, following the victory at Ninety Six, Lt. Col. Richard Cruger offered to resettle Loyalist families from the area around the Ninety Six, Hard Labor Creek, and Long Cane, on plantations in the low country. David was almost certainly among the more than eight hundred men who had served the Loyalist cause in the Ninety Six District and left the area with their families in June 1781—many bringing along with them horses and wagons filled with their provisions. The Loyalist evacuation also included many widows and young children. The group gathered at the Star Fort and then began their journey along the Charleston Road, which is still visible today. Many of the Loyalist Palatines followed the Loyalist troops to Charleston, fleeing first to Rawdontown, and then under the leadership of Col. John Hamilton, second in command of the Stevens Creek Militia Regiment, went on to Halifax, Nova Scotia. A few who stayed were also among the distressed refugees with David Pressly in Charleston.

Most of these loyalists, including David, ended up in refugee camps in Charleston rather than the promised plantations, where they lived in destitute conditions, with many dying of disease.[4] The largest group of refugees came from the Ninety Six District. David's son, "Samuel Presley," probably did not join him because he later served in Brigadier General Robert Cunningham's Brigade from June 14 to December 13, 1782. When David fled to Charleston with his family, two of his deceased brother John's children were almost certainly with him. We don't know if John's wife, Elizabeth, was still alive and also with them. However, by July 1782, the children were listed as orphans. The Report of Distressed refugees from the Ninety Six District, under the inspection of Thomas Edghill, Thomas Fletchall, and John Hamilton, Charleston, July 1782, lists as #38, "Pressley, John, dead, left 2 children orphans" and as #5, "Pressley, David, with a wife and 5 children." On this same list was David's neighbor, "William Dorris, left orphan, one child."[5] The Report ordered five dollars to be paid to each man and woman and two dollars to each child. In another list of "distressed refugees," David and his wife, Hester, are listed as #60 and "Presly, John's orphans with payment rec'd by Hester Presly" as #61. Also on this list were neighbors George McComb, #47, Henry Wyley, #84, William Dorris's son, James, #20, and Arthur Reid, #62.[6] Distressed refugees were the lowest and largest class of refugees and received the least amount of available money. John's children, Martha and John Pressly, were registered at John Bell's Refugee School from November 1, 1781, to January 31, 1782, and from February 1 to April 30, 1782. David's two youngest sons, John and William Pressly, are listed for the periods April 30 to August 1, 1782, and August 1 to September 31, 1782.[7] John Bell, a farmer from Hard Labor Creek and a militiaman in Richard King's Regiment, conducted a school for refugees during an eleven-month period from November 1781 through September 1782.

The British left Charleston on December 14, 1782. The Pressly name does not appear on the Confiscated Lists, published in the Royal Gazette Confiscation lists of March 20, 1782, but a "David Pressly" Sr. and Jr. and "Samuel Pressly" appear on Col. Robert Anderson's Patriots' Enemies list of 1783.[8] The only other thing that we know about David from this period is that, after the British retreat, he may have tried to serve as a merchant of sorts, lending money with interest, or that he was selling his own holdings, including one slave. In 1783, he had a transaction with a Dickinson Watkins for thirty pounds sterling for Watkins to purchase "diverse goods, wares, and merchandise," and a Roan horse and a black man for a fixed amount of interest. This transaction was later part of a legal dispute that was not settled until 1794, with David's estate losing and being forced to pay fifty pounds sterling in damages.[9]

David died on January 5, 1785, in Charleston, and his will was probated on January 15, 1785, when son, David Jr., and three Loyalists friends, Henry Geddes, and George and Henry "McCombe," were appointed executors. By this time, his wife, Esther, was presumably dead, because she is not mentioned in his will. His son-in-law, Henry Wyly, along with Casimer Patrick and John Pattison, witnessed his will, in which "David Pressly, Long Cane settlement, Ninety Six District, planter, now residing in Charleston" left "Sons: eldest Samuel, plantation of W branch of Stephens Creek; 2nd David, land on S branch Hard Laebuor [*sic*] Creek next land laid out to me, William Pressly and William Drise's [*sic*] survey." Another transcription of this passage reads, "2nd David, a tract on the Southern branch at Hard Labour Creek, bounded on land laid out to me and William Pressly to have full right to that side nixt [*sic*] to William Drises [*sic*] survey." (Drises was his neighbor Dorris) He left his "Daus: eldest Agnes [Wyly], alias Agnes Pressly, (fifty acres) land on any square or corner of the survey where on I lived, except that part already mentioned to my second son David, then to her (eldest) dau. Elizabeth Wyly . . . remaining lands divided among my children Mary Ann, William, John, and Esther; residue of estate to said children and son-in-law."[10]

After David's death, his youngest children returned to the land where their life had first begun in the Colonies and lived with their older brothers, Samuel and David Pressly Jr, both of whom were married and were to remain in Abbeville County in the succeeding decades. We can also be fairly confident that by 1785 all of John's (imm 1772) children were also living nearby on or near their father's bounty land. Now, all orphaned, they would have had the comfort of their cousins as the two families regrouped after the loss of their parents, painful separations, and the chaos of the war.

Notes

Preface

1. In 1996, my father-in-law, Dr. William L. Pressly (1908–2001), president and founder of The Westminster Schools, Atlanta, wrote an unpublished *Pressly Family History and Memoir* mainly devoted to Reverend E. E. Pressly and subsequent generations. He also wrote a memoir about his father, Reverend Paul Adam Pressly (1979) and worked extensively on the family ancestry tree.

2. Jim Gettys has shared his research with family members and in 2005, he distributed a draft of an unpublished eighteen-page article, "The Pressly Family of Ninety Six Judicial District in the Eighteenth Century." It provided a brief history of the family's arrival in the 1760s and 1770s and gave me a helpful introduction to South Carolina backcountry history. He has also provided me with copies of some of the articles that he and Lowry Ware have found in nineteenth-century publications. I am immensely grateful to him for so generously sharing information. I am also grateful to Paul Gettys for looking at the Hart archives in Rock Hill, South Carolina.

3. In 1930, Prof. William Pressly, son of John Bonner Pressly (a brother of Reverend Paul Adam Pressly), received documents from Dr. William A. Pressly (WAP) of Rock Hill, South Carolina, a descendant of David Pressly (imm 1767). These documents were originally owned by his uncle, Judge Benjamin Chapman Pressley (1815–1896), son of David's (imm 1767) son, William Pressly, who lived in York County. He also received some material from Charles Payson Pressly, a grandson of Dr. George W. Pressly. The current whereabouts of these documents is not known. Prof. Pressly's *The Pressly Family* (ca. 1980) is the most complete genealogy of the family to date, although it contains misinformation about the family's arrival in South Carolina and some errors regarding dates, names, and how family members are related.

4. John S. Pressly's (JSP's) unpublished three-page *A Brief Memoir of the Pressly Family in the United States* was written in the decade before his death in 1863. It was later appended to by either Charles Payson Pressly (the son of Dr. Joseph Lowry Pressly) of Cedar Springs and Augusta or Professor Pressly of Due West sometime before 1940. The typewritten transcript of this memoir is in the Williamsburg County Historical Society, Kingstree, South Carolina. It is also reprinted in John Renning Phillips, *The Good Intent* (New York, 2007, Magnolia Group Press, pp. 393–7). JSP also wrote several other short articles/memoirs about himself and members of the family.

5. Historical and Archaeological Report—Robert W. Benson, *Cultural Resources Overview of the Sumter National Forest,* April 2006, Southeastern Archaeological Services, Inc.

6. This type of phonetic spelling is common for the period. The surname Hearst, for example, was also spelled Hurst, Harse, Hearse, Herst, and Herse; and a neighboring land owner identified as William Drise in David Pressly's (imm 1767) 1785 will also appears in records as Doris, Dorris (his actual name), and Darrisse. Misspellings also occurred on gravestones.

7. Judge B. C. Pressley noted in his letter dated January 30, 1882, to J. N. Miller, "You will see I spell my name Pressley. It was so on my Father's Tombstone (William, son of David, imm 1767) but I think a mistake of his Executor" reprinted in Phillips, *The Good Intent* (New York, 2007, Magnolia Group Press, pp. 390–1). This same type of mistake also occurred on Dr. George W. Pressly's tombstone when he was buried in Cedar Springs

Church cemetery in 1870 and on that of his cousin, Reverend Samuel Patterson Pressly, who is buried in Athens, Georgia. Both mistakenly read "Pressley."

Prologue

Chapter 1: Ancestral Roots: Searching for Connections

1. Joan Pressly Kirk discovered this material while researching her family and shared it with Jim Gettys circa 2005. I returned to these Scottish Parish records and uncovered additional information that provides a small window into David's life in the late 1750s and early 1760s. At the time, Kirk believed her Aberdeen ancestors were a different family line. Subsequent DNA information supports this assessment. Her family was descended from a George Pressly (b. 1798), who lived near Aberdeen and whose descendants moved to Glasgow in the nineteenth century.

2. The current whereabouts of the Bible is unknown. David Pressly Jr., the son of David Pressly (imm 1767), refers to the Bible in his 1830s affidavit requesting a Revolutionary War Pension (W24917) noting it belonged to his first cousin David Pressly, Sr. (1756–1818), already dead.

3. This brick wall is shared by all of the families with whom I have corresponded that are in the same DNA subgroup mentioned in this chapter. No one has been able to identify conclusive family connections prior to emigrating.

4. Additionally, a William "Presly" is baptized December 30, 1753, in the Parish of Halifax, St. John the Baptist, West Yorkshire. There were also several clusters of "Priestley" families living in Brodsworth, Yorkshire, including the family of Joseph Priestley. There are also several families in Wiltshire that merit further research as well as one in Nottinghamshire. A Samuel "Presly" was baptized February 8, 1712, in Great Yarmouth, Norfolk. His parents were probably the same William and Mary listed two years later, on August 26 (24), 1716, when a Samuel "Presey" is baptized in Bishopstrow (stone), Wiltshire. There are other interesting seventeenth- and eighteenth-century Wiltshire references that need further investigation, including the marriage of John Pressly and Elizabeth Hall on August 30, 1738, in Salisbury, Wiltshire, and the arrival in the American Colonies in 1740s of an indentured Wiltshire servant named John Presley.

5. Test results within this surname project were initially sorted into four distinct DNA subgroups (A to D), with a fifth subgroup listing members with insufficient representation to fit into a distinct line. Although this project is no longer current, new Family Tree DNA tests results are still added if an individual joins this list. Bill's test result fit into subgroup C composed mainly of descendants of James Presley and of immigrants David and John Pressly.

6. There is a thirty-six out of thirty-seven-marker match (one genetic distance removed) with Brad Thomas Presley, and a thirty-five out of thirty-seven-marker match (two genetic markers removed; the latter in sequences where mutations frequently occur) with William Cameron Presley. Both also identify James Presley as the father of their most distantly known ancestor.

7. M. J. Green, compiled by, *Family Marriages & Bonds, 1780–1790—Rockbridge Co., VA,* lists a marriage bond for September 18, 1780, between "William Presley and Esther Cowen"—bondsman: Robert Ewing. Augusta, Rockbridge, and Russell counties' archives merit further research. Orange County was formed in 1734, and Augusta County was formed from it in

1738. Later, in 1770, Boutecourt County was formed from a part of Augusta; and in 1778, Rockbridge was formed from Augusta and Boutecourt. For some time, these names were used interchangeably.

8. The Mountain Kin Family Tree proposes that a "James Presley" (father or grandfather of the James Presley born in 1783) came from Yorkshire to the Colonies with two brothers. He went first to Richmond, and then to Winchester, before settling in Russell County at Forks of Indian Creek. The Turner/Farber/Horton Tree suggests that William Presley, father of James Presley, was born in Yorkshire (ca. 1765) and died in 1835 and that he was the son of Andrew Presley. This is not substantiated by Yorkshire birth records. Additionally, Norma Jean Crabtree, in *Leaving a Trail: Crabtree, Bale, Jackson, Presley*, Printt Press, 1987, pp 70–71, notes that a James Presley came to the Colonies from Yorkshire, landed in eastern Virginia in what is now Dickson County, buried a daughter near a store on Coney Fork of Indian Creek and then went to Hurricane Creek. The fact these three account link their ancestor to Yorkshire is of particular interest in terms of tracking our own family roots. Once again, we have the story of three brothers.

9. This William appeared on a different day in the collector's journals than William Pressly (Priestley) Sr. and Jr., so presumably he wasn't living adjacent to them. See Appendix A for a discussion about them and the possibility that William, Sr., could be James's father. James appeared in the 1810 tax lists with one tithe and "Hester Presley" appeared with zero, which suggests that they were living in different dwellings.

10. Other early baptisms in the Aberdeen area include seven children of "Andrew Pressley" born between 1714 and 1727 in Lomnay Parish; John, son of "William Pressly" and Elizabeth Forrest, baptized in 1714 in Logie Buchan Parish; John, son of "William Presly," baptized in 1727 in Ellon Parish and his son, William, in 1757; and William and Elizabeth "Presly" who had several children during the 1760s. These families seemed to have remained in this area well into the twentieth century.

11. David Hackett Fischer, *Albion's Seed: Four British Folkways in America,* New York, 1989, Oxford University Press.

12. Further research needs to be undertaken in Ireland especially in the PROVO archives and the Belfast Library, where some original Seceder and Covenanter records are deposited. I retained a PROVO researcher to search the Rosemary Street Third Presbyterian Church records from 1726–1800 but she did not find any further reference to the Pressly surname. She looked at the Second and Third Church Pew Rent records (1726–73), and Communicant (1728–42), Baptism, and Marriage (1741–1846) records.

13. John Witherspoon and his wife, Janet, had seven children, including sons James, David, Gavin, and Robert. The family plantation, *Thorntree,* which was built in 1749 in Kingstree, South Carolina, survives. William Willis Boddie: *History of Williamsburg, South Carolina,* Columbia, SC, 1923, pp. 10–12. The Witherspoons came from the Parish of Drumbo in County Down.

14. Vol. VIII, 1993, no. 3, pp. 45–48. Jim Gettys was the first in our family to demonstrate conclusively that the three Williamsburg brothers, who settled near the Santee River and Kingstree, were a different family line (although perhaps descended from an earlier common ancestor) than the David Pressly and his brother, John Pressly, who arrived in Charleston in 1767 and 1772, respectively. In *The Good Intent* (New York, 2007, Magnolia Group Press), John Renning Phillips recounts the history of his ancestors beginning with their voyage on the ship, the *Good Intent.* He, through a nineteenth-century marriage, is linked to both the

Williamsburg Pressleys and to David Pressly's (imm 1767) granddaughter, Ann Esther Pressly Anderson. After the Civil War, almost all of the Williamsburg Pressley descendants moved as a group to California. Hopefully, DNA testing can be undertaken with descendants of this family to see if there is a similar DNA mapping and a close relationship. Connected with the Williamsburg Pressley family is a well-documented African-American "Presley" family, whose nineteenth-century ancestors were probably their slaves. John Gotea Pressly, who also wrote about the Williamsburg Pressleys, states that John and Mary B. Pressley emigrated from Scotland to Ireland, and their name in Scotland was Priestly.

15. John names his brother, William, in his will, which helps confirm the three were brothers. See Caroline T. Moore, *Abstracts of the Wills of the State of South* Carolina, 1740–1760, 1964.

PART I

1. Samuel Johnson, *A Journey to the Western Isles of Scotland*, London 1775, vol. 2, image no. 29. Johnson traveled with Boswell to the Hebrides in 1773. He commented with concern about the number of immigrants from the Scottish Highlands who had left for the Colonies.

Chapter 2: Historical Overview: Life in the Backcountry of South Carolina

1. The old Ninety Six District was originally part of Granville and Colleton Counties that extended from one end of the state to the other until 1769 when the Ninety Six District was formed.

2. Gouedy was one of the most successful white traders with the Indians in the backcountry and later expanded his commercial enterprises to include money-lending and farming before he died in 1775. At the time of his death he had a plantation with over 1500 acres and thirty-four slaves.

3. John H. Logan, *History of the Upper Country of South Carolina*, 1859, vol. 1, Winsborough, SC, reprint 2009, Southern Historical Press, pp. 448–9.

4. The Calhoun settlement was about nine-and-a-half miles from the village of Abbeville.

5. Bobby F. Edmonds, *Destiny of the Scots-Irish: A Family Saga*, McCormick, SC, 2004, Cedar Hill, Unltd, notes this palisade on p.17.

6. Two helpful accounts of Clark's congregations and this voyage are as follows: Hugh McGough, "Presbyterian Emigrations from Ulster to South Carolina: The Cahans Exodus from Ballbay to Abbeville in 1764," available online at http://www.pennywind.com/Genealogy/Migration/presbyterian_emigrations.htm; and James H. and Peadar Murname, *At the Fords of the Birches: The History of Ballbay, Its People and Vicinity* (Ballybay, 1999). The latter has not been seen by the author and is no longer on the shelves at the Library of Congress.

7. Jean Stephenson, *Scottish-Irish Migration to South Carolina, 1772: Reverend William Martin and His Five Shiploads of Settlers*, Bronx, NY, 2013, reprinted Ishi Press International.

Chapter 3: Glasgow and the Ulster Migrations: John and David Pressly, Emigrating to America, 1767–1772

1. Reverend Hamilton (1707–1788) was the son of Hugh Hamilton, a merchant in Ayr. Dr. Robert Clark, brother of Reverend Dr. Thomas Clark, who was later to play an important role in Abbeville, was living in Ayr at the time.

2. Richard Pococke & Daniel William Kemp, *Tours in Scotland 1747, 1750, 1760,* October 1887, Scottish History Society, p. 58.

3. An advertisement for the ship *Prince of Wales,* which was to sail for Charlestown, appeared in the *Belfast Newsletter and General Advertiser,* Belfast, Ireland, on December 19, 1766 cited R. J. Dickson, *Ulster Emigration to Colonia America 1718–1775* (Belfast, 1966, Ulster Historical Foundation, p. 3 This is an immensely helpful book on late eighteenth-century sailings to the Colonies. It also stated, "In which Ship a Passage will be given without any Payment or Consideration other than the Bounty granted by the Governor and Assembly of the said Province, for the Encouragement of Protestant Settlers. Therefore those who incline to embrace this Opportunity are desired to come in immediately and engage with Valentine Jones, George Black, or David Tomb, at the Office of Thomas Bateson and Company, and to bring Certificates of their being Protestants, signed by the Minister or Curate, and Church Wardens of the Parish, or by the Minister and two of the Elders of the Congregation to which they belong."

4. The *Earl of Hillsborough* sailed for South Carolina from Belfast on Christmas Eve 1766. It reached Charleston on February 19, 1767, *South Carolina and American General Gazette,* February 20, 1767).

5. The *Nancy* brought 291 passengers to Charleston in June 1767. It was designed to hold a maximum of eighty adult passengers. As of a result of the overcrowding, many arrived sick and dying. Among those on the *Nancy* were John Foster and his brother James, later leaders in the Cedar Spring ARP Church.

6. Janie Revill's book, *A Compilation of the Original Lists of Protestant Immigrants to South Carolina, 1763–1773* pp. 120–21 (for David Pressly), 1999. The Colony of South Carolina paid passages for those who could not pay. The process of securing land was complicated and involved fees. The applicant had to appear in person before the Council to request a warrant for survey, then he had to take the warrant to the Surveyor General to secure a survey and prepare plat, and lastly he had to apply for a grant of land.

7. Vol. 9, p. 261, his survey was certified May 5, 1767, on a "branch of the Western bank of Stephenson Creek in Belfast Township bounded on southern corner by land laid out to James Crosier." According to his plat, Crozier's one hundred acres were "on a small branch of the Western Fork of Stevens Creek" [an early name for Hard Labor Creek] known as Calabash Branch. This helps locate David's plat.

8. This could be Esther. Her tombstone indicates she was about eighty when she died, which would make her approximate birth year 1767–1768. She is buried in Generostee ARP Church Cemetery in Anderson County, South Carolina. This would mean the children were not listed in their birth order in David's (immigrant 67) will.

9. The following year, the Council awarded plats to John Pressly and his daughter, Mary Patterson Pressly, adjacent to Samuel Pressly's land. Mary's land was next to John Hearst. Revill, pp. 169–70.

10. On May 17, 1774, "David Pressley" petitioned to have certified an elapsed plat on the bounty for one hundred acres in Granville County as shown in *Petitions for Land from South Carolina Council Journals,* Volume VII: 1771–1774 (Columbia: SCMAR, 1999, p. 272). "David Pressly, 7 Oct. 1774: one hundred acres in Granville County on waters of Stevenson's Creek. Survey certified 16 Jan 1773. It was granted 25 May 1774. Quit rent in ten years. Pat Cunningham, DS. Delivered 12 Dec. 1774 to David Presly" [13–44:2]. It is also possible, but

not likely, that David sailed alone on The *James and Mary,* which sailed from Larne on August 25, 1772, arriving at Charleston on October 18, 1772. It was quarantined for seven weeks because of an outbreak of small pox. Also on this ship were Reverend Robert McClintock, Timothy and John McClintock, John and James Peddan, Joseph Lowry, James Stinson, James Young, and Robert Neile (also referred to as Neel and Neeland) whose land was to border John Pressly. The *James and Mary* warrants for passengers were prepared earlier but were not issued until Reverend Martin's ship arrived. The passengers were able to go freely from the ship to the hospital on shore, and it is possible that David was able get away.

11. A Margaret McQueen was born in Girvan, Ayr, on the June 17, 1743. If this is the same Margaret, she would have been approximately fifteen years old when she gave birth.

12. The use of the wife's maiden name as the middle name was a common practice and frequently used by our family.

13. A brigantine is a type of sailing ship with two masts, at least one of which is square rigged. The *Free Mason* may have been the sixteen-gun privateer American brigantine that later fought in the Revolutionary War and caught fire and sunk in Marblehead Harbor in 1779. John Semple was the master of the *Free Mason,* and the ship advertised J., W., G., Glenny, Hill Wilson, Geo. Anderson, and Wm. Beath Merchants as owners.

14. Other passengers on the *Free Mason* granted land in the same Hard Labor Creek community were James and William Foster (later elders in the Cedar Spring Church), Reynolds, and Andrew Taylor. Also nearby were Thomas McDill, Robert Neiles, and John Wilson who came on another Martin ship, the *James and Mary.* The advertisement stated prospective passengers "must give earnestly before September 5 to enable owners to victual ship." The ship was initially supposed to sail on September 20, and it finally sailed on October 27.

15. South Carolina Council meeting January 6, 1773 (p. 96 #419). It is interesting to speculate as to whether the sizeable group of Seceders on these ships were coming to join Reverend Clark's community. In addition to the *Free Mason,* passengers on three other ships with Martin's parishioners also received warrants that day. With passenger ships going back and forth to Ulster, there was possibility of some communication, so David could have known about John's arrival.

Chapter 4: Building a Community in the Ninety Six District

1. Available online. Thompson and others that helped him overlaid the colonial plats onto a modern map that shows, albeit faintly, major roads and waterways. http://www.bfthompson.com/abbeville_colonial_plats/AbbePlats_home.htm

2. Dr. Anton Wachsel became the first pastor of St. George's Lutheran Church.

3. William L. Anderson, "Cherokee Clay From Duche to Wedgewood: The Journal of Thomas Griffiths, 1767–68," *North Carolina Historical Review,* Vol LIII, no. 4, October, 1986, p. 501.

4. Quoted in *A History of Londonborough Township, South Carolina.* www.Carolina.com/sc/towns/Londonbortough_township.

5. Anderson, "Cherokee Clay."

6. Morris House is described and illustrated in Bobby F. Edmonds, *The Making of McCormick County,* Cedar Hill Unltd., McCormick, 1999, pp. 39–40.

7. My thanks to Jim Bates for sharing this photo and information with me.

8. Nora Marshall Davis: *An Historical Sketch of the Long Cane Associate Reformed Presbyterian Church.* Available online http://www.longcanearp.org/noradavis.html.

9. Reverend Robert Latham, *History of the Associate Reformed Synod of the South: To which is Prefixed a History of the Associate Reformed and Reformed Presbyterian Churches,* Harrisburg, 1882, Associate Reformed Presbyterian Center, p. 438.

10. Nora Marshall Davis: *An Historical History of the Cedar Spring Church,* Typescript, McCain Library, Erskine College, Due West, South Carolina.

11. Upper Long Cane Presbyterian Church cemetery is an important early cemetery with many gravestones carved by some of the most important Charleston carvers.

12. A wood-frame building succeeded the log house—the current church is a few miles away. The historic cemetery is located on an unpaved road some five and a half miles southeast of Lowndesville.

13. January 26, 1786, land surveyed by William Lesly—series S213190, vol. 0003, p. 00285 and Estate Packet: Box 24, package 557, Probate Records, Abbeville County Courthouse. It is unlikely this is John's (imm 1772) son—especially because the land offices were closed between 1775 and 1784, and the land bequeathed to William when his father died in 1778 was more than a mile away. William "Presly's" name appears again in a land reference the following year, in 1786, when he purchased seventy-nine acres immediately adjacent to his homestead and to James Crozier and "David Presly." This same James Crozier, in 1778, named "William Prestly" as one of the executors of his will. Although once again, this could have been John's (imm 1772) son, who would have been between sixteen and twenty years old in 1778, it is more likely that Crozier appointed his neighbor, William Pressly, as an executor along with his brother, Thomas Crozier. James Crozier will, Probate Records, Abbeville County Courthouse, Box 24, Pack 557, the will was proven in 1789 so William Pressly still alive. Lastly, another reason (although circumstantial) William was his given name is that his daughter, Elizabeth, who married Andrew Paul, named her second son, William Pressly Paul, perhaps in keeping with the Scottish custom of naming the second son after the wife's father.

14. David's will is included in *Abstracts of the Wills of Charleston District, South Carolina, and Other Wills Recorded in the District, 1783–1786,* Compiled and edited by Caroline T. Moore, 1974. p. 76.

15. South Carolina Council Meeting (October 26, 1766) refers to delays in awarding bounty grants because of the Stamp Act. "Jon Hearse" produced the appropriate certificates and receipts of passage and was paid what the Bounty allowed on October 2, 1767. He received 252 pounds. He probably came on the *Belfast Pacquet.* The spelling of the Hearst name appears in various legal documents as Harser, Herse, Hurst, Hearse, and Hears. John Hearst, Sr. had several additional children with his second (or third?) wife after settling here, all of whom are listed in his will dated September 9, 1780, and probated August 23, 1782. His stepdaughter, Eloner O'Bryan, is also listed.

16. John S. Pressly states in his "Family History" that he was "personally acquainted" with all of John's children except Mary Patterson Pressly, who may have died before 1810. Phillips, *The Good Intent,* p. 395.

17. Find A Grave identified three other graves at this site, two of which, members of the Foster Family are actually buried elsewhere. Jim and Paul Gettys and my husband, Bill, and I tried unsuccessfully to find John's grave. The wooded area had been logged within

the past few years. It is also possible someone picked up the marker. William L. Pressly in his book, *The Pressly Family* (p. 2), also suggests that "His grave is unmarked but he is probably buried in the Old Cedar Spring Cemetery about two miles from the present site of the Cedar Springs Church."

18. Jim Bates, archaeologist with of the US Forest Service, Department of Agriculture, kindly provided me with a copy of this archaeological report along with several other sites in the area.

19. While many early cemeteries have been identified, there has been little interpretative analysis related to them. Some were undoubtedly communal and may also mark the existence of early meeting houses. There are other cemeteries, many like the Wideman-Patterson Cemetery near *Ivy Gates,* that document plantation families.

Chapter 5: The Revolutionary War: Chaos and Upheaval, 1778–1785

1. In 1778 and 1779, the Whig General Assembly of South Carolina passed legislation establishing new lists of jurors from each of the seven Judicial Districts created in 1769, one for petit juries and one for grand juries. The Legislation for the Ninety Six District passed in February 1779, and the lists were broken down by geographical subdivisions to identify where the jurors lived. (*The 1778–1779 Jury Lists of South Carolina,* compiled by Gelee Corley Hendrix and Morn McKoy Lindsay, pp. 78, 86.) He is listed in 1779 census as "Presley" David.

2. John W. Gordon, *South Carolina and the American Revolution: A Battlefield History,* Columbia, SC, 2006, University of South Carolina Press, p. 97.

3. Jim Gettys says this battle probably took place at Hogskin Creek, a tributary of Little River.

4. Robert Stansbury Lambert, *South Carolina Loyalists in the American Revolution,* Clemson University Digital Press, 2011.

5. Murtie June Clark, *Loyalists in the Southern Campaign of the Revolutionary War,* Vol. 1, p. 517 and again on p. 518, Report of Distressed Refugees from Ninety Six District, Charleston, SC, under the inspection of Thomas Edghill, Thomas Fletchall, and John Hamilton.

6. Clark, *Loyalists in the Southern Campaign of the Revolutionary War,* 1981, vol. 1, p. 59.

7. No parent certificate was signed for John's children; David Pressly appears on the list of parents for his children.

8. The Confiscation Act of February 26, 1782, confiscated the real and personal property of more than two hundred persons. The 1783 Enemies List, Ordinance No. 1189, had minimal practical impact and apparently no additional estates were confiscated as a result of being named on the militia commanders returns. The list, however, had close to three times as many names as the 1782 confiscation list. *Loyalists in Southern Campaign of the Revolutionary War,* vol. 1 p. 29.

9. David's estate litigation judgment—Roll Series L10018 1794, Item 0388a, David Pressly, Jr., Henry Geddes, and George McComb, Exors Dickinson Watkins. This information was found in the South Carolina Archives in Columbia, South Carolina.

10. David's will is included in *Abstracts of the Wills of Charleston District, South Carolina, and Other Wills Recorded in the District, 1783–1786,* Compiled and edited by Caroline T. Moore, 1974. p. 76.

PART II

Establishing a Significant Presence in Abbeville District, York District, and Charleston, 1785–1820

Chapter 6

The Aftermath of the War: Healing and Rebuilding

The Revolutionary War was particularly vicious in the Ninety Six District, and the aftermath left devastation. Departing Loyalists in 1781 torched the landscape, burning farms and fields and houses, destroying stored grain, and setting cattle loose. Areas of the backcountry were a wasteland. Many farmers had to rebuild their homes and plow new fields, and widows with young children faced similar difficulties. The first years after the British departed were not an easy period of transition. The Circuit Courts did not open until 1783, and it took some time to reestablish order as raiding parties of bandits and horse thieves were widespread, making recovery difficult. There was also initial resistance to allowing Loyalists, who had fled to Charleston, to return, and some confiscated land was given to Whig supporters. However, despite some early retaliatory incidents, the area started to recover, as neighbors and families once divided by conflicting loyalties began to rebuild their community.

This was also a period of dramatic land expansion and speculation. Many settlers took advantage of the availability of confiscated and vacated land as well as the Land Act of 1784, which reopened the Land Office (closed for over eight years), to expand and consolidate their holdings. Other families, mainly widows with small children, sold their land and relocated. The Land Act also lifted restraints on large scale engrossment and land speculation, and many in the Hard Labor Section took advantage of this opportunity to expand significantly their holdings, including the Hearsts, Benjamin Tutt, the Perrins, the Stieffels, and Henry Wideman, surnames that were to form part of a core group of wealthy planters in this area for several decades to come.[1] The area also saw a new influx of settlers from Virginia, including the Chiles family, and from the South Carolina low country. The sheer number of recorded land transactions in 1785 and 1786 alone document the scale of this expansion, and land speculation became a serious concern. The road infrastructure was strengthened after the war with important commercial wagon routes being added in the immediate vicinity of where the Pressly family lived. In 1784, the General Assembly authorized the Barksdale Ferry Road, a public road from the Savannah River, near Fort Charlotte, to Ninety Six and Cambridge, and also, around the same time, the Abbeville to Charleston Road, which passed close to the Pressly farms. This last merged with the Long Cane Road, which passed in front of John Pressly's home. Foot and bridle paths still remained transportation routes and frequently appear on surveys from this period. There were also major legislative changes. The Court Act of 1785 divided South Carolina into thirty-four counties, setting up new administrative structures, with six counties being formed out of the Ninety Six District: Abbeville, Edgefield, Laurens, Newberry, Spartanburg and Union, with Pendleton and Greenville added a few years later (Figure 6-1).

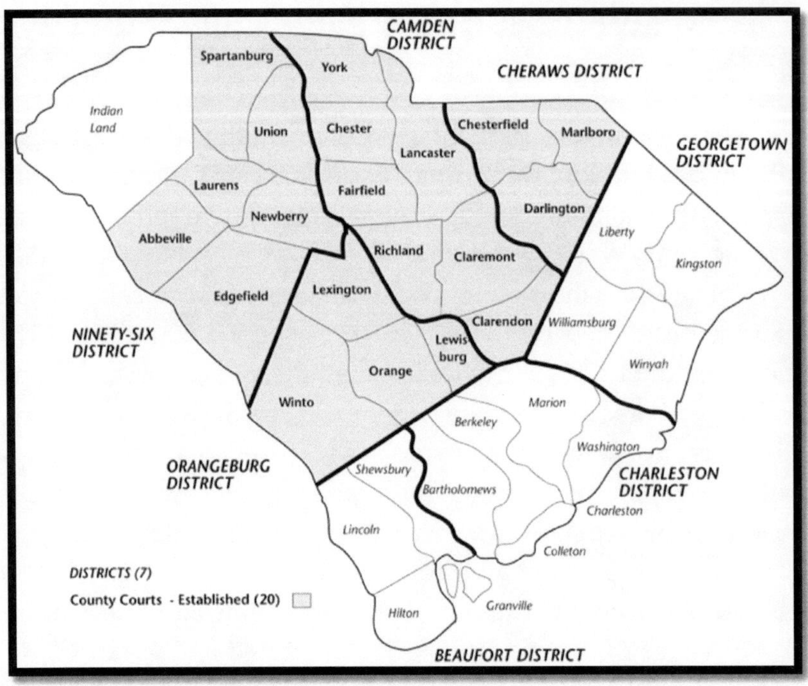

Figure 6-1. South Carolina districts established by the Court Act of 1785.

Despite these changes and the turmoil of the war, there was also remarkable continuity in the Long Cane and Hard Labor Creek area of lower Abbeville District. Neighborhoods had been closely linked by kinship, religion, and shared histories, and as a result many Loyalists, even those on enemies lists, were able to return to the area where the Presslys lived; some were even able to return to the land that they owned before the war. They mended severed relationships and picked up their lives. David's son, Samuel Pressly, and John's son, David Pressly, were among those who returned. Land plats, census data, marriages among neighbors, and other legal documents, such as wills and estate papers, reveal the continued interconnectedness of families and neighbors over the next decades. These records open up a window into understanding the social fabric of this close-knit rural farming community and its remarkable insularity, which, although hardly unique, is notable. Numerous marriages over several generations among neighbors' children created new alliances and resulted in an expanding and interconnected grid of kinship groups. This was particularly the case for the Hearst and Pressly families, not only for the descendants of John Pressly, but also for those of Jane Pressly and her husband, William, the third Pressly family living in the immediate area.

Community bonds in this mainly Scotch-Irish community were further cemented by the close connection between the Lower Long Cane Church, organized in 1771, and Cedar Creek (later Cedar Spring) Church, which was organized circa 1779–1780 but probably functioned earlier—both founded by settlers who emigrated from Ireland with Reverend Thomas Clark in 1764. Clark returned to the area in 1782 and served as an interim supply for both churches until late 1783, when he went to Philadelphia to affiliate himself with the newly formed Associate Reformed Presbyterian Church, the result of a merger between the Reformed Presbytery (Covenanters) and the Associate Presbytery (Seceders). In May 1785, the combined Lower Long Cane, Little Run (Little River), and Cedar Creek (Cedar Spring) churches petitioned to Philadelphia to become part of the new Synod of the Associate Reformed Presbyterian Church and sent a call for Reverend Clark to become their appointed supply. According to tradition, the petition was signed by Robert Foster, the son of John Foster, and John Cochran, who had accompanied Clark from Ireland in 1764, and by Elijah Sinclair and "Mr. Patterson." John Cochran and Robert Foster, who married Arthur Patton's sister, Nancy, and several members of his family, later served as elders under Reverend Clark, who returned permanently to the area in late 1785 and served as minister of these congregations until his death in December 1791. Clark's presence was of significant import for our family and for Scotch-Irish Seceder and Covenanter settlers in the area as well as for the history of the Associate Reformed Presbyterian Church in the South. He brought these settlers together to form a strong core group of Associate Reformed Presbyterians who embraced their own distinct faith within the larger Presbyterian community in the backcountry. This was also a time when other denominations began to strengthen their presence in the Hard Labor Section, in particular the Baptists who established Siloam Baptist Church in 1810 and Mt. Moriah Baptist Church in 1810.

Like so many of their neighbors, the Pressly cousins had to reconcile their differences and begin anew without their parents in an area ravaged by war. They continued to live near each other for many years, educating younger siblings and their own children. Many of these cousins went on to lead extraordinarily successful lives, becoming leaders in new professions and in the ARP church, and together they built an expanding kinship network that helped keep the families close over the next several decades. John's (imm 1772) son, David, who probably fought briefly as a Loyalist during the Revolutionary War, was not among the refugees who fled to Charleston, and there is no record of any further military service after 1780. He and his brother, William, divided the three hundred acres they inherited from their father in 1778. Their sister, Mary, who married Robert Martin, inherited one hundred acres adjacent to them and to her cousin, Samuel Pressly, and John Hearst. Mary and her brothers cared for their younger siblings, John, Joseph, and Martha, who would have been between nine and fourteen years old in 1785, all of whom remained in the area until at least 1810.

Four of immigrant David's children also remained in the Ninety Six district after the Revolutionary War. Samuel, a Loyalist like his father, presumably was able to resume living on the one hundred acres he left behind before the war as he is listed in the 1790 census living near his cousins. His younger sister (Mary Ann) and brother (either William or John) were living with him and his wife, Elizabeth Thompson, whom he married circa 1782–83. Samuel's brother, David Pressly, Jr., a Patriot during the Revolutionary War, married Ann Edmiston on November 16, 1784, and after his father's death in 1785, settled on the 135 acres of land bequeathed to him. Their sister, Esther, who remained a spinster, lived with his family for the rest of her life. There is little information about their sister, Agnes, who was already married to the Loyalist, Henry Wyly, at the time of her father's death, except that she had at least one daughter, Elizabeth, and that she and her husband returned to the area after 1785 and settled near Generostee Creek.[2] Immigrant David's three other children eventually left the Hard Labor Creek area; Mary Ann probably accompanied her brother, William, back to Charleston, where on December 13, 1804 he married Eliza Eleanor Adams and established residences in Charleston and York County.[3] Mary Ann married Stephen Thomas on April 25, 1811, in what may have been her second marriage.[4] Their youngest brother, John, married Isabella Brown sometime before 1800, and they lived for most of their lives in the area around Rock Hill, in York County, South Carolina (see p. 86). William and John and their descendants built a large kinship group in York County, South Carolina, with connections to Darlington County and Charleston.

The Hearst family, who owned land adjacent to immigrant John Pressly, was central in the lives of John's descendants over the next fifty years. After the Revolutionary War, two of immigrant John Hearst's sons, John Jr. and Joseph, both of whom had served as Patriots in the war, took advantage of the availability of confiscated and vacated land as well as the Land Act of 1784 to expand their holdings. Their neighbors, the Perrin family, also Patriots, rapidly expanded their land holdings, as well, and both families became large plantation owners within a couple of decades. Immigrant John Hearst dies in 1782, and several of his other children stay in the neighborhood, including William, Joseph, John, and Nancy. Thomas Hearst and his brother, George, later settle in Missouri. John, known as Major Hearst, married Martha Carson in 1775, and became a man of significant wealth for his day. He expanded his land holdings through numerous purchases, and when he died in 1806 his probate and estate sale records detail his extensive holdings.[5] Josiah Patterson, who came on the *Earl of Hillsborough* with David Pressly in 1767 and lived near him, was Hearst's brother-in-law and served as the administrator of his will.

Major Hearst's brother, Joseph, married in 1784 Jane Pressly, identified in some accounts as the daughter of John Pressly (imm 1772), although, as we shall see, this is almost certainly not the case. He, too, made several land acquisitions, including 933 acres in 1802, on Rocky Creek, a portion of which was part his siblings distribution share of their father's estate. William Pressly and his wife, Elizabeth Hearst, Joseph's sister, owned adjacent land. By the time Joseph died in 1814, his significant holdings comprised some 2,020 acres, including his father's four-hundred-acre bounty plat. The children of these three families grew up together and would have gone to the same neighborhood common school. Three of Joseph's daughters married David Pressly's sons, and a granddaughter married a fourth son. The Hearst and Pressly family relationship was further strengthened by the fact that both belonged to the combined Lower Long Cane and Cedar Spring Associate Reformed Presbyterian congregations, a bond of faith and identity that became increasingly important in the first decades of the nineteenth century. Many members of the two families were buried near one another in the Cedar Spring ARP Church cemetery.

The Hearst family also had a close connection with Widow Pressly: Jane (her daughter) married George Hearst, Joseph Hearst's brother, sometime before 1790, when their first child, Martha, was born. They had three other children and lived (at least initially) on George's father's original bounty land, near his brother, Joseph, and William and David Pressly. George left the area sometime around 1808, for Illinois, as part of the migration west taking place at the time (see p. 92), and eventually settled in the Meramec Valley in Missouri near his brother, Thomas Hearst. Martha remained behind and married her first cousin, Lewis Hearst, son of her father's brother, Major John Hearst. By the time of his death in 1822, George had become one of the wealthiest men in Meramec Township in Franklin County.[6] His grandson (the son of William George Hearst, born ca. 1796) was George Hearst (1820–1891) who became a very wealthy rancher and miner. He eventually moved to California where he bought, among other properties, San Simeon in 1865, and in 1862 married Phoebe Apperson. Their only child was the immensely wealthy and well-known newspaper magnate, William Randolph Hearst. Widow Pressly's daughter, Mary (died 1821), married Joseph McCord (ca. 1755–1816), who migrated from Orange County, Virginia, with his family before the Revolutionary War, and a third daughter, Elizabeth, married Andrew Paul, a member of the Cedar Spring Congregation, with whom she had six children.

Jane Pressly's husband died sometime before 1790, when she is recorded in the Abbeville census as "Jane Pressly," head of household with one male under sixteen and one over sixteen, and three females, including herself. A woman of some wealth, she received on May 27, 1791, a survey for an additional sixty-eight acres (certified on October 19, 1793) located on the "new Longe [*sic*] Cane Road from Abbeville Courthouse to Charleston" that bordered land she already owned next to David Pressly, Jr., Benjamin Tutt, and James Crozier.[7] By 1800, Jane was living with her son, John, who is listed in the census as head of household, between sixteen and twenty-five, and with three slaves and one female over forty-five. She died in 1805, and her sons-in-law, George Hearst and Joseph McCord, along with Joseph Hearst and "Greggery" Caudle, witnessed her will, in which her son, John, is named executor.[8] Widow Pressly's probate records reveal a woman of some considerable means who could be considered part of "the featherbed aristocracy" in the upcountry, and a substantial sum of $10,000 was placed in bond. Her estate inventory appraised for over $2,000, excluding land. Circa 1800, an estate valued over $1,000 reflected considerable wealth and a comfortable standard of living. Her sale included extensive home furnishings, furniture, books, luxury items (such as tablecloths, silverware, and sheets), several beds, a loom, farm animals and equipment, and four slaves which sold for a total of $1,293. It also reveals she held notes for various neighbors and family members including Joseph Hearst and James Devlin. Her son, John, died four years later in 1809, and with his death, the paternal line died out. This may be why the family is not referred to in JSP's later *Brief Memoir*. John's estate sale offered many of the items in his mother's sale, including the slaves.[9]

The close familial connections between Widow Pressly and Joseph Hearst and his family extended beyond the marriage of her daughter to Joseph's brother, George. When Joseph died in 1814, two of Jane's sons-in-law, Andrew Paul and Joseph McCord, were among the executors of his estate and eight years later, when Andrew Paul died, he appointed John "Whitehall" Hearst (Major John Hearst, Jr's son) as one his executors.[10] This family intimacy led me to reconsider the identity of Joseph Hearst's wife, Jane Pressly, who died in 1828 at age sixty-six and is buried next to him in Cedar Springs ARP Cemetery. Her origins are particularly relevant here because three of Joseph and Jane's daughters were to marry David Pressly's (died 1818) sons, and a granddaughter a fourth son. Although it has been assumed until now that Joseph's wife was John Pressly's (imm 1772) daughter, there was no reference to a daughter, Jane, in John Pressly's will, and she was not included as one of John's daughters in John S. Pressly's *Brief Memoir.* Considering that JSP would have known her as he was living in the area and she did not die until 1828, the fact she is not included is significant. Given Joseph Hearst's close connection with widow Pressly, it is a plausible hypothesis to suggest that his wife may been a relation of widow Pressly's husband, William, possibly a younger sister, cousin, or niece. It was common custom among early settlers to marry close friends, second cousins, siblings, and relations of people already married into a family. Her son-in-law, Joseph McCord's, brother had married a Catherine "Pressley," who was the daughter of Robert and Mary Elizabeth Pressley of Orange County, Virginia. Catherine and her husband, William McCord, both from Virginia, also settled in the Abbeville District.[11] While admittedly speculative, it is possible that Widow Pressly's husband, almost certainly a close relation of immigrants John and David, was also related to Robert Pressley of Orange County. And, if so, it is possible this could lead us back to William Presley, the father of James Presley, with whose descendants we have an identical DNA match. Whatever these connections may be, Widow Pressly and her family were very much part of the Pressly and Hearst circle in the decades following the war and they enjoyed a level of comfort in a fast-changing society.

Chapter 7

Choosing Paths: Transition from a Frontier Economy and the Central Presence of the Cedar Spring ARP Church

Many of John and David's children and grandchildren went on to live extraordinary lives. Their stories, along with those of some of their neighbors, especially the Hearst family, are representative of a larger story of life in the Abbeville District and nearby districts in the backcountry of South Carolina in the first decades after the Revolutionary War. As the area slowly transitioned from a frontier, yeoman economy, and as slavery became more a way of life, we see the emergence of larger farms and a planter class, different from the coastal planter elite. The small farmer also understood the necessity of accumulating more land and slaves as a means to wealth and enhanced social standing. To this end with the advent of the cotton gin, many risked growing cotton as their cash crop. This opened up new opportunities for the merchant, a profession adopted by several Pressly cousins who were also farmers. The merchant became a critical player in community economics: crops yielded income once a year, and the country store merchant provided the credit for the rest of the year for purchasing dry goods, groceries, and so on. We also see the beginnings of a new, educated middle class where merchants and professionals, such as physicians, clergy, and lawyers, began to take their place within the backcountry social strata. In terms of the Pressly family, this it is also the story of the growth of the Associate Reformed Presbyterian Church in the South, a small and insular denomination, in which the Pressly family members were to become leaders.

Successful Merchant: David Pressly (ca. 1756–1818) "A man of uncommon energy and business tact."

David Pressly, immigrant John's eldest son, became a successful and wealthy merchant and as such was part of an emerging middle class in the South Carolina backcountry, where, at the time, being a merchant was a more respectable occupation than it was in Charleston. He rose to wealth and some prominence within the household economy of the times by providing a variety of essential services to his increasingly prosperous farming neighbors. David was able to take advantage of a changing economy as the growth of short staple cotton took hold in the backcountry in the late 1790s with his neighbors expanding their land holdings. Many were subsistence farmers or yeomen farmers with less than five slaves who seized every opportunity to increase their land holdings, with some becoming planters within a generation. By 1820, these families owned much of the land west of Hard Labor Creek that had belonged to the Palatine settlers. The number of planters (farmers owning more than twenty slaves) also began to steadily increase.

David married Jane Patterson sometime between 1787 and 1789, when he was thirty-two or thirty-three years old, presumably with Reverend Thomas Clark officiating. She was the daughter of Samuel Patterson, who sailed on the same ship as David's father. Their first child, Samuel Patterson Pressly, was born in 1792. They had nine children, seven of whom survived into adulthood, and together they nurtured an exceptional family. The family probably lived on the 150 acres David inherited as his distribution share of his father's estate. It was on an important transportation route, the old Long Cane to Charleston Road, and was also near the Barksdale Ferry Road (authorized in 1784), which passed through what is today the village of Troy. According to the 1790 census, David already had seven slaves, which means that very early on he had acquired some wealth and probably additional land, placing him in a relatively elite group in his neighborhood and in Abbeville District.

At some point, with his success secured, David built his home, the Brick House, which was one of the first brick homes in the district. It was almost certainly built on his distribution share of his father's land, which would correspond to Nora Davis's description of it near the old Long Cane to Charleston Road and Rocky Creek.[1] When David and William divided their father's land, David probably received the section closest to John Hearst. A recent exploration into the dense underbrush of this site, with the help of John Calvin Grier, its current owner, revealed large field foundation stones and also some small piles of handmade nineteenth-century bricks that could have been from David's home.[2] Brick began to be used more frequently in stores and merchant warehouses, as it offered greater protection from fires than

Figure 7-1. Stoney Point, begun in 1818 by William Smith and finished by his son, Joel. Greenwood County, South Carolina. Photograph courtesy of author.

wood-framed buildings. Although still rare at this time, there were other brick houses built in the area between 1800 and 1820. Stoney Point (Figure 7-1), located northeast of Greenwood, South Carolina, may give us some idea of what an early brick house looked like. It was begun somewhat later in 1818 by William Smith, also a merchant and storekeeper. Smith opened a store on the site possibly as early as 1800, and a post office in 1808, and it is marked on Robert Mills's map of Abbeville County. Undoubtedly more elegant and imposing than David's home, Stoney Point was completed in 1828 by William's son, Joel Smith (1798–1855), who became one of the wealthiest men in the state outside of Charleston. It was decorated with hand-painted ceilings and walls in both the entry hall and drawing room and survives in good condition (see p. 152).

David was clearly entrepreneurial and forward-thinking for his time. He recognized early on the importance of education not only as a cornerstone of his faith, but also as a critical tool in the path to success and status in the first decades of the nineteenth century. His focus was unusual among his farming neighbors. Given the limited opportunities for secondary schooling in the backcountry at the time, it is a testament to their values and ambitions that David and his wife made education a priority, ensuring that all of their sons were able to attend university and secure an upwardly mobile place in the social structure of the day. It is remarkable to think that, as early as circa 1808, their eldest son, Samuel Patterson Pressly (b. 1792), went to Transylvania University in Lexington, Kentucky, and became a physician and later an elder in the Cedar Spring ARP Church. Samuel was joined at Transylvania two years later by his brother, John Taylor Pressly (b. 1795), who, after graduating circa 1813, went to study at the Associate Reformed Seminary in New York and was ordained in 1816. Another son, George William Pressly (b. 1803), attended Transylvania and also became a physician and elder at Cedar Spring ARP Church, graduating in 1824, six years after his father's death, from the University of Pennsylvania, which was the best medical school in the country at the time. The two youngest sons, James Patterson Pressly (b. 1808) and William Patterson Pressly (b. 1811), both attended Miami University in Oxford, Ohio. James was an ordained minister, who later taught at Erskine College, in Due West, and William was a successful merchant and wealthy landowner in Illinois and elder in the ARP church. David and Jane's twin daughters (b. 1797) also married professionals: Mary married a minister, Reverend Joseph Lowry, and lived in Jefferson County, Georgia. Elizabeth (Jane) married a physician, Dr. George Brown, in Preble County, Ohio, where she remained for the rest of her life.

Being a merchant was a demanding profession, and David, like his brother, William, was almost certainly also well-educated and literate. As a merchant, he would have engaged in a complex system of barter and credit, providing basic supplies in exchange for produce. David would have had to have connections with Charleston wholesalers and even factor merchants, and it is very likely that he had some kind of working relationship with his cousin, William Pressly (David's imm

1767 son), a successful factor merchant in Charleston who owned several stores in South and North Carolina.

Stores, like David's, kept careful accounts of credit extended to customers. An account book from 1806, in the South Caroliniana Library, from an unknown store, from the Hard Labor Section, provides a valuable insight into how a store from the period functioned.[3] The account book contains the names of numerous individuals from the area, including John and George Hearst, Reuben Chiles, James Adamson, Elijah Lyon, John McClinton, William Gaston, William Chiles, Jr., and James Devlin, Jr. John, David, and Joseph Pressly also made modest purchases: for example, John Pressly bought whiskey and paid for it with corn meal. This store may have belonged to Robert Perrin, a successful merchant and shopkeeper who lived nearby in the area later known as Winterseat, close to Swamp Meeting House. The store ledger was organized by customer and included, on the left side, the date and what was purchased, and on the right side, how it was settled. Most entries were short, with people making purchases four or five times a year. Purchases included whiskey (the most frequent purchase), wine, brandy, sundries, shoes, cotton cards, Bateman drops, black silk, cotton bagging, chamber pots, castor oil, sugar, coffee, and paper. Accounts were settled in cash, by notes, and with bartered goods such as cotton, whiskey, corn, butter, cheese, bees' wax, broad cloth, fodder, corn meal, and potatoes. The largest and most frequently used accounts in this ledger were for John Hearst and John McClinton. Reverend Alexander Porter, pastor at Cedar Spring Church—also bought a sizeable amount of sundries, which he paid for in cash. Also listed in the ledger were numerous judgments before "Esq. Chiles" to settle accounts. By not relying totally on farming, the store owner could also lend money to support a cyclical economy, extending credit to farmers who could produce more cash crops. During the first decades of the nineteenth century, the small farmer with cash crops relied wholly on the local store for supplies. This dependency gave shopkeepers some leverage, because customers who failed to pay their bills could be denied credit.

David also owned other tracts of land, including nineteen acres on Reedy Branch, adjacent to William Buck, which he purchased in 1799, and forty-one acres near little Curtail Creek, which he acquired in 1802. Because he was later a land speculator in Preble County, Ohio, he may have also owned additional parcels in the neighborhood, acquired either through purchase or as a merchant through exchange of goods for land. Because so many land records were destroyed in the disastrous Abbeville Courthouse fires in 1872, we have no way of tracking land transfers, but it would appear he focused more on being a merchant than on being a large-scale land owner.

Probate records after David's death in 1818 show the extent of his business dealings, and the fact that he held many notes for neighbors, friends, and family members for short periods of time, including his brother-in-law, Joseph Lowry, Col. John Hearst, James Boyce, Elijah Lyon, and Matthew Shanks. At some point he may have owned a store with his neighbor, Samuel McClinton, as a Pressly and

McClinton store is mentioned in the probate records of his son, Dr. Samuel Patterson Pressly.[4] In terms of his character and success as a businessman, General P. H. Bradley later described David as, "a man of uncommon energy and business tact, and he succeeded in amassing a considerable fortune for his day." He also was a respected neighbor, and his name appeared in several of his neighbors' wills either as an executor or witness. Concerning his wife, Jane, Bradley wrote, "For strength of character and keen perception she had few equals."[5] Although not an elder like his brother, William, David was active in the Cedar Spring Church, where he served as treasurer in 1803, at a time before deacons were appointed.

Patterns of Slave Ownership

One of the reasons David was able to educate his sons so well and allow them to become professionals was that he was wealthy and successful enough to have slaves. Slaves allowed him to devote his attention to his merchant business, acquire more land, and increase his wealth. According to census data, David had seven slaves in 1790, three in 1800, and seven in 1810. Even for the yeoman farmer, a farmer with less than five slaves, slaves represented some status and freedom from more menial tasks. They provided the ability to expand production, acquire more land, and increase their wealth, allowing their sons to attend school and improve their prospects. If we look at some of David's neighbors in 1810, Major John Chiles had eleven slaves, Joseph Hearst had fifteen, Thomas Chiles had thirteen, Robert Perrin had eleven, and John Foster, a leading elder of the Cedar Spring Church, had twenty-four, all of them expanding their wealth as the cotton economy took hold.

Discussing the issue of slavery in any depth is clearly beyond the scope of this effort. However, a brief overview is appropriate to understanding the values and norms in the backcountry that existed in the decades following the Revolutionary War, and thus the context for our family's choices. The slave trade in Charleston in the years leading up to the Revolutionary War was extremely active, as the indigo and rice market boomed, and wealthy low country planters and more modest backcountry plantation owners and farmers expanded their holdings. Some successful backcountry Indian traders and plantation owners had a large number of slaves prior to the Revolutionary War. Robert Gouedy, for example, had thirty-four slaves at the time of his death in 1775, and the very wealthy George Galphin of Silver Bluff who had over 120 slaves and gave them their freedom when he died in 1780.

Despite the terrible conditions slaves endured during their journey and the degradations suffered upon their arrival, which were witnessed by planters and yeoman farmers alike, slavery became a way of life. It was embraced in the backcountry by 1790 and especially after 1800, when the short staple cotton crop became a profitable export item. Abbeville and Edgefield, in particular, were counties where there were a large number of slaves. Pro-slavery sentiments supported the growing market-driven economy for yeomen farmers and planters. Rachael Klein, in her book, *Unification of a Slave State,* argues that the South Carolina backcountry planters' and yeoman farmers' need for slavery, especially with the expansion of the cotton culture, helped unify the state. Indeed, she suggests that their desire to emulate their low country fellow citizens and enhance their economic status may have been one of the reasons many backcountry men became Patriots, knowingly or unknowingly throwing their support for slavery in the process.[6]

Being a planter was a desirable occupation, more prestigious than being a merchant, and successful plantation owners would have had at least twenty slaves. In 1790, one-fourth of the families in Abbeville (333 of 1,338) owned slaves, and fifty percent of this group, including David's brother, William Pressly, our direct ancestor, owned three or less. David, with seven slaves, represented a smaller and more elite group of slave holders. By 1800, the percentage of slave owners grew, and over one-third of Abbeville County families owned slaves (604 of the 1827) in the Abbeville census. During this same period, the percentage of families owning five to nineteen slaves was up from 28 percent to 35 percent, and those with twenty or more slaves was up from 3 percent to 5 percent. Slaves were personal property that was either bequeathed to specific individuals or sold at estate auctions. Between the years 1790 and 1810, the slave population in the South Carolina backcountry grew from 29,094 to 85,654, with most slaves working for yeoman farmers who owned fewer than five.

Beginning January 1, 1808, the United States Constitution prohibited the importing of slaves, and some hoped that slavery would slowly diminish. However, South Carolina's position with regards to slavery, and the willingness of planters throughout the state to safeguard it after January 1808, was made unequivocally clear when the State voted to implement a constitutional amendment which established a system of apportionment based on population and taxable property. This ensured that power would remain in the hands of representatives who were least subject to the influence of non-slave holding voters and most sensitive to the potential of a slave majority. Following the Great Revival in the early part of the first decade of the nineteenth century, most religious leaders accommodated the need for slavery in the context of God's ordained hierarchy, and many, including ARP ministers, were slaveholders. The issue of slavery became more of a focal point in the Associate Reformed Synod of the South in the 1830s, but even then it revolved more around congregations defending a Master's right to educate his household, including his slaves, than in an abolitionist stance. Many ARP ministers, however, did champion the sanctity of marriage and keeping the slave family together. Beginning in 1810, as farmers began to expand their land holdings, Abbeville County supported a large number of slaveholding families, especially the lower half of the county. The Presslys were, at least until 1830s, for the most part, slave owners, and some were eventually wealthy enough to have more than thirty slaves. David's son, Dr. George William Pressly, the only member of the family to remain in the Hard Labor Section after 1840, became a wealthy land owner with as many as sixty-six slaves in 1860. In 1860, Abbeville District had the highest percentage of families owning slaves in both the upper and lower piedmont.

Respected Elder: William Pressly (ca. 1758/62–1809/10), "He was in his day one of the leading men in his Cedar Spring congregation and a man among men."[7]

While immigrant John's son, David, was a wealthy merchant and a man probably of some influence in the economic growth of the backcountry, his brother, William, devoted his life to the Cedar Spring Associate Reformed Presbyterian Church, where he served many years as a respected elder. By all accounts, William was well educated for his day. As noted earlier, most of his formal education would have had to have taken place before he emigrated in 1772 (when he was between twelve and fifteen years old) and from his father after he arrived, because schooling in the backcountry at this time was minimal. It is very possible that William was educated from an early age to serve in the ministry, something that was cut short by the move to America. It is clear that William's father instilled in his sons the importance of piety and Christian service, and the value of education. Reverend J. I. Bonner, in his *Biographical Sketch* of William's son, Reverend Ebenezer Erskine Pressly, provided the fullest description we have of William, noting that "He was from his youth remarkable for his prudence and piety" and "Possessed of a strong mind, well cultivated, for those days, and an amiable disposition."[8]

The years after his father's death in 1778 must have been difficult for William, who, as a young man without parents, and caring for younger siblings, had to build a new life in the aftermath of the Revolutionary War. He was not listed in the 1779 census and Jurors Lists for the Ninety Six District, and there is no record of him serving in the Revolutionary War. Because his name does not appear in Refugee Lists, it is unlikely that he was among the refugees who fled to Charleston in 1781. After their parents' death, he presumably shared responsibility with David and their sister, Mary Pressly Martin, for caring for their younger siblings. Later, his unmarried sister, Martha, lived alternatively with him and their sister. Martha was with Mary in the 1790 census and with William in 1800. According to the 1810 census, she was living (after William's death) with his widow, Elizabeth.

The Influence of Reverend Thomas Clark

It is interesting to speculate about the influences on William's life during the decade of the 1780s, and especially on the role that Reverend Thomas Clark most likely played as an influential mentor after his father died. A controversial and charismatic figure, Clark returned in 1782 to the Long Cane area and became a major force in the community, where many of his Scotch-Irish parishioners had earlier settled. He was a tall, gaunt man who is said to have had a brilliant mind and organizational skills, and he is frequently referred to as the father of the Associate Reformed Presbyterian Church in the South. His importance and influence were acknowledged some forty years later, when the Synod of the South created Clark and Erskine Academy in Due West, later changed to Erskine Seminary. Clark was a zealous missionary who, according to George Howe in his *History of the Presbyterian Church,* "By violently opposing everything else in public praise besides the Psalms of David, and by wittingly, as is charged, admitting to stealing ordinances members of the neighboring churches under suspension for immoralities [by inviting them to join his congregation], he somewhat interrupted the strength and peace of the Church."[9] Howe also noted that Clark expressed himself in broad Scotch and that "He possessed quite a polemic spirit even to his death. He was peculiarly odd and uncouth, even sometimes ridiculously so in the pulpit." Despite these comments, it is difficult to overstate Clark's importance. During the 1780s, a period of enormous change and renewal, he brought a zealous belief in preserving the purist position with regards to the orthodoxy of Scottish traditions and nurtured the growth of the newly formed Associate Reformed Presbyterian Church in the South Carolina backcountry.

In thinking about William's involvement with the Associate Reformed Presbyterian Church during the first decades of its history, and the formative and zealous role played by Reverend Clark, it is important to understand the beliefs of this denomination, whose origins trace back to the Scottish Covenanters and Seceders. In Ireland, these groups disagreed on many small things, and theological squabbles were the public face of the Presbyterian fringe—as they were regarded. They were an ultraconservative group, and they embraced their orthodoxy; making themselves rigidly distinct in their worship validated their outsider sense of their special history. They saw themselves as a people set apart from all other Protestants, and they embraced this exclusivity. They brought this conviction with them to the Colonies as well as the desire to maintain some of the unique characteristics of their Scotch-Irish past and resist assimilation persisted into the twentieth century.[10]

After they petitioned to become part of the newly formed Associate Reformed Presbyterian Church in 1785, the Cedar Creek/Cedar Spring and Lower Long Cane congregations were joined and led by one bench of ruling elders. This lasted until 1803, when the two churches separated. The years between 1785 and 1800 were a period of tremendous growth and change for these young congregations. The charismatic and zealous presence of Reverend Clark coalesced many of the Scotch-Irish settlers into strong and devout congregations that attracted the attention of the Synod. On February 24, 1790, the Associate Reformed Presbyterian Church created the First Presbytery of the Carolinas and Georgia at the original Cedar Creek Church, which was a modest log structure. In attendance were Reverend Thomas Clark, Reverend John Boyce of Hopewell in Chester, Reverend Peter McMullen, Reverend James Rogers, and Reverend David Bothwell—the latter two were new arrivals from Scotland.[11] According to Reverend Latham, Clark celebrated this occasion "clad in canonical robes" and he noted people were astonished to see him "attired in a powdered wig, cocked head, and clergyman's gown."[12]

Figure 7-2. Waxhaw Presbyterian Church, Lancaster County, South Carolina; built circa 1800. Courtesy of Nancy Crockett. "Background Legends of a Minister's Death," Daniel W. Patterson, *Southern Spaces*, published October 30, 2012.

Before his death in December 1791, Clark also achieved the remarkable and strategic feat of erecting two new church buildings, which was a clear statement that he was strengthening the Synod's presence within the larger Presbyterian community in the area. At the Lower Long Cane Congregation, he replaced the log structure with a larger church building on the same site. Around the same time in 1791, he moved the newly named Cedar Spring congregation to its present site, where he built a larger frame structure.[13] It was not until the 1850s that both buildings were replaced, when Reverend Hempwell was pastor. The remarkably preserved Old Brick Church, also known as the Ebenezer ARP Church in Fairfield County, from the same period (1788), and the wood-frame Waxhaw Presbyterian Church (ca. 1800), in Lancaster County, give us some idea what the church may have looked like (Figures 7-2 and 7-3). Clark was one of the first people to be buried in the new Cedar Spring

Figure 7-3. Old Brick Church, also known as Ebenezer ARP Church, in Fairfield County, South Carolina, 1788.

church's cemetery, which is still used today. His gravestone inscription mistakenly gives the year of his death as 1792.

From the 1790 census, we know that William was not yet married, he had two slaves, and one of his brothers, either Joseph or John, was under sixteen years old and living with him. He almost certainly lived on the 150 acres inherited from his father in 1778.[14] In addition to his brother, David, his immediate neighbors included Thomas, George, Joseph, and William Hearst, his cousin, Samuel Pressly, Andrew Paul, who married Widow Pressly's daughter, and his sister Mary Pressly Martin. His cousin, David Pressly Jr., widow Jane Pressly, William Dorris, and Samuel Crozier (son of James Crozier), Elizabeth Kirkwood, Samuel McClinton, Mouchet, and John Gaston were nearby, closer to Calabash Branch.

Sometime after 1790, William married Elizabeth (Betsy) Hearst, the daughter of immigrant John Hearst. They had four children: John (b. ca. 1794), Martha (baptized November 29, 1801), Jane, and Ebenezer Erskine (b. December of 1808). The 1800 census lists William with one male under ten years old (John), one male aged twenty-six to forty-four, one female under ten years old, one female aged sixteen to twenty-five, and one female aged twenty-six to forty-four—the latter is probably his sister, Martha. He maintained a working farm of subsistence crops for the household and possibly some cash crops, because he had two slaves in 1790, placing him among the one-third of yeoman farmers living in Abbeville who owned slaves. He had no slaves at the time of his death circa 1809–10. In addition to his home, which was probably a log cabin that was enlarged over time, William may have had a few outbuildings, such as a kitchen and sheds. It was within this familiar world that William spent the rest of his life. We know little about his secular life except for occasional references to him in contemporary wills and land plats.

Seceder Traditions and Cedar Spring ARP Church

William's life, as best we can conjecture, was mainly devoted to the Cedar Spring Church; his role as a ruling elder for the combined Lower Long Cane and Cedar Spring Church was probably the most central activity of his life. Posthumous comments on his piety and goodness and the few anecdotal stories that survive suggest that he was an extremely devout and "pious" man, well versed in the scriptures and deeply involved with the Cedar Spring congregation. Once again, we turn to Bonner for information about William, who he described as a "man of deep toned, practical piety" who was "one of the leading men in his Cedar Spring congregation and a man among men . . . His memory is embalmed in the hearts of the older members of Cedar Spring and Long Cane, to this day . . . and the influence of his holy life will be felt there for a long time to come." Bonner described William's wife, Elizabeth, as "kind, affectionate, and devotedly pious. She was of a somewhat gloomy turn of mind."[15]

William was almost certainly elected an elder while Reverend Clark was still alive, as there are no records of elders being appointed between Clark's death in December 1791 and the appointment of Reverend Alexander Porter in 1797. Because one set of elders served both congregations, this group would have played a particularly important role during the five years that the congregations were without a minister. The other elders during this period, along with William, were James McBride, Alexander Smith, Robert Foster, James Foster, Samuel Foster, Andrew Jones, Robert Gibson, Arthur Morrow, and James Cochran. Reverend Clark was not replaced until 1797, which was when the call for the Reverend Alexander Porter on March 22 was sent to the Synod in Philadelphia and recorded in the Session Book. This call is an extremely important record of this community at the end of the eighteenth century. Some 237 names signed this call, including David, William, John, and Samuel Pressly.[16]

One of the distinguishing characteristics of the Covenanters and Seceders orthodoxy was the importance of literacy and the idea of an empowered laity. Ruling elders regarded exercising discipline as a divine responsibility. They were the keepers of peace and purity, and they addressed issues of morality, including drinking, stealing, and adultery, as well as civil disagreements in a trial-like setting. Parishioners could be denied Communion until they repented publically before the congregation. The Cedar Spring Church Session books that survive reveal the enormous disciplinary power elders, like William, wielded. Each case was considered individually at regular Session meetings, which served as church courts, and the transgression and punishment were recorded in session records, where William's name, as elder, faithfully appears.[17] Elders also played an important role in preparing communicants for Communion. In between Communion seasons, one day a month was set aside for examination and instruction, in preparation for Communion, with this study generally held at elders' homes.

Another aspect of old-world traditions brought to America was the idea of Scottish-inspired holy fair-styled Communion occasions that involved a large numbers of worshippers who attended from other ARP churches, including Due West Corner, Rocky Springs, and Generostee (the latter in the Anderson District), which was a reminder of the communal nature of their faith. These occasions held a very special place in Scottish Seceder and Covenanter ritual and were described as great spiritual feasts that covered five days. Latham in his *History of the Associate Reformed Presbyterian Church* describes Thursday as the fast day and Friday as the day applicants for membership were received or kept back. Saturday and Sabbath were especially devoted to the sacrament. On Saturday tokens were given to church members intending to take Communion as evidence as their right to receive Communion, which elders would then retrieve the next day. Communicants sat at long tables in a grove outside to take Communion. Monday was thanksgiving.[18]

By the turn of the nineteenth century, the combined Cedar Spring and Long Cane churches emerged as the leading ARP congregation in the region. It had more than 260 families and 520 communicants. In 1801, an addition was made to the Cedar Spring wood-frame church, extending the length of the building to accommodate its growth. As an elder, William would have also been involved in important meetings, such as when the Second Presbytery of the Carolinas and Georgia was organized at Cedar Spring on April 8, 1801. More significant was the decision by the Associate Reformed Presbyterian Synod on October 22, 1802, to dissolve the Synod and, in its place, to organize four Synods with the headquarters for the General Synod remaining in Philadelphia. The Synod of the Carolinas (one of the new Synods formed), included the First and Second Presbyteries of South Carolina and Georgia. It was formally organized at Ebenezer Church, now the Old Brick Church in Fairfield County, on May 9, 1803. The other Synods were those of Pennsylvania, New York, and Scioto Valley, Ohio.

The creation of the Synod of the Carolinas began a period of growing unrest for the Cedar Spring and Lower Long Cane congregations and perhaps also for the Associate Reformed Presbyterian Church as a whole. Shortly after the Synod met in 1803, Reverend Porter requested to be relieved of his duties as pastor of Lower Long Cane due to ill health. In 1804, he became Minister of the Gospel for Cedar Spring (which at some point later in the century became known as Cedar Springs); and under his leadership, it became the leading church in the area. This separation created a significant division between the two congregations, which had previously been closely linked. This was also the time of the Great Revival and the large interdenominational camp meetings. The increasing strength of the Methodist and Baptist denominations in the area added to the growing insularity of the ARP church. Nearby were Mt. Creek Baptist (1798), Siloam Baptist (1799), Bethany Baptist Church (1800), and Mount Moriah Baptist (1810). As noted earlier, in 1805, the Methodists took over the St. George Lutheran Church at the junction of what is today Millway Road and Eden Hall Road and renamed it Tranquil Church. (Swamp Meeting House on Robert Mills's 1820 map of Abbeville District.) The issue of denominational integrity became increasingly important, and preserving the purist position with regards to the orthodoxy of Scottish traditions would have certainly occupied William's thoughts. Indeed, the Synod's concern about denominational integrity was sufficiently great enough that in 1797 it urged its ministers to abstain from "promiscuous" Communion because it implies "a coalescence with other denominations." Quarrels and factions that developed over small points of interpretation were part of the history of both the Associate Church and the Reformed Church in Ireland. However, the contemporary debate over the exclusive use of the psalms of David from the Old Scottish Psalter of 1650 was not a minor disagreement. It was an essential element of the Scottish Covenanter and Seceder beliefs. In Scotland and Ireland, they chose to worship apart from the more moderate Presbyterian Church of Scotland; and once in America, they maintained exclusive psalm singing, which helped sustain their reputation as the most zealous and pure element of Scotch-Irish Presbyterianism. Over time twelve psalm tunes or metric melodies were used for the entire body of the psalm texts. Because so many members could not read and prayer books were expensive, a clerk would first sing, "lining out" a line, and then the congregation would repeat it unharmonized and without instrumental accompaniment. Psalm singers would slow the tempo of their singing and developed an intense, highly ornamental performance style that, combined with lining out, made Psalmody very distinct from secular song. It was an essential part of the communal Associate Reformed Presbyterian experience.[19]

Weakened without a spiritual leader, tensions intensified at the Lower Long Cane congregation between those strictly committed to Psalmody and exclusive use of the *Psalms of David* as translated in the Scottish Psalter, and those who wished to admit Hymn singing and the use of Isaac Watt's *Imitation of the Psalms of David,* (first published in 1719), which, in some editions, included hymns. Ministers from other congregations, who served as temporary supplies, sometimes preached half-day psalmody and half-day hymns, which further heightened divisions within the congregation. The influence of Watts's psalms even insinuated itself into church graveyards, where quotes from his translation began to appear on gravestones.[20] These intense debates were one of the issues behind the exodus to Ohio, Illinois, and other states of so many Associate Reformed Presbyterian parishioners over the next ten years (see Chapter 10).

The last decade of William's life was certainly deeply affected by these discussions. The last description we have of him before his death (ca. 1809) appears in a brief article by JSP, published in the *Due West Telescope* on October 9, 1857, entitled "That Friendly Visit." JSP lived with his uncle, David Pressly Jr., William's first cousin, whose home was said to be about a mile from Lowndesville in the northwest part of Abbeville County. JSP described William's visit as follows: "About the year 1809 or '10, a gentleman, plainly dressed, rode up one afternoon, to the residence of my uncle . . . the individual in question remained there during the evening, the next day entire, and the night following." He goes on to say William's conversation with his cousin David and his wife was "almost exclusively of a religious cast." They discussed Reverend Alexander Porter, Reverend Ebenezer Erskine's sermons (he was the Scottish minister who helped form the Associate denomination in 1733), and numerous other religious texts and, according to JSP, "seemingly to realize a spiritual feast."

William appears to have died unexpectedly soon after, and no will or estate papers are known to have survived. Although we do not know for certain where he was buried, he was most likely laid to rest in Cedar Spring Cemetery, at the church where he served as an elder for so many years. His tombstone does not survive. However, his brother David's remarkably well-preserved gravestone is in the church cemetery. David died eight years after William, in 1818, and one has to assume that he would have wanted to have been buried next to his brother. Next to David's gravestone are the remnants of a head and foot stone for another grave placed in the same alignment as his (Figure 7-4). Both are close to the burial site of Reverend Clark and are also in a relatively parallel alignment to it. This is, with a high degree of probability, William's grave. Additionally, the 1978 to 1979 Inventory of the Cemetery noted that four graves marked with fieldstones were found next to David's grave and that many broken tombstones in the cemetery had been previously removed by workers cleaning up the site. It is also very possible that William's wife, Elizabeth, and their son, John, who died in 1826, were buried next to him. John Taylor Pressly's infant son, John Mason, who died in 1821, is buried next to his uncle on the other side of David's tombstone. Numerous members of the Hearst family are buried very close by.

Figure 7-4. View of David Pressly's (died 1818) gravestone and the remnants of a head and foot stone for another grave placed in the same alignment, most likely that of his brother, William Pressly. Cedar Springs ARP Church Cemetery, Bradley, South Carolina. Photograph courtesy of author.

William left behind four children: John, who married Martha Devlin and died young in 1826, five weeks before his son, John Ebenezer Pressly, was born; Martha (Patsy), who married John Lindsey and moved to Lincoln County, Tennessee; Jane, about whom nothing is known; and Ebenezer Erskine Pressly, who married Elizabeth Agnew and became pastor of the Due West ARP Church and the first president of Erskine College in Due West (see Chapter 13).[21] William's widow is almost certainly the "Eliza Prisly," who appeared on the same 1810 census page as "Robt. Pressly" and "Da[vid] Pressly." She is recorded as having one male under ten years old (Ebenezer Erskine); one male aged sixteen to twenty-five (John); three females under ten years old (Martha, Jane, and possibly a third daughter who died); and two females aged twenty-six to forty-five, Elizabeth and most probably William's sister, Martha. She had no slaves. After William's death, his family continued to live on the family homestead, adjacent to the old Hearst plantation, which was then owned by John Hearst's son, Joseph, Elizabeth's brother.

Like his siblings, immigrant John Pressly's son, John (ca. 1775–1836), also remained in the Hard Labor Creek area, possibly living on a portion of his father's land. He married Margaret Patterson, another daughter of Samuel Patterson, on November 15, 1798, at Cedar Spring Church, with the newly installed Reverend Porter officiating. Their first child, Samuel Patterson Pressly, probably named after Margaret's father (although Samuel was also a Pressly family name) was born in 1799. John and Margaret are listed in the 1800 census as being between sixteen and twenty-five years old, which meant that John was born no earlier than 1775. They had no slaves. John and his wife and brother, William, served as witnesses to the 1805 will of James McCullough, who appointed his "three friends John Devlin, James Stinson, and John Pressly" as executors. John was not in the 1810 Abbeville census. Despite the fact that he lived in the area for close to sixty years, we know little about him. His name appears occasionally in estate inventories and neighbors' wills, and he was most likely a subsistence farmer and was an elder in the ARP church. New to our knowledge about John is the likelihood that, in addition to Reverend Samuel Patterson Pressly, he and first wife, Margaret, had other children. The 1820 census data strongly implies that John had at least two other children with his first wife: he is listed with one male aged eighteen, two males aged sixteen to twenty-two, and two male children and one female child under ten years old. One son would have been John Brown Pressly (1805–1832) and the other probably William P. Pressly (died 1831). Margaret probably died circa 1812 to 1814, although the date and place of her death are not known. In 1816, John married for the second time, Elizabeth Weed, daughter of Nathaniel Weed, in Preble County, Ohio, and had several more children.

There are no references to immigrant John's youngest son, Joseph, from this period apart from the fact that he married before 1799, when their son, James, was born; he married a "Beckie Pressly," who was baptized as an adult at Cedar Spring Church in 1801. Joseph's name first appears in Preble County, Ohio, records circa 1812, and he will be discussed in the following chapter. In terms of John's (imm 1772) daughters, Mary probably died before 1810, and Martha went to Preble County, Ohio, with her brothers, where she eventually married (see p. 90).

Successful Farmer and Postmaster of Pressly's Station: David Pressly, Jr. (1760–1834)

Two of immigrant David's sons also remained in Abbeville District. We know little about David and Esther's eldest son, Samuel, who, like his father, was a Tory. He married Elizabeth Thompson, whose family were Associate Reformed Presbyterians, and they had four children: Robert, Mary, Nancy, and John S. Pressly (JSP). After the war, he was able to return to the Hard Labor Creek area and lived next to his cousins, immigrant John's sons. He was a subsistence farmer, and he almost certainly died before 1810, which is when he is no longer in the census. Sometime after his wife died circa 1798, their children were separated, and JSP went to live with his uncle, David Pressly, Jr. In 1809, Samuel's son, Robert, married Elizabeth Clark, a granddaughter of Reverend Clark, and, according to the 1810 census, his sister, Mary Ann, who later married John Baird, was living with them. Another sister, Nancy Pressly, married Andrew Weed in 1809 and moved soon thereafter to Preble County, Ohio, where so many Abbeville family members were later to join them. JSP and Robert were to retain close connections with the Hard Labor Section most of their lives.

David Pressly, Jr., David's second oldest son, and the cousin William visited in Lowndesville shortly before his death, was a Patriot during the Revolutionary War. He married Ann Edmiston on November 16, 1784, and his sister, Esther, who remained a spinster, lived with them for the rest of her life. There has been some confusion over David's birth date. According to Scottish parish records, he was baptized in Lochwinnoch (near Glasgow) in 1760, and he is listed as being six years old in South Carolina Council records when he arrived in Charleston, in 1767. However, David states in his 1832 Revolutionary War Petition (W24917) and interrogatory that he was born on January 12, 1764, in the city of Glasgow and "was brought thence to America when he was an infant in the nurses drews [*sic*]."[22] He also noted in the interrogatory that his birth was recorded in a missing family Bible that had belonged to his first cousin, David Pressly, John's (imm 1772) son.[23] The inscription on his tombstone in Generostee Church Cemetery in Anderson County, South Carolina, further confuses the issue, because it reads: "In Memory of David Pressly, Sen. Who died May 11, 1834, aged about seventy-eight years," which suggests he could have been born as early as 1756.

After his father's death in 1785, David immediately took possession of the 135 acres bequeathed to him on the South Branch of Hard Labor Creek, recording his deed less than two weeks after he died. He lived near Calabash Branch, close to Jane Pressly and her family, and less than two miles from his brother Samuel, his cousins, and the Hearsts. He was, in these first years, a yeoman farmer with one slave in 1790 and in 1800. Sometime in the early 1800s, he acquired land in northwest Abbeville District, near the present day town of Lowndesville and the Rocky River, and moved there circa 1802–03. His sister, Agnes, married to Henry Wyly, may have lived nearby as her husband bought land in 1785, near Generostee Creek, in Anderson District. We know nothing about their lives except, as noted earlier, she had one child, Elizabeth, before her father died in 1785.

We don't know what prompted David's move to Lowndesville or what happened to his father's adjacent 350 acres. The land could have been confiscated after the war, or sold to the Hearst or Chiles families, whose holdings eventually

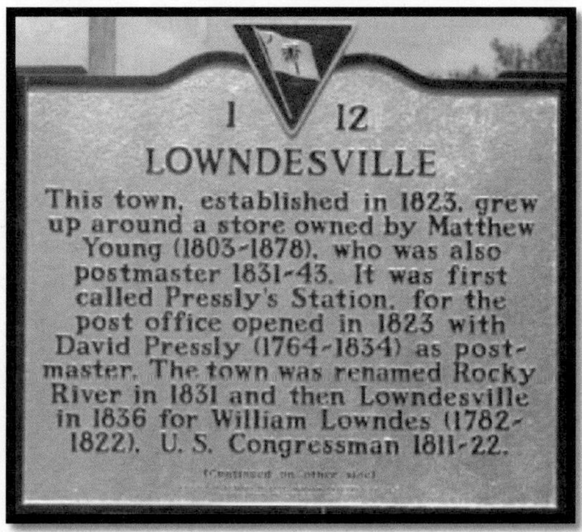

Figure 7-5. Historical marker in Lowndesville, South Carolina. Photograph courtesy of author.

encompassed this land. David, Jr. may have initially retained his 135 inherited acres, but we know he sold eighty acres to Reuben Chiles in 1807. David soon established a presence in the Rocky River area and owned sufficient land to be able to give his sons, James and David, each their own farmsteads by eighteen. His home is clearly marked on Robert Mills's map of Abbeville District surveyed in 1820 by William Robertson and published in Mills's *Atlas of the State of South Carolina* in 1825 (see Figure 7-5). The fact that his homestead was included on this map suggests that he owned sizeable property and had a dwelling of some substance. In 1823, he was named the first postmaster of Pressly's Station, a village named after him (Figure 7-5). The post office was probably in a general store, which he probably owned, as was often the case during this period. Located inside the main entrance, post offices were frequently named after the store or plantation owner who often served as the postmaster. As postmaster, David would have been at the center of communication for this area, and presumably a man of trust and some social status. The town was renamed Rocky River in 1831, and then Lowndesville in 1836, at which time it had between 150 and 350 inhabitants. David's home survived into the 1980s, when it was destroyed by fire. Pressly Creek, presumably near his home, flows into Rocky River.

David and his wife had a large family with three sons and five daughters surviving into adulthood. All but one daughter married, and there were numerous grand-children. David appears to have been a generous man, raising his brother Samuel's son, John S. Pressly, with whom he maintained a loving relationship throughout his life. He was also responsible for overseeing the welfare of the orphaned children of Robert Martin and his wife, Janet, after her death in 1811. It is possible that Robert Martin is the son of his cousin, Mary Pressly Martin, and her husband Robert Martin. David remained close to the children of his uncle, John Pressly (imm

1772), throughout his life, especially to William and his son, Reverend Ebenezer Erskine Pressly. The best description we have of David appears in a memoir about JSP, published in the 1860s: "His uncle [referring to David Pressly], to whom his youthful training was committed, though not highly educated, was conscientious and devoutly pious and was strict, in his attention to the religious training of those who were subjected to his authority and dependent upon him."[24]

Figure 7-6. David Pressly's gravestone. Generostee ARP Church Cemetery, Iva, Anderson County, South Carolina. Courtesy of Bill Cash.

In 1832, David moved to the Anderson District, near the town of Moffitsville, some six and a half miles from Lowndesville, sometime after his nephew, Reverend E. E. Pressly (William's son), became the second pastor (1830–1838) of Generostee ARP church. David and his family attended Generostee Church while living in Pressly Station, some seven miles away. E. E.'s son, Reverend William Laurens Pressly, as well as several other Pressly family members, later served as pastors there. David died in 1834 and was buried in Generostee Church cemetery as were, later, his wife, Anne, sister, Esther, and nephew, JSP (Figure 7-6). He appointed his "good friend and beloved cousin," E. E. Pressly, as one of his executors.[25] David's will spoke to his love of his children and their spouses, and his grandchildren, six of whom were named "David," after him. In it, he asked his family to make every effort to divide the estate equally so as not to expose the property to public sale. He appeared to have had close relationships with his sons-in-law and daughter-in-law, Elizabeth Ardley Pressly, the second wife of his eldest son, James; David took care of her and designated a portion of land for her to live on after his death. Her son, William Ardley Pressly (1816–1865), remained in Abbeville County and married Arabella Hardin in 1838, and was a successful farmer with a large family. Appointed a magistrate at the Abbeville Courthouse in 1856, he had sixteen slaves, and his combined real estate and personal estate worth was $21,465.00. He died in the Civil War in 1865, writing a moving letter to his wife shortly before his death.[26] Most of David's other children remained in the area, although his son, Alexander, returned to the Hard Labor Section circa 1815 and married Tabitha Thompson, the daughter of Moses Thompson.

Charleston Factor Merchant and York District Farmer: William Pressly (ca. 1778–1820)

David's, brother, William, was also a success story in the mercantile world, becoming a wealthy factor merchant and plantation owner with stores in York and Charleston, and in Mecklenburg, North Carolina. He married on December 13, 1804, Eliza Eleanor Adams, whose father was also a factor merchant, and he is listed in the Charleston Directory for 1809 as a store keeper at 177 King Street. This was presumably also his home, because he is described as living at King and Woolfe Street in his death notice in 1820. Mainly retained by large plantation owners, factor merchants were generally located in urban areas and were a critical link in the post-war plantation economy. They often served as their bankers, lending money and paying bills, and acted as agents for planters, both selling their staple goods and purchasing supplies on commission. They sometimes also advanced credit to backcountry stores in return for the opportunity to market staple crops received from smaller farmers. As noted earlier, it is very likely William had a working relationship with his cousin, David, in the Hard Labor section. William would have known many of the Hard Labor farmers from his youth, and we know that he had dealings with Major John Chiles, winning a suit against him for the sizeable amount of $4,299.08, with a final settlement of $2,104.34.[27]

William was successful enough to have a plantation and summer home known as *Hicklin Place* in Santuc, near Neely's Creek in eastern York County. He was also an elder and member of the Second Presbyterian Church in Charleston, where he is buried, and of the Bible and Fellowship Society. His wife, Eliza, died in 1818 and is buried in Ebenezer Cemetery in Rock Hill, South Carolina, where many members of William's family were later buried. William died two years later in Charleston, leaving sufficient funds to ensure that his orphaned children would be well educated and cared for. In his will, he requested his wife's body to be moved and buried next to him at the Second Presbyterian Church, but this did not happen. One of his executors and later guardian of his children was Stephen Thomas, the husband of his sister, Mary Ann. William's children were remarkably successful; they left a distinguished record of professional accomplishment, all the more extraordinary given the fact they were orphaned by 1820. Most retained a close commitment to the

Associate Reformed Presbyterian Church, although two joined the Baptist Church (Samuel and Benjamin). Like his cousin, David, all of William's sons were well educated, which was unusual for the time, and most remained in York County, South Carolina, or in nearby Mecklenburg, North Carolina (see pp. 194–195). Two sons became physicians: Samuel Henry (1817–1885), in Darlington County, South Carolina, and William Adams (1813–1874), in Mecklenburg. Another son, David Adams (1807–1841), was an attorney who studied at Yale and in Scotland, who died young at *Hicklin Place,* and a fourth son, Benjamin Chapin Pressly (1815–1896), was a ward of his maternal uncle, Reverend James Adams, of the Bethel Presbyterian Church in York County, after his father's death. He went to school in Newberry, possibly studying under his cousin, Reverend Samuel Patterson Pressly (see p. 195), and then to the University of Georgia. He was a well-known Charleston lawyer (Pressly, Lord, and Ingelesby), and, in 1877, became a distinguished judge of the First Circuit Court. William's daughter, Ann Esther (1809–1874) married a professor, George Anderson, and eventually moved to Georgia, and another daughter, Mary Adams (1812–1884), married Dr. Archibald Ingram Barron, a distinguished and wealthy physician and planter (see p. 195).

William's brother John also lived in the York District, probably near its border with Mecklenburg County, North Carolina. He was a member of the Tirzah ARP Church in what is today Rock Hill, and was most likely a small subsistence farmer. He and his wife, Isabella Brown, had eight children who survived into adulthood, and most remained in the area with two also marrying into the Barron Family.

Chapter 8

Upheaval and Change, 1810–1820: A Community Migration to Preble County, Ohio

As noted earlier, the first decade of the nineteenth century was a period of significant change for the Associate Reformed Presbyterian Synod, which divided into four Synods in 1802. It was also a period of significant change within the Lower Long Cane and Cedar Spring congregations and in nearby congregations, including Hopewell Church, in Chester, the Old Brick Church in Fairfield, and Duet's Corner (Due West). This was due in part to the Great Revival and the growing strength of other denominations in the area, especially of the Baptist Church. Camp meetings, with their emphasis on vital piety, and the experience of intense feelings of guilt and unworthiness transformed into redemptive grace, were in dramatic contrast to the rigid structure of old world Seceder and Covenanter traditions. These profoundly different religious orientations began to divide congregations and helped polarize the controversy between psalms and hymns. Psalms embodied the Associate Reformed Presbyterians' zealous desire to protect old world traditions and the commitment to the Westminster Confession of Faith. The threat to denominational integrity only intensified their commitment to preserve the exclusivity of their beliefs. In considering the move to Ohio over the next decade of so many members of the Cedar Spring congregation, and nearby sister congregations in the backcountry, and the impetus behind it, one needs to keep in mind the zealous nature of the early ARP Church and its desire to be rigidly distinct from other denominations. This was also a period of economic change as short staple cotton expansion began to increase the percentage of slaveholding families and enlarge the planter class. The fact that much of the top soil was exhausted by 1800, prompting the need for more fertile land, also helped inspire the first major wave of westward migration from this area to Ohio and as far as Illinois.

Some settlers moved to Ohio, which was a free state, because of their opposition to slavery. In 1801, land west of the Miami River in Ohio was opened to settlement. In 1806, the first settlers, mainly Seceders of Scotch-Irish descent, began arriving from Kentucky, South Carolina, and Pennsylvania. Ohio was to grow rapidly from a population of 45,000 people in 1800, to 581,434 in 1820. Hopewell Associate Reformed Presbyterian Church, in Israel Township, Preble County, Ohio, was later to become a very vocal supporter of the abolitionist movement. Sometime around 1806, a small group, including parishioners and elders from Hopewell Church near Chester and the Old Brick Church (Ebenezer) in Fairfield, moved to Preble County, Ohio. They settled in Israel Township, a new township, which was one of eleven in Preble County, located near the current Indiana border. These townships were laid out in an orderly fashion, with a basic infrastructure in place. Among the new arrivals in 1806 were Ebenezer E. Elliot, Robert Martin, William McCreary, and William Ramsey. In 1807, they were followed by John Patterson, son of immigrant Samuel Patterson, who had been an elder in the combined Long Cane and Cedar Spring Church; Hugh McQuiston, from Cedar Spring, Andrew McQuiston, from Ebenezer Church; and David and Hugh McDill, and Robert Boyce from Little River.[1] Boyce was married to John Patterson's niece, Jane "Jencey" McGaw, the daughter of his sister, Mary Patterson McGaw. They were joined the following year by another small group from the Cedar Spring congregation, including Robert Boyce's brother, James Boyce, who was married to Mary, another daughter of Mary Patterson McGaw. These first settlers, several of whom were elders in their former congregations, formed the Hopewell ARP Church in Israel Township in 1808. John Patterson and James Boyce were among the first elected elders. The newly organized Hopewell congregation erected its first church building just west of the present church. It was a log structure thirty feet square, to which an addition of thirty feet was later added to accommodate the growing congregation. The seats were made of slabs hewed from logs, and had stiff, upright backs.[2] Once again, Waxhaw Presbyterian Church may give us some idea of what this first church may have looked like. In 1822, after the Hopewell congregation had sufficiently grown, it decided to build a new church building, which is still in use (Figure 8-1).

Figure 8-1. Hopewell ARP Church, Israel Township, Preble County, Ohio. Built 1822.

This was the beginning of a communal migration. These first settlers from Cedar Spring and Lower Long Cane congregations traveled mainly in small groups under difficult conditions, riding horseback or in wagons pulled by cows, oxen, and horses. The route they took probably passed through the Saluda Gap, at the tip of Greenville County, where they would then pick up the Catawba Trail (shown in blue) which eventually connected with the Wilderness Trail (Figure 8-2). Many settlers shared religious and secular kinships, and they more or less transferred a community and a way of life, helping to ensure a fundamental element of communal cohesiveness and security, and the ability to succeed in their new homes.

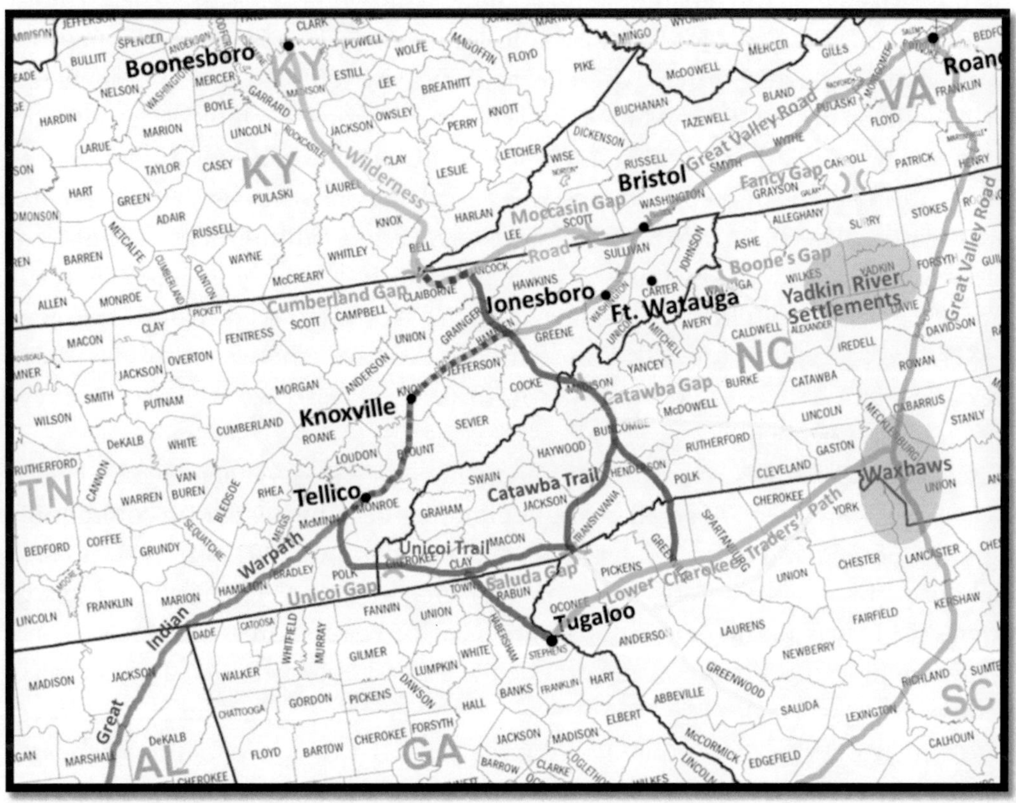

Figure 8-2. Map showing the Catwaba Trail and Wilderness Trail. Courtesy of Familysearch website.

In 1812, Samuel Patterson, Jr., a brother of David Pressly's wife, Jane Patterson, and also of John Pressly's wife Margaret, moved most of his family to Preble County, Ohio, including two daughters and their husbands, and a third daughter, Margaret, who later married in Ohio. Here, they joined his brother, John Patterson, and his sister, Mary Patterson McGaw. One of Samuel's sons-in-law, William McGaw, an elder of the combined Long Cane and Cedar Spring churches in 1800, also became a ruling elder. The fact that so many members of the Patterson family settled in Ohio is surely one of the reasons David Pressly (died 1818) and his family joined this exodus. He and his wife arrived, probably in early 1813, with at least five of their children, including their eldest son, Samuel Pressly, a physician, and his new wife, Elizabeth Hearst, who he married on September 11, 1812. Samuel later served in Ohio as a surgical mate in the War of 1812. He returned to Abbeville, probably by 1816, and no later than June 1817. Also with David and Jane were their other children, James Patterson (b. 1809), George William (b. 1803), Elizabeth Jane (b. 1797), who was to marry George Brown of Newberry County, and the infant William (b. 1811). Their other son, John T. Pressly, had graduated from Transylvania University in 1812, and had gone on to seminary school in New York City. Their daughter, Mary, remained behind, having married Reverend Joseph Lowry before they departed. Mary and Joseph moved to Louisville, Georgia, where he became pastor of the Ebenezer Church. Also joining David in Preble County was his sister, Martha, who is probably the Martha Pressly who married Archibald Hamilton in 1815, with Reverend Porter officiating.[3] Their brother, Joseph Pressly, whom we meet for the first time in Preble County, was already in Ohio. Also with them in Ohio were their cousins, all four of Samuel Pressly's (David's [imm 1767] son) children, who lived near them in Abbeville District: Robert Pressly and his wife, Elizabeth Clark, JSP, Nancy Jane Pressly and her husband Andrew Weed, who were there by 1811; and Mary Pressly and her husband, John Baird, who was a brother of the wife of Reuben Weed, Andrew's brother.[4] In 1816, John Pressly was to marry Andrew Weed's sister, Elizabeth.

By any standards, this was an extraordinary family exodus. What may have begun as a sporadic movement of small groups of families became, by 1813, a community migration of secular and sacred kin. It speaks to the strong pull of family ties and neighborly friendships intertwined through marriage and nurtured over many decades. This was particularly true for the Clark, Weed, Patterson, McGaw, and Pressly families, whose children and grandchildren had already forged a complicated web of marriages. The Preble sojourn was now to bind them together in new ways.

It is interesting to contemplate all the reasons for this move and the personal sacrifices the Pressly family made, leaving comfortable homes and well-cultivated land and, in the case of David, a very successful business. This may have also been a period of regrouping, fueled by all the reasons cited earlier, but also because between 1808 and 1812, the family had suffered the loss of several members. William died in 1809/10, leaving four young children. His sister, Mary Patterson Pressly, married to Robert Martin, also died sometime before 1810, which is when she no longer appears in census records. Their brother, John Pressly, lost his young wife, Margaret Patterson, sometime during this period, and their first cousin, Samuel Pressly, the eldest son of David (imm 1767), died between 1807 and 1810. Because most of the Presslys were slave owners and continued to be after they returned, it is unlikely that antislavery sentiments contributed to the decision, but the opportunities of land expansion may have.

Between 1808 and 1813, the community grew considerably, including a large influx from the Cedar Spring and Lower Long Cane congregations. For its first years,

Hopewell Church had a series of visiting ministers, including Reverend Alexander Porter, who preached there in early 1814, after he had resigned from the Cedar Spring congregation. Late that year, the Hopewell congregation presented to the Presbytery of Kentucky a call for Reverend Porter, signed by some seventy individuals, including John and Samuel Patterson, Jr., and, most importantly for our story, John, Joseph, David, and his son Samuel Pressly, and Robert Pressly, and Reuben and Andrew Weed.[5] Reverend Porter accepted the call in October 1814, and left for Ohio with thirty-four members of his congregation. They were later joined in 1815 by at least fifty other Abbeville families who followed him to Preble County.

The Preble sojourn provides us information for the first time on John's (imm 1772) youngest son, Joseph Pressly. The only mention of him in family histories is that he is said "to have gone north." He is not in the 1800 or 1810 Abbeville census, although he could have been living with one of his brothers. He married his wife, Becky, sometime before 1801, which was when Reverend Porter baptized her at the Cedar Spring Church. Before moving to Preble County, Joseph may have had two or more children: James, born in 1799 (died in Indiana in 1849), and possibly Mary (Polly), born in 1805. He and his family were probably in Preble before 1810, but certainly by 1813, when his son, John Newton Pressly, was baptized on October 20, 1813. Joseph was also listed, along with Robert Pressly, Andrew Weed, and Samuel and John Pressly, in the roster of Ohio soldiers in the War of 1812, under Capt. William Ramsey's Company, October 11, 1813, to April 7, 1814. This may have been part of Lanier's Independent Battalion, Ohio Militias.

Joseph Pressly had a large family. We know from the August 7, 1820, census that he had five male children under ten years old (including John Newton): one male aged sixteen to twenty-five (probably his son, James, who married Eliza Hamilton in 1823), three females aged ten to fifteen (one daughter, Mary, married Michael Harris on June 23, 1825; daughters Deborah and Sally may have married William and James Shirley, respectively); and one male (himself) and one female aged twenty-six to forty-four. His first wife died sometime before April 5, 1825, when he married Mary Ann Stuart, with Reverend Porter officiating. According to the 1830 census, Joseph was between fifty and fifty-nine, living in Dixon Township, just north of Israel Township, with one male aged five to nine, one male aged fifteen to nineteen, one female aged five to nine, and one female aged twenty to twenty-nine, his young new wife. He and his wife, Mary Ann, later petition for a pension for his War of 1812 service in Capt. William Ramsey's Company Ohio Militia WC—petition #30862. In the late 1830s, they moved across the border to Rush County, Indiana, where his son, Rev. John Newton Pressly, became a pastor for three congregations in 1838. Little else is known about him except that his brother, David, deeded him several pieces of land in Preble County between 1815 and 1817.

John Pressly married his second wife, Elizabeth Weed, in Preble on April 4, 1816, with Rev. Porter officiating. He served as an elder in the Hopewell Church and remained in Ohio until 1818, returning to Abbeville sometime after the death of his father-in-law, Nathaniel Weed, and possibly before the death of his brother, David. While in Ohio, John purchased at least two parcels of land in Israel Township and was also a witness to several family-related land transactions. David Pressly also speculated in land, acquiring and selling numerous parcels, including several to family members. He sold several parcels of land as late as October 18, 1817, shortly before he and his wife returned to Abbeville. At the time of his death, he still owned some 733 acres in Preble County.[7] There is no other information on his five-year stay in Ohio. David may have returned to Abbeville because of ill health or because the "experiment" in Preble had run its course, but surely one of the reasons he returned had to do with the appointment of his son, Reverend John Taylor Pressly, as Pastor of the Gospel at Cedar Spring Associate Reformed Church. In addition, his son, Dr. Samuel Pressly, had returned to Abbeville by March 1817, which was when he witnessed Robert Giles's will.

The move to Ohio was a permanent one, however, for many Cedar Spring and Lower Long Cane parishioners, including the Gilmores, Pattersons, and some members of the Weed family, creating a new extended family cluster. Most of the Patterson family never returned. David's son, William Patterson Pressly, returned to Ohio and studied at Miami University from 1826 to 1830 and married Mary Ann Gilmore in 1833; she is buried in Hopewell Church Cemetery. He was a successful farmer there for some twenty years before moving to Illinois. Robert Pressly and his family stayed for several more years before returning to South Carolina in the mid-1820s. He and his family later moved to Randolph County, Illinois, where his mother's relatives, the Thompsons, lived.

The migration to Preble County was not an isolated move. It was among the first of several significant migrations of members of several ARP congregations including Lower Long Cane, Cedar Spring, Little River/Due West, and Hopewell Church in Chester, starting in the first decade of the nineteenth century and up until the Civil War. As early as 1802, a small group of Cedar Spring parishioners, including James Patterson (1802), John and Samuel McClinton Jr. (1805), Archibald and John Thompson, William and Thomas McBride (1804), and Samuel Crozier Jr. (1806), along with several sons, began to settle as far west as Randolph County, Illinois, near Plum Creek. This community of Scotch-Irish settlers continued to grow and several Pressly kin, including members of Robert Pressly's family, were to settle there in the 1830s. Some of these moves were fueled in part by opposition to slavery and by political events like the nullification crisis; others by missionary zeal and the promise of better land. Many of these parishioners directly linked back to Reverend Thomas Clark and the core group of Scotch-Irish immigrants who first worshipped at Long Cane and Cedar Creek. They went on to form the nucleus of many new ARP churches later established in Illinois, Rush County and Marion County in Indiana, and Guernsey County in Ohio, which all later became part of the Associate Reformed

Synod of the West. Others from this initial core group moved to Arkansas, Mississippi, Alabama, and Texas, and remained part of the Associate Reformed Synod of the South and what is today the Associate Reformed Presbyterian Church.

When David moved to Preble County, Ohio, in 1813, he is said to have left his house and plantation in the care of Mrs. Marsh (Samuel Leard's grandmother), while the McClintons presumably continued to run the store. He returned to the Hard Labor Section in late 1817 or early 1818 with his wife Jane and younger sons, James Patterson and William, and possibly also his son, George, who by this time was ready for university and might have accompanied his family as far as Transylvania University in Lexington, Kentucky. His oldest son, Samuel, and his wife were already living in the Brick House, while his daughter, Elizabeth, remained in Ohio with her husband, Dr. George Brown.

David died on September 24, 1818, and was buried in Cedar Spring Cemetery probably next to his brother, William, who had died eight years earlier. This was also near the grave of his neighbor and friend, Joseph Hearst, who had died in 1814 while he was away. From the inscription on the beautifully engraved tombstone, it is clear that David embraced the values of Christian service. Deacons were specially charged with ministry and mercy, especially toward the sick and poor, and his tombstone speaks to this ministry: "The memory of David Pressly who departed this life 21 September 1818 aged sixty-two years. Eminently [*sic*] distinguished as the friend of the poor *blessed is he that considers the poor, the Lord will deliver him in time of trouble Ps 41.1.*" Headstones were a point of pride for a family, and his tombstone acknowledges his social and economic status (Figure 8-3). David's tombstone

Figure 8-3. David Pressly's tombstone carved by T. W. Walker. Cedar Springs ARP Church Cemetery, Bradley, South Carolina. Photograph courtesy of author.

was made by Thomas Walker of Charleston, a master stone carver from Scotland, who came to Charleston shortly after the Revolution. Walker was an active carver from 1790 to 1836, and established a business with his sons and later with his son-in-law, John White. According to the Historical Marker Database, the Walkers' stones were usually cut from high-quality Italian marble and carved with "a grace and sophistication surpassing most other gravestone art in South Carolina and the rest of the region for this period."

David's estate was probated on February 12, 1819, and his two eldest sons, Dr. Samuel Pressly and Reverend John T. Pressly, along with his close friends, John Devlin and John "Hard Labour" Hearst, were appointed administrators (not executors) indicating he did not leave a will. A sum of $20,000 was bound to Moses Taggart.[7] Most likely, David gifted to his children and/or sold off much of his personal property, including slaves, farm equipment, household furnishing and utensils, and farm animals, before his death, because the inventory and appraisal of his personal estate was modest. It consisted of only a basic household inventory of three beds, a spinning wheel, one bay mare, two cows and calves, a yearling, and a few miscellaneous items that totaled only $396.25. Estate records, however, reveal the extent of notes held for money loaned, presumably as part of his merchant business, which he continued while in Ohio and upon his return. Many notes had due dates from 1815 to 1821, and note holders included his sons-in-law and other relatives and Abbeville neighbors as well as Reverend Alexander Porter and elders in the Hopewell Church. The largest note was from a Hopewell Church Elder, James Boyce, with $2,000 due August 1819. David's administrators designated these notes as paid, expected, and not expected to be paid. The 1820 estate records listed $5345.87½ as the amount of money on hand, excluding many large outstanding notes expected to be paid. Estate records for the next several years listed taxes paid on land both in Abbeville and Ohio through at least 1826, with expenditures for the estate between January 1, 1821, and December 30, 1826, totaling $209.92¼.

His widow and legatees received a portion of the estate from notes collected in 1821 and another large sum on December 30, 1826. The estate remained open until at least 1830, when his sons Samuel and John filed a Petition for Partition in Common Pleas Court in Ohio relating to the partition of the Preble property of 733 acres that consisted of seven parcels and its distribution to David's heirs.[8]

Notes

Chapter 6: The Aftermath of the War: Healing and Rebuilding

1. Major land transactions of 1,000 acres or more took place in the immediate area around Calabash Branch and Hard Labor Creek including Benjamin Tutt's purchase on January 3, 1786, of 2,638 acres bordering, among others, Abner Perrin and John Steiffle. There were also many small transactions, such as Benjamin Tutt purchasing 312 acres on November 24, 1784, near James Crozier and David Pressly, and Nicholas Bigel purchasing fifty-seven acres on Steiffles [*sic*] Creek, also near David Pressly.

2. Wyly returned to the Ninety Six District and purchased two hundred acres near Generostee Creek in 1785. (S213190 vol. 0015, p. 222, South Carolina Department of Archives and History.)

3. Their marriage was reported in the *Charleston Courier* on December 15, 1804.

4. Stephen Thomas was one of the executors of David Pressly's estate in 1785. He or his son by the same name married Mary Ann and was an executor of her brother, William's, estate when he died in 1820.

5. Major Hearst's will, Box 47, pack 1060, Probate Records, Abbeville County Courthouse.

6. George Hearst owned nineteen of the forty-one slaves in the township. He died intestate, and his estate was administered by his brother, William Hearst, and by William Gibson, a brother of his second wife. He may have had a daughter, Eveline Hearst, with his second wife.

7. Jane's 1791 survey. "William Presly" received a plat for seventy-nine acres on "branches of Hard Labour Creek" January 26, 1786, adjacent to David Pressly and James Crosier.

8. Box 74, Pack 1805, Probate Records, Abbeville County Courthouse: Estate administered December 3, 1805, and paid out July 18, 1807. Her estate records are detailed enough to include the fact that on December 23, 1805, Dr. Robert Smyth, a neighbor, is reimbursed for providing eight gallons of whiskey, two glass tumblers, and two blank books for the funeral. Drinking at funerals and estate sales was commonplace at the time. Probate records reveal that she held notes for numerous neighbors and family members, including James Adamson, Katherine Mark, Robert and John Smyth, and her son and sons-in-law. The notes held for her son, John, totaled close to $1,800. He is referred to as "John Pressly Jr." in some estate-related transactions, probably (as was often the custom) to distinguish him from immigrant John Pressly's son, John. Among buyers at the sale were neighbors Samuel Perrin, Williams Chiles, George Hearst, Katherine Mark, and William Pressly, the latter purchased knives and forks for $0.32. (Box 74, Pack 1805, Probate Records, Abbeville County Courthouse.) Widow Pressly's son and her three sons-in-law, Joseph McCord, Andrew Paul, and George Hearst, were the designated legatees; each received between $561.56 and $587.

9. John's will, dated November 6, 1808, was recorded March 20, 1809. Neighbors James Adamson and his wife, Lydia, and Fanny Shatten witnessed his will. His widow, Nancy, of whom nothing more is known, was named executor. (Box 74, Pack 1817, Probate Records, Abbeville County Courthouse).

10. After Paul's death, his wife, Elizabeth, married John Gray and when he died John Pressly was an executor. Probate Records, Abbeville County Courthouse, Box 40, Pack 1895. Proven August 23, 1827.

11. Robert Pressly is thought to have been born circa 1735 in Orange County; his daughter, Catherine, was born circa 1761 and her sister, Elizabeth, circa 1773, possibly in Rockbridge. This needs further research. Joseph McCord died in 1816, and his wife in 1821. A detailed McCord genealogy can be found on the McCord Angel Fire website.

Chapter 7: Choosing Paths: Transition from a Frontier Economy and the Central Presence of the Cedar Spring ARP Church

1. Nora Davis, *A History of Cedar Spring Associate Reformed Presbyterian Church,* manuscript typescript, McCain Library, Erskine College, Due West, SC. In the 1870s, J. I. Bonner describes the Brick House where Dr. Samuel Pressly had lived as some three miles from the Cedar Spring Church.

2. I would like to thank John Calvin Grier, distant relative, for sharing the 1933 plat with me and for guiding us through dense brush on the site in a successful search for foundation field stones and several scattered piles of bricks on the property. His father, F. E. Grier, purchased the land from Dr. Pressly Neel.

3. South Caroliniana Library, University of South Carolina, Columbia, Anonymous Abbeville Store Ledger 1804–06, OCLC # 726207437.

4. The close connections of these two families was clearly expressed in Samuel McClinton's will (his property was adjacent to David Pressly [imm 1767]) of December 7, 1807, where he appoints "my Loving friend" Robert Gilmore (whose daughter later marries David's youngest son, William) and David Pressly to be executors.

5. Quoted in *Centennial History of the Presbyterian Church,* p. 300.

6. Rachel N. Klein, *Unification of a Slave State: The Rise of the Planter Class in the South Carolina Backcountry 1760–1808,* Chapel Hill, 1990, University of North Carolina Press.

7. J. I. Bonner in his "Biographical Sketch of Dr. E.E. Pressly" in the *Due-West Telescope,* December 20, 1861.

8. Bonner, "Biographical Sketch."

9. George Howe, *History of the Presbyterian Church,* 1883, pp. 555–556. Clark was known to have done this in Ireland as well.

10. See Joseph S. Moore, *Scottish Phanaticks: Toleration, Seceders and Slavery, 1689–1800,* and his dissertation, *Irish Radicals, Southern Conservatives: Slavery, Religious Liberty and the Presbyterian Fringe in the Atlantic World, 1637–1877,* directed by Robert M Calhoon, University of North Carolina at Greensboro, 2011, for an excellent discussion about Seceders in Ireland and America.

11. Other churches that formed part of this First Presbytery included Rocky Creek Meeting House (later Union), Indian Creek (later King's Creek), Prosperity, Long Cane, Little Run (Little River in Abbeville County), Generostee, Duet's Corner (later Due West Corner), Diamond Hill, Crystal Spring, Rocky Spring (in Abbeville county), and Little River (in Laurens county). Reverend Peter McMullen became Pastor for Due West in 1794.

12. Latham, p. 287. Clark estate records and inventory include several items of dress clothes and a very extensive library including literary and theological books; Box 17 Pack 349, Probate Records, Abbeville County Courthouse, along with those of his son, Dr. Benjamin Clark, who died in 1796.

13. On July 25, 1790, Mary Black sold five acres for the new church site. Arthur Morrow, Robert Gibson, and James Foster Sr., as elders and trustees, made the purchase.

14. Reverend J. I. Bonner, "Biographical Sketch of Dr. E. E. Pressly," 1861. "William settled on the road leading from Abbeville to Augusta about one mile below Chiles Cross Road, and about 4 miles above Hard Labor [*sic*] Creek." This would roughly correspond with his father's bounty plat located (see Figure 3-8) on what is today Eden Hall Road located in the present-day town of Troy in McCormick County.

15. Bonner, "Biographical Sketch," 1861.

16. George, John, Joseph, Robert, and Thomas Hearst; Nathaniel Weed Sr.; John Devlin; Alexander Clark; Andrew Paul; William Clark; James, John, and Alexander Patterson; John Gaston; Hugh and John McCullough; Thomas Wiley; James, Robert, William, Samuel, and John Foster; Thomas and John Lindsey; and Samuel McClinton were among those who signed the call. Among the new elders added on February 24, 1800, were William McGaw, John Patterson, John Young, Archibald Thompson, Samuel Leard, and Hugh McBride. Four years later, John Pressly, John's (imm 1772) son, was appointed an elder, along with John Devlin, William Dale Sr., and Joseph McCreary.

17. Session Records, Cedar Spring Church, copy in McCain Library, Erskine College, Due West, South Carolina.

18. Latham, and also see H. Leonard Porter III, *Destiny of the Scotch-Irish an account of a migration from Ballybay, Ireland, to Washington County, New York, Abbeville District, South Carolina, Pittsburgh, Pennsylvania, Preble County, Ohio, Randolph County, Illinois, and the central Illinois prairie, 1720–1853,* The Porter Company, 1990, pp. 34–48; and Moore, *Scottish Phanatics* pp. 23–26.

19. Daniel W. Patterson, *The True Image: Gravestone Art and the Culture of Scotch Irish Settlers in the Pennsylvania and Carolina Back Country*, University of North Carolina Press, 2012, p. 72 and pp. 211–213.

20. Patterson, *The True Image*, pp. 215–216.

21. Martha "Patsy" Pressly marries Thomas Lindsay Jr. who was one-year-old when he arrived in Charleston on the same ship as David Pressly, in 1767. William Pressly in his *Family History* (1980) notes that Jane Pressly married Captain John Drennan, but there is no documentary material to support this conclusion. The only known connection between the families is that James L. Drennan married Margaret Devlin, a sister to John Pressly's (d. 1826) wife, Martha. James and Margaret's son, John Lewis Drennan, had a daughter named Jane Pressly Drennan.

22. David Pressly Revolutionary War Pension Application and Interrogatory 1833, W24917. Published in Bobby Gilmer Moss, *Roster of South Carolina Patriots in the American Revolution*, Baltimore, Genealogical Publishing, Inc., 1983.

23. The Bible also lists the birthdates for all of David and Ann's children. H. A. Carlisle briefly discussed David in his book, *The History of Lowndesville, S.C.*, Danielsville, GA, 1987, Heritage Papers, p. 9.

24. Unknown author, "Memoir of the Reverend John S. Pressly," prepared after his death for the *Associate Reformed Presbyterian* found in Samuel Agnew's scrapbook, Erskine College McCain Library; Jim Gettys shared a transcript of the "Memoir" with me.

25. David Pressly estate, filed in Anderson County, SC, will dated January 12, 1834; filed June 14, 1834, Will Book A; p. 508, Estate pkg 536.

26. One of his sons, Ralph A. Pressly (1839–1912), eventually settled in Atlanta and was confined to an insane asylum late in life. It is not known where he is buried. Members of

his family, including his sister, Rosa Rebecca Pressly (1845–1915), and his son, Robert Henry Pressly (1868–1930) and his family, are buried in a family plot in Old Casey Cemetery, which is now part of Crestlawn Cemetery in Atlanta. Robert Henry Pressly was married to his first cousin Willie P. Cater, daughter of Rosa Rebecca.

27. William Pressly vs John Chiles, Judgement Rolls, South Carolina Department of Archives and History, Series L10018, 1809, 0030a.

Chapter 8: Upheaval and Change, 1810–1820: A Community Migration to Preble County, Ohio

1. Porter, *Destiny of Scotch-Irish.*

2. *History of Preble County, Ohio.* Cleveland: 1881, pp. 233–234.

3. Archibald Hamilton is listed in the 1830 census as in Preble County, Ohio, but the original page is mostly illegible. He and his wife are listed again in 1840 between the ages of sixty and sixty-nine, which corresponds with Martha's age.

4. Robert Pressly married Elizabeth on December 14, 1809. In the 1810 census, he has one sister aged ten to sixteen living with him. John S. Pressly (JSP) states in his *Brief History* that "[a]bout the year 1812 he accompanied his brother [Robert] and family to the state of Ohio and remained there three years."

5. Other members signing the call from Cedar Spring and Long Cane included William, James and Moses McGaw, James and Robert Boyce, George Brown, John Foster, Alexander Hamilton, James Giles, Robert Gamble.

6. In 1816, David sells land to his brother, Joseph, a transaction witnessed by John Pressly. Robert, David, Samuel, and Joseph Pressly are listed in the tax lists for 1816. There were other land transfers among family members including David and his wife, Jane, to Joseph, John, and Robert Pressly.

7. David estate papers Box 75 Package 1842 Probate Records Office, Abbeville County Courthouse. Legatees received the first installment "according to their acts": Joseph Lowry (husband of Mary Pressly), $936.90; George Brown (husband of Elizabeth Pressly), $835.00; Samuel Pressly, $800.00; and John T. Pressly, $150.00. Appraisal done by John Pressly (his brother) and William Hearst.

8. Preble petition, filed 10-13-1828. Samuel and John T. Pressly (as executors) vs James Pressly and others to Petition for David Pressly's land holdings in Ohio to be "Petitioned" so they could be divided among heirs.

PART III

Abbeville District and the Hard Labor Section: The Secular World, 1820–1850

Introduction

Part III deals with the years 1820 to 1850 and focuses primarily on the secular world of the grandchildren of immigrants John and David Pressly. These grandchildren were the first generation in which all of its members were born in America. The primary emphasis is on John's (imm 1772) descendants who remained in Abbeville District, where the family first settled. While many of David's grandchildren enjoyed a similar trajectory of success, they are not treated here in the same depth because their adult years were spent in a different "place," mainly York County, Darlington County, and Charleston, South Carolina—each with its own history. By 1820, the cast of characters has expanded greatly since this story began some fifty years earlier. From two brothers, their wives, and thirteen children between them, there were now over sixty grandchildren (see Appendix B) many of whom distinguished themselves as ministers, educators, medical doctors, prosperous merchants, political leaders, and elders in the Associate Reformed Presbyterian Church throughout the South. This section also considers the Hearst family and the lives of other Pressly neighbors, including the Chileses, Perrins, Devlins, Cothrans, Widemans, Marshalls, and Sproulls, within the context of the secular plantation world and the thriving rural farming community around Hard Labor Creek. Today this encompasses the towns of Troy and Bradley, the Cedar Springs Historic District, Winterseat, and, further to the east, Whitehall, now forming parts of modern day Abbeville, Greenwood, Edgefield and McCormick counties. Part III attempts to open a window into this world during the period 1820 to 1850.

Chapter 9

The Hard Labor Section: A Prosperous, Rural Farming Community

The 1820s: An Overview and Laying out the Immediate Neighborhood

Like other lower Piedmont districts, Abbeville District's long growing season and climate were ideal for subsistence crops and especially for growing short staple cotton, which was its main export crop.[1] According to the 1820 census, the district had nearly doubled its number of inhabitants since 1800 (13,500 to 23,103) and more than tripled the number of slaves (2,964 to 9,615). In his *Atlas of the State of South Carolina,* and the accompanying *Statistics of South Carolina,* published in 1825,[2] the architect, Robert Mills, provided an overview of what South Carolina was like in the early 1820s, capturing a moment in time as he and his assistants traveled throughout the state. He described Abbeville as "a pleasant village laid out with some order; containing besides a courthouse and a jail, about forty houses, and a population of four hundred souls; an arsenal and magazine are located here the latter is some little distance from town." It was still a relatively small village compared to Cambridge, which had more than ten stores and four hotels, or an upcountry town like Yorkville, which (according to Mills) had fifty-two mechanics (skilled, generally white laborers), eight lawyers, two physicians, eight stores, and five taverns, a male and a female academy, a printing office with two papers weekly, and some eighty houses.[3] Mills's *Atlas* included detailed maps of each district, locating key roads, towns, rivers and creeks, taverns, mills, post offices, churches and meeting houses, and larger home sites (Figure 9-1).

By the 1820s, Abbeville District and the adjacent Edgefield District had transitioned from a frontier, yeoman farmer economy, to a larger farmstead and small plantation culture with active links to commercial ports and export centers, such as Vienna, Hamburg, Augusta, Camden and Charleston. In 1833 a railroad opened up between Hamburg and Charleston, greatly facilitating the transport of cotton. A strong middle class of well-educated professionals began to emerge in the South Carolina backcountry, many of whom worked as lawyers, educators, merchants, skilled artisans, clergy, and physicians. Most middle-class professionals, however, shared a desire to increase land holdings. It was not uncommon for them to hold dual occupations, working also in agriculture, some eventually becoming wealthy planters while maintaining their professional status. The movement across social strata was more seamless in the backcountry, and even merchants had an ease of

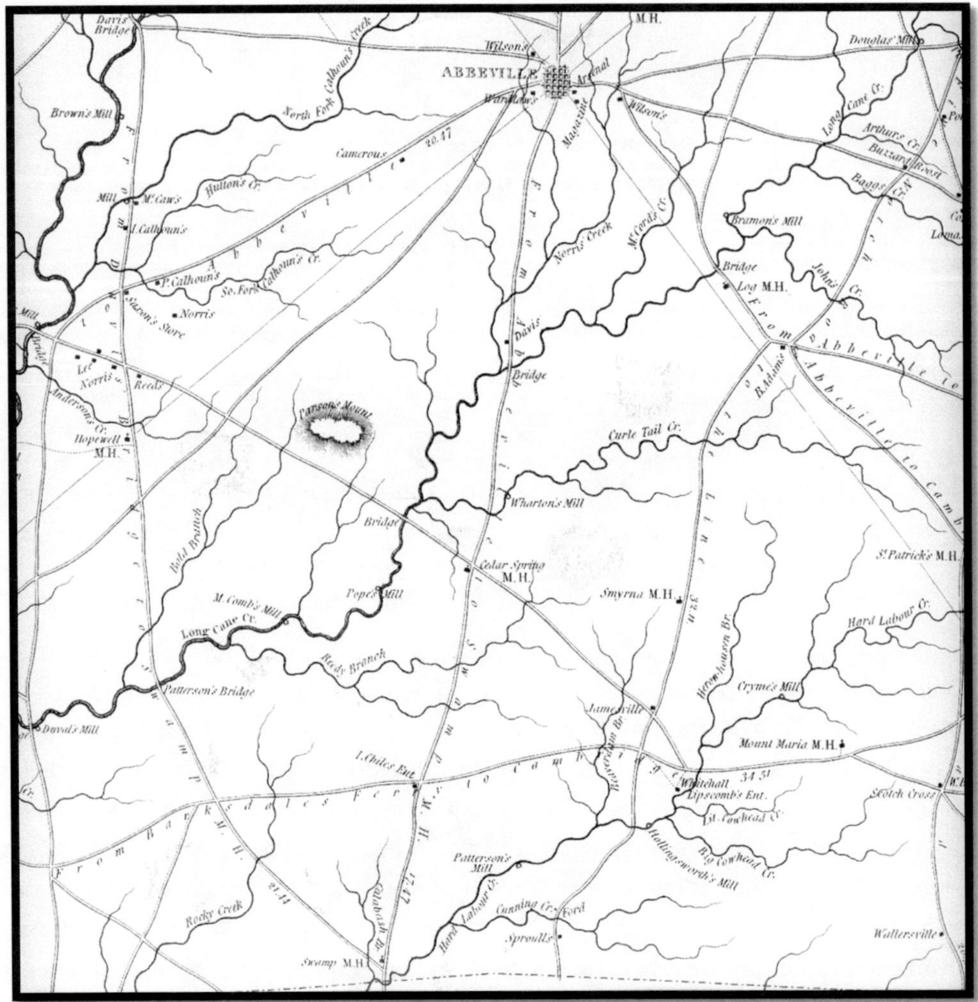

Figure 9-1. Detail of Robert Mills's map of Abbeville District showing Hard Labor section, executed by William Robinson, 1820. Robert Mills, *Atlas of the State South Carolina*, Baltimore, *1825*. Scanned by author from purchased facsimile.

access denied their low-country counterparts, particularly in the first decades of the nineteenth century. This was especially true in areas like Abbeville and Edgefield districts, where small communities were bound together by ties of friendship and kinship that extended over several generations.

By 1820, following the death of David Pressly, in 1818, and the return of most of the family from Preble County, Ohio, the Pressly kin regrouped in the Hard Labor Section, where the family first settled. This was to remain the center of family life for the next fifteen years. The Pressly family's extended neighborhood encompassed the area between the Lower Long Cane ARP Church, the Hard Labor Section where they lived (including Whitehall and Winterseat), and the Cedar Spring ARP Church where they worshiped. This nineteenth-century community was strategically located (some ten to fourteen miles from the village of Abbeville) at the intersections of several major public roads (authorized by the State Assembly) leading from Abbeville to Camden, Cambridge, and Charleston and from Vienna, Augusta, and Hamburg on the Savannah River. These included the Barksdale Ferry Road, the Abbeville Road to Charleston, and the Long Cane Road to Charleston, the latter passing by John Pressly's land. A few miles to the east was Five Notch Road, which was an important transportation route from the area to Hamburg and Augusta. During crop season, these roads were heavily trafficked with wagons loaded with crops for sale. Along these routes were a number of stores, inns, and taverns, the latter identified by *Ent* (presumably an abbreviation for entertainment) on William Robinson's 1820 map of Abbeville District, prepared for Robert Mills's *Atlas,* as well as plantation homes like Chiles Crossroads and White Hall Place, which also served as inns. An early nineteenth-century inn, circa 1825, next door to Cedar Spring ARP Church, and probably built solely for the purpose of serving travelers, can still be seen in the Cedar Springs Historic District (Figure 9-2). Taverns and stores also served as neighborhood gathering places where information was shared, bartering and business deals were negotiated, and politics were debated.

Figure 9-2. Stage Coach Inn, circa 1825 on the Abbeville to Charleston Road (now Cedar Springs Road). Cedar Springs Historical District, Bradley, South Carolina. Photograph courtesy of author.

In the decades leading up to the Civil War, plantations, large farmsteads, and small farms filled the area around Hard Labor Creek. Between 1815 and 1835, several large working plantation homes were built in the immediate neighborhood as planters reaped the benefit of the first cotton boom. Unlike the planter elite of the low country, who did not "dirty their hands," many of these upcountry farmers worked hands on in the fields, sometimes side-by-side with their slaves. Mainly cotton farmers, they continued to consolidate and enlarge their land holdings, frequently owning several tracts of land managed by family members. Securing land wealth remained an important aspiration and planters often reinvested their profits to secure more land. This community became a center of wealth and power. By 1860, at least ten of the twenty wealthiest individuals in the entire Abbeville District lived here, including Dr. George W. Pressly.

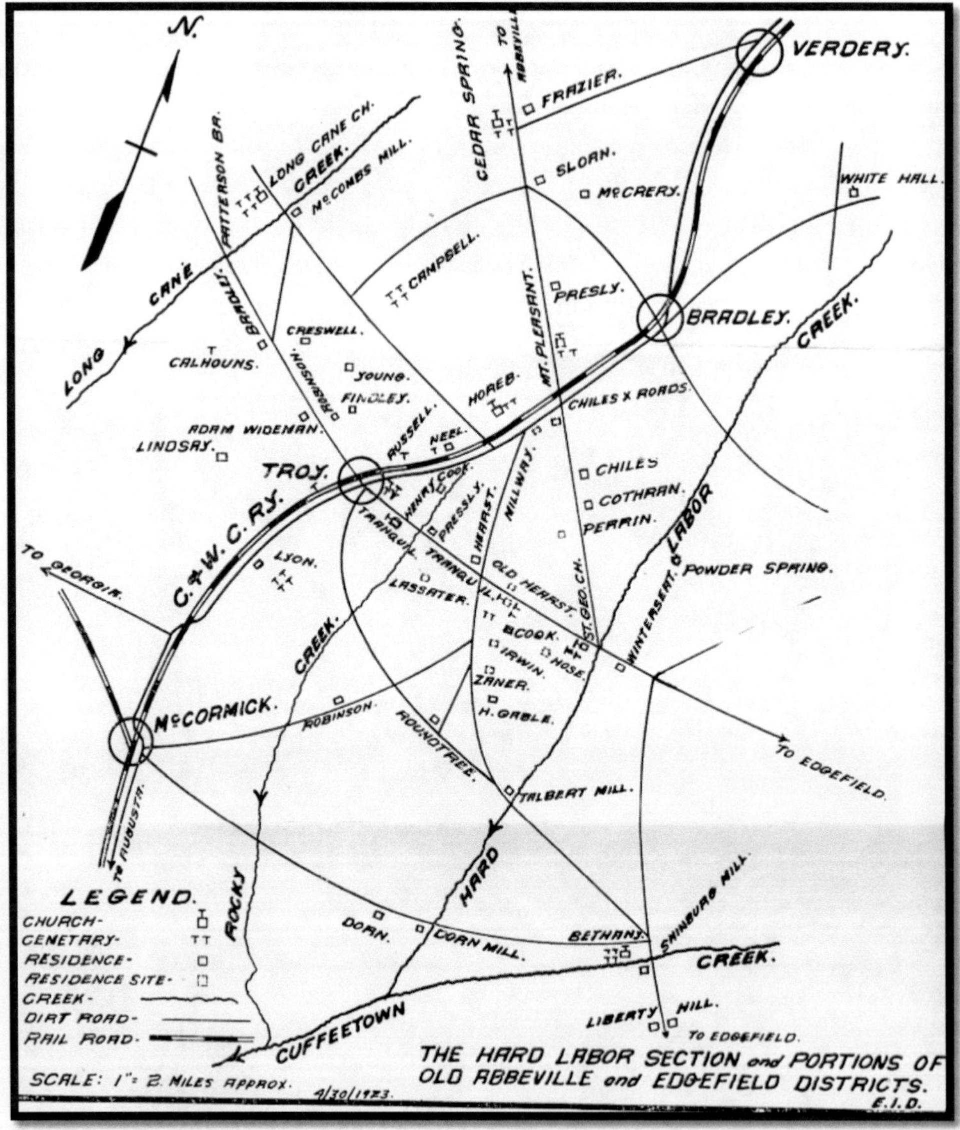

Figure 9-3. Emmett J. Davis's 1923 reconstruction of the Hard Labor Section, published in Harvey Toliver Cook, *The Hard Labor Section*, 1924. Greenville, South Carolina. Privately published.

Today this is a sparsely populated area that includes the late nineteenth-century towns of Troy and Bradley. Only a small number of antebellum homes and churches survive and for the most part, crumbled foundation stones and forgotten cemeteries, hidden or barely visible in the Long Cane Section of Sumter National Forest, are the lone reminders of the once vital community that flourished here before 1860. Robert Mills's 1820 map and Emmett J. Davis's 1923 reconstruction of the Hard Labor Section, which shows how the area may have looked in the first half of the nineteenth century, (Figure 9-3) provide a starting point for reconstructing this community during the period between 1820 and 1850. Although these maps are not entirely accurate, they provide important details locating home sites, roads, churches, and meeting places. Paul Grier's 1894 topographical map for Abbeville County is also a valuable resource for identifying midcentury home sites (Figure 9-4). If we integrate information from these maps and from nineteenth-century survey plats and local histories as well as from recent archaeological surveys, it is possible to recreate (at least partially) a picture of this neighborhood in the first half of the nineteenth century. I took the further step of superimposing this data, along with location of Pressly family home sites and those of their immediate neighbors, the Hearst family, onto a contemporary map of the area. By locating relevant eighteenth- and nineteenth-century reference points, including farmsteads, plantations, small home sites, taverns, churches, cemeteries, important roads as well as old sunken road beds on today's terrain, it is possible to assess distances and adjacencies (Figure 9-5). This brought the area to life in extraordinary ways. This nineteenth-century world suddenly became real. I was able literally to walk the ground where our ancestors lived.

Figure 9-4. Detail from official topographical map of Abbeville County, South Carolina, executed by Paul L. Grier and W. P. Bullock, 1895.

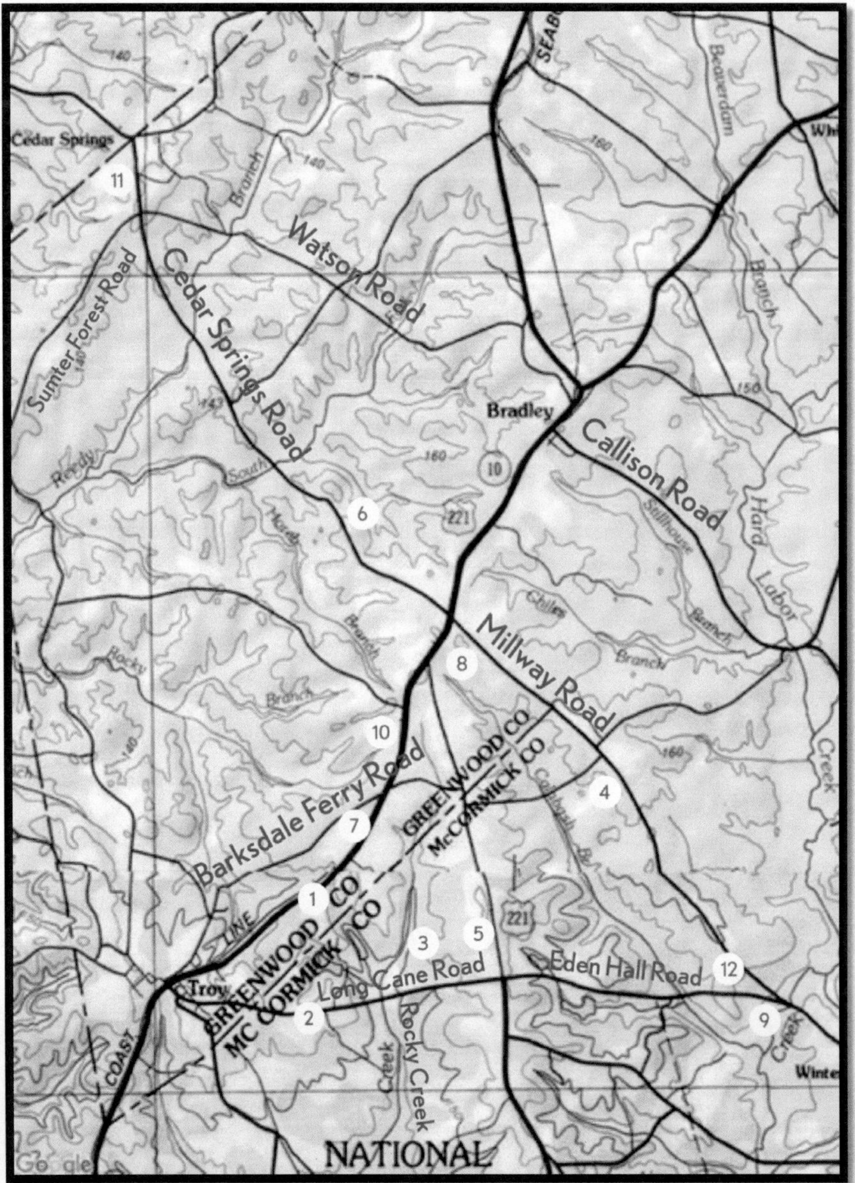

Figure 9-5. ACME map of location of homes of some plantation owners and key sites in the Hard Labor section, 1820–1850.

1. Reverend John Taylor Pressly
2. John Pressly and Dr. Samuel Pressly
3. Col. John Hearst and his mother Jane Hearst
4. Sylvania (Col. John Hearst)
5. Eden Hall (Dr. John Wardlaw Hearst)
6. Dr. George W. Pressly Farmstead
7. Dr. George Pressly Home
8. Chiles Crossroads (Major John Chiles)
9. Swamp Meeting House
10. Horeb Baptist Church
11. Cedar Spring ARP Church
12. Perrin land

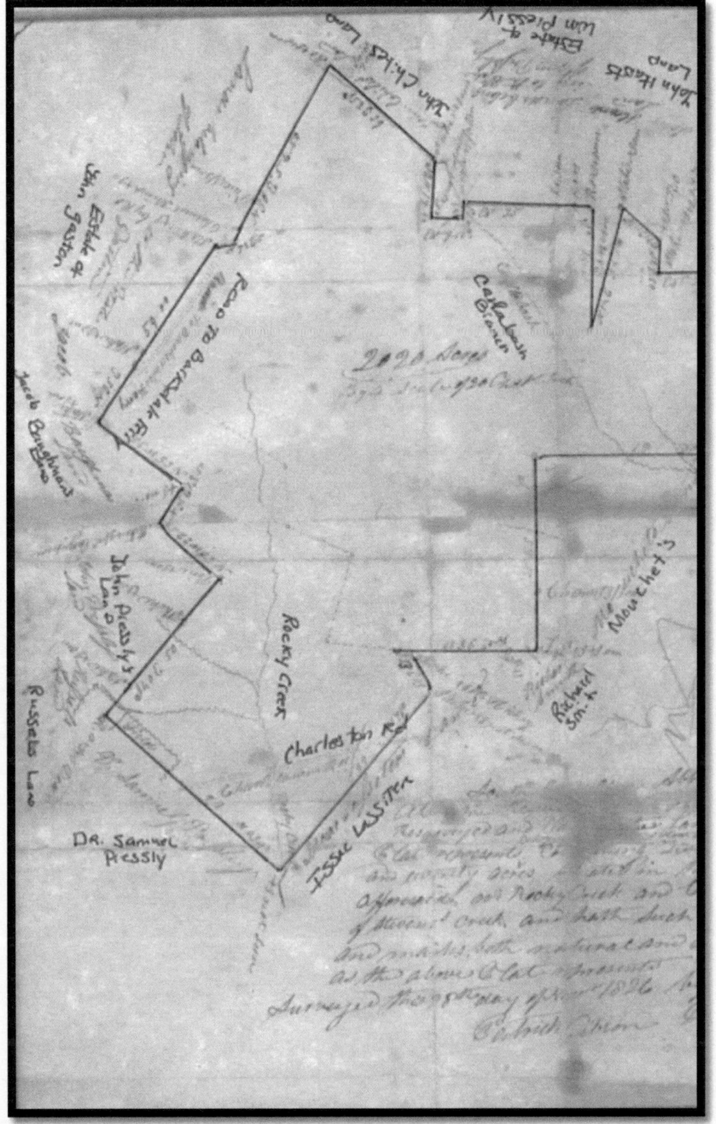

Figure 9-6. Detail of 1826 survey with boundaries and neighboring landowners highlighted. Courtesy of Wideman Family Papers. Bradley, South Carolina.

After his death circa 1809–10, William Pressly's widow, Elizabeth Hearst, and their four children remained on the home track, and their eldest son, John, took over the homestead when he came of age. John is listed in the 1820 census as head of household with one male aged ten to fifteen (his brother, Ebenezer Erskine), one male aged sixteen to twenty-five (himself), one female aged ten to sixteen (his sister, Jane), one female aged sixteen to twenty-five (his sister, Martha), one female aged twenty-six to forty-four (his mother), and no slaves. The family lived next to Elizabeth's brother, Joseph Hearst, and his wife Jane who, after his death in 1814, continued to live on their large plantation with her younger children and her son,

Col. John "Hard Labour" Hearst, who was their guardian, and his wife, Sarah Wardlaw. John Pressly was a subsistence farmer whose land essentially served the household with some cash crops like corn and cotton. After his father's death, he would have had little choice but to take over the farm and help support his family rather than get a university education and pursue a professional career like his brother and many cousins. In 1823, John married Martha Devlin, daughter of John Devlin (1771–1850), who was a leading elder in the Cedar Spring ARP congregation and a close friend of the Pressly family, having served in 1818 as one of the executors of David Pressly's estate. John Pressly died in 1826, five weeks before his son, John E. Pressly, was born most likely at the home of his grandfather, John Devlin.[4] His wife, her father, and her brother-in-law, James Drennan (husband of Martha's sister, Mary Devlin) served as executors of his estate. The estate inventory was typical of a small farmer with some cash crops, and Martha purchased many things from her husband's estate (see pp. 175–176). Their neighbor, Col. Hearst, rented the plantation for a year and also made numerous purchases, including a field of cotton. Other buyers were John T. Pressly, James Tutt, Samuel Perrin, William Chiles, Joseph Lindsay, John Devlin, and Jacob Gable.[5]

Living next to John Pressly were his cousins, Dr. Samuel Pressly and his wife, Elizabeth Knox Hearst, and Reverend John Taylor Pressly (JTP), pastor of the Cedar Spring ARP Church who was married to Jane Hearst, Elizabeth's sister. Samuel resided in the Brick House located next to John Pressly, which had belonged to his father and where, presumably, he also had his physician's office.[6] It is unclear how much additional land Samuel owned, but given the fact he had twenty-nine slaves by 1830, it was likely that he owned more than his father's 150 acres. JTP, who also owned land next to him, lived nearby in Henry Cook's home, which was on Barksdale Ferry Road, on land that later belonged to James Madison Chiles and then to his brother, Dr. George Pressly. According to the 1830 census, his mother was living with him. Nora Davis states that JTP's home was located "2 miles east of Troy on a bluff on the west side of Rocky Creek about one-third of a mile above its intersection with the old Long Cane-Charleston Road, about one-third of a mile upstream from his brother Dr. Samuel Pressly."[7]

Also in the immediate area, were several of David Pressly's (imm 1767) grandchildren, including Robert Pressly and JSP (Samuel's sons) who were able to hold on to their father's land after his death. JSP noted, in an account of his life, that he was born near a rivulet known as Indian Branch, about a half-a-mile from Josiah Patterson, probably a tributary of Rocky Creek with its headwaters near the town of Troy. This is the approximate location of the land Robert and JSP sold in 1819 to Moses Thompson (1762–1831), who was probably their mother's brother.[8] Around 1815, David Pressly, Jr.'s son, Alexander (1793–1863) returned to the area from Lowndesville and married Moses Thompson's daughter, Tabitha Cothran Thompson. He lived next to Moses Thompson and his name appears on a March 15, 1827, survey for his neighbor, Abner Perrin, on Rocky Creek as a chain bearer, indicating he was authorized to hold the chains for the surveyor, a common practice for adjacent landowners. Alexander was very much part of this community into the 1840s. He was included in the 1830 Abbeville census with one slave and in 1840 in the Edgefield census with none. Several of his children were still in the area as late as 1843 when they appear in Horeb Baptist Church records. Alexander eventually moved to Lowndes County, Mississippi.

The family group also included, John Pressly, the only child of John Pressly (imm 1772) still in the area, and until 1826, his son, Reverend Samuel Patterson Pressly (see pp. 171–176). Returning from Ohio to Hard Labor section around 1818, John was probably a subsistence farmer who occasionally served as a tutor. We know he was appointed as executor or estate appraiser for neighbors on several occasions and that he was listed in the 1830 census with his second wife, Elizabeth Weed Pressly, and six children under fourteen and one slave. It is unclear where they lived, but the family moved to Rush County, Indiana, in 1835, shortly before his death (ca. 1836/37; some descendants still live there). His nephew, George Pressly, administered his estate.[9]

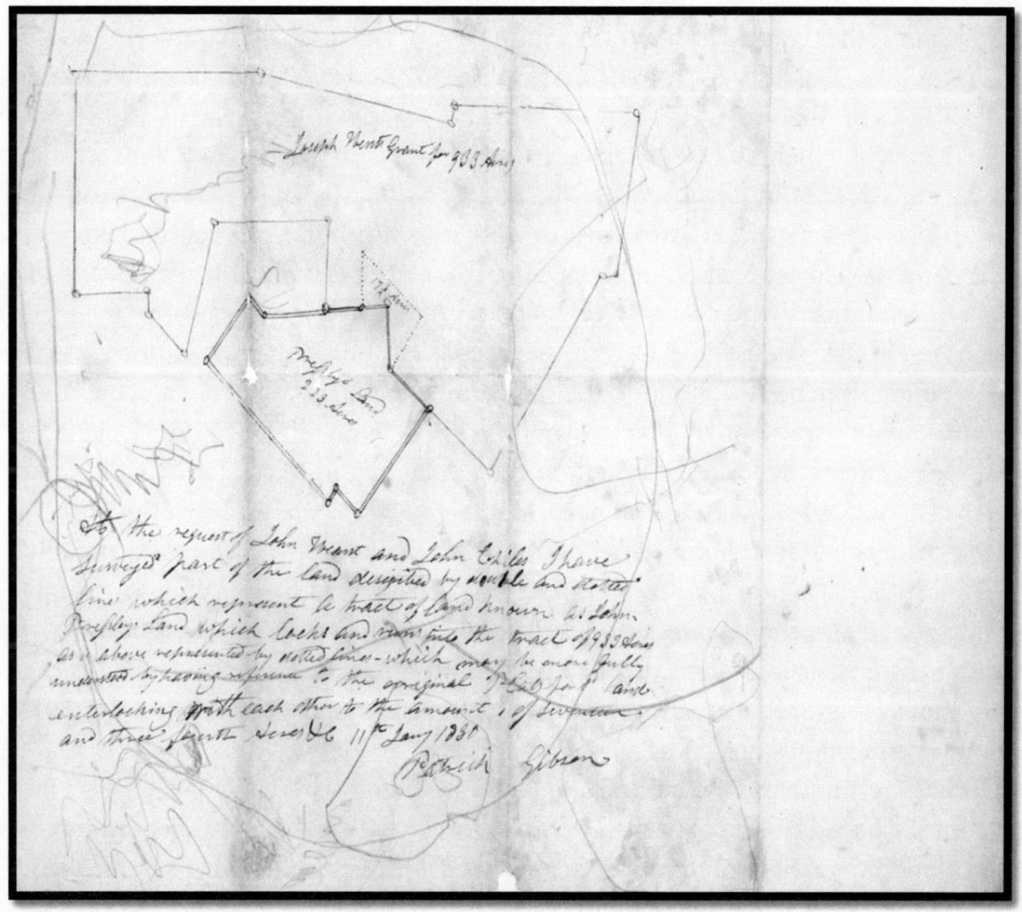

Figure 9-7. Detail of survey related to "Pressly's land" prepared by Patrick Gibson fin 1882 or Col. John Hearst and Major John Chiles. Courtesy of Wideman Family Papers, Bradley, South Carolina.

Among the Presslys' closest neighbors were the Hearst family. By the time of his death in 1814, Joseph Hearst's holdings included much of the land between his father's and John Pressly's (imm 1772) bounty plats and the area some one-and-a-half miles northeast, where Calabash Road intersects the old Abbeville to Charleston Road including the land where his son, Col. John "Hard Labour" Hearst, was to build Sylvania circa 1825. During the late teens and 1820s, Col. Hearst continued to enlarge his land holdings, buying neighbors land (including 312 acres from Benjamin Tutt) and buying out his siblings' shares of their father's estate, which included the 933 acres Joseph Hearst had purchased in 1802.[10] Joseph and Elizabeth Hearst's brother, William, who never married, also lived nearby and was deeply involved with the Cedar Spring Church.[11] After his brother-in-law, William Pressly, died he took a special interest in his sister's son, Ebenezer Erskine Pressly. He paid for his books and tuition at Union Academy, which was established in 1820, and was sufficiently involved with E. E.'s life to leave him in his will "a suffitiantey [*sic*] to pay for his present steadys [*sic*] for his colegiate [*sic*] course his theological steadies or other profession to the amount of $1000."[12] Dr. Samuel Pressly, Reverend John Taylor Pressly, and John S. Pressly, along with William B. Wardlaw (Col. Hearst's brother-in-law) witnessed William Hearst's will.

In 1826, Col. Hearst had Patrick Gibson prepare a survey of his father's estate and his own land holdings (Figures 9-6), and in 1829, after their mother's death, his brother, Joseph Hearst, had Gibson prepare a survey of the 933 acres that belonged to him and his siblings.[13] These surveys are important documents in terms of Pressly neighborhood history and are the most accurate record we have of neighbor adjacencies in 1826 and 1829. They allow us for the first time to situate various Pressly family members in the 1820s within the context of their neighbors. The land closest to Sylvania included or was adjacent to David Pressly's (imm 67) 1767 bounty plat. Col. Hearst's neighbors in 1826, as shown on the survey, were Major John Chiles, John Pressly, Dr. Samuel Pressly, Russell, Isaac Lassiter, "Pressly's land," Reverend John T. Pressly, Mouchet, Jacob Baughman, estate of John Gastin, R. Smyth, and estate of William Pressly. There are several references to Pressly land in the Wideman Family Papers: one relates to the John Pressly tract which included two sketches drawn by Patrick Gibson, one for a 223-acre tract and the other for 17 acres which were adjacent to the above mentioned 933 acres (Figure 9-7). The second reference is to another track of land comprising 99 acres that was part of 223 acres that belonged to the estate of William Pressly and his wife Jane (the third Pressly family). Col. Hearst acquired this land in 1829 for $280.68 from his neighbor, Major John Chiles, who purchased it from a Court of Ordinary sale of the estate of William Pressly, presumably after the deaths of his widow and son, John Pressly, the latter dying in 1809.[14] The Wideman Family Papers include numerous other surveys and deeds that document transactions among neighbors including the Hearsts, Leonard Wideman, Moses Thompson, and Abner Perrin, among others.

Also living in the immediate area along with the Presslys and Hearsts were a number of large plantation owners including the Perrins, Chileses, Cothrans, Wardlaws, and Widemans, most of whom had been in the neighborhood for several generations. Interspersed among these plantation homes were smaller farmsteads of twenty or fewer slaves and subsistence farms belonging to families who had also been in the area for decades, including James and Phillip Stieffle, Alexander Pressly and his father-in-law, Moses Thompson, Samuel Mouchet, the Dorris family, and the Robinsons, Russells, Dowtins, Holloways, Devlins, Gables, and Adamsons.

Educating Young Farmers: The Founding of Union Academy, 1820

For small farmers, especially, it was hard to rise above the status of yeoman farmers without an education. By the 1820s, many upcountry farmers' sons were also aspiring middle class professionals and a university education became an increasingly critical component to upward mobility in the backcountry. Samuel Pressly and his brother, JTP, were both university graduates and among the first professionals in their peer group. As noted earlier, what was so remarkable in this environment was the fact that all five of David Pressly's (died 1818) sons received a university education—three of them before Union Academy even began. Samuel graduated circa 1809 from Transylvania University (founded in 1780 and moved to Lexington in 1789) and went on to become the first physician in the family, a very young profession in the backcountry at the time. JTP graduated in 1812, at age seventeen, also from Transylvania University, and then went to New York City to study under Dr. John Mitchell Mason at the Associate Reformed Theological Seminary. He was ordained on July 3, 1816, at the Cedar Spring Associate Reformed Church, where he had been baptized, and he married Jane Hearst the following day. From the early 1820s the Pressly family name was to be linked with education and intellectual endeavors and JTP played a key role in setting this course. Well educated and worldly, he developed a reputation early in his career as a gifted educator, and he played an extremely important role in the education of the young farmers in this relatively rural area and in the success of Union Academy. By 1825, he also was Professor at the ARP Synod of the South's newly formed Seminary with his home serving as a classroom.

According to John S. Pressly (JSP), "About the year 1820 a little company of plain farmers met, to consult regarding the propriety of getting up a classical school."[15] They met at the residence of Col. John Hearst and decided to build a school that consisted of a very basic log structure with two apartments, each about twenty square feet. It was described as "located near Chiles' Cross Roads [*sic*], on the premises of the late John Hearst." The school opened in February of 1820 with Job Swift as its first teacher. JSP identifies the "plain" farmers as Capt. Samuel Perrin, Major John Chiles (Chiles Crossroads), Col. John Hearst (Sylvania), William Hearst, John Holloway, Philip Stieffle, and Capt. John Pressly. The pupils for the first year were, for the most part, children of these families, including Thomas C. Perrin (Samuel Perrin), James P. Pressly (David Pressly's [died 1818] son), Ebenezer E. Pressly (William's son), and James M. Chiles (Major John Chiles), who, according to JSP, were "companions since childhood having grown up in the same neighborhood and attending primary school together [common schools in the neighborhood]." They studied a classical education for about four years. As we shall see, these "plain farmers" were in actuality wealthy planters who wanted their sons to have a traditional classical education and the opportunity to go to university and perhaps even the prestige of going to northern schools. Every one of the first students at Union Academy went to university, becoming successful professionals and planters.

Union Academy was one of many classical academies developed in the early nineteenth century and often run privately by preachers.[16] These academies were comparable to middle or secondary schools, often preparing students to enter the junior year of college. Reverend Moses Waddel's Willington Academy, started in 1804, is probably the largest and best known.[17] Located four miles west of Vienna (a major export town on the Savannah River in Abbeville District) it was initially laid out with a forty-foot-wide street, and twelve houses and log huts. Sometimes referred to as "Eton in the Woods," it had between 150 and 200 students at its peak, some of whom were boarding students. In 1819, Waddel, whose first wife was a sister of John C. Calhoun, left to head the University of Georgia in Athens.

Soon after Union Academy opened, Reverend JTP assumed teaching duties with the assistance of his cousins, John S. Pressly and Samuel Patterson Pressly (son of John Pressly's [imm 1772] son John), also a graduate of Transylvania University; Samuel also studied theology under JTP during this period before going on to Princeton Seminary to complete his theological studies. Little information survives regarding Union Academy or how long it remained active. J. I. Bonner, in his 1861 sketch of Reverend E. E. Pressly, described Union Academy as a high school and of "higher grade than most of its contemporaries in the country."[18] Because private academies, often established by Presbyterian ministers, assumed much of the responsibility for educating sons of the low country elite and wealthy upcountry farmers, it was not unusual for JTP to have assumed this role. His cousins, Reverend Samuel Pressly and JSP, were to do the same later in their careers. A few years later, Reverend Richard Furman helped establish the Village Academy in Edgefield in 1826, in preparation for a Baptist seminary.

Chapter 10

The Presslys and Hearsts: Physicians, Planters, and the Nullification Crisis

As noted previously, living in the immediate area with the Presslys and Hearsts were a number of other large plantation owners, including the Perrins, Chileses, Cothrans, Wardlaws, Pattersons, and Widemans, most of whom had been in the neighborhood for several generations. Many were key players in state politics and in financial, legal, and commercial circles. Nearby were other wealthy planters, including on Five Notch Road, James Sproull, and in Whitehall, the Marshalls, Lipscombs, and John "Whitehall" Hearst. While this was a more informal culture than in the low country and most backcountry plantation homes were smaller,[1] many of the homes of these "plain farmers" began to reveal a more fashionable and cultured side of backcountry life as they acquired some of the polish of a more mature, upland gentry. They were entrepreneurial and ambitious with some also professionally engaged as lawyers and physicians and merchants, the latter frequently also served as postmasters of post offices located in their stores. The community became a center of wealth and power in the decades before the Civil War. By 1860, at least ten of the twenty wealthiest individuals in the entire Abbeville District live here, including Dr. George W. Pressly. Fortunately, several well-preserved homes and outbuildings survive, and, along with descriptions and old photographs of other homes since destroyed, they allow us to better understand the character of life this notably independent group of Scotch-Irish planters, farmers, and professionals enjoyed.

The next two chapters examine in some detail the lives of many of the families in this close-knit community, beginning with the Pressly and Hearst families who, in addition to their physical proximity, were intimately intertwined through marriage and a shared faith with both families attending the Cedar Spring ARP Church. This bond was further deepened by the mid-1820s, by which time three of Colonel Hearst's sisters were married to David Pressly's (died 1818) sons: Samuel married Elizabeth Knox Hearst in 1811–12; John Taylor married Jane Hearst in 1816; and Dr. George W. Pressly married Isabella in the early 1820s. In 1830, Col. Hearst's daughter, Jane, married another of David's sons, the newly ordained Reverend James Patterson Pressly.

Dr. Samuel Patterson Pressly and Dr. George William Pressly

Samuel Pressly and his brother George were very much part of this world. They were able to capitalize on their father's early success and wealth to become successful professionals who rose to the status of planter. As noted previously, they were among the first of their peers to receive a university education and an advanced degree. During the first three decades of the nineteenth century, medicine was still a loosely supervised profession, and in 1810 there were only seven medical schools in the country, with 650 students in attendance, 406 of which were at the University of Pennsylvania. Student instruction was mainly limited to books and lectures, and young doctors received their clinical experience as apprentices. Samuel may have studied medicine under a Charleston physician, as had, around the same time, Dr. Samuel Steen Marshall who later practiced in nearby Whitehall. He could also have continued to study at Transylvania Medical College, which opened in 1799 and had several highly regarded physicians on the teaching staff at the time. However, it was not fully operational until 1817, so he would have also apprenticed under an established physician. Within a short time after his return from Ohio (by 1816), Samuel became a successful physician and a man of considerable wealth. He was also the first in his family to become a planter. His plantation bordered Col. Hearst's and Thomas Chiles's, and his name, along with Chiles, is highlighted as a chain bearer in Gibson's 1829 survey for Joseph Hearst Jr.[2] By the late 1820s, Samuel probably had, in addition to his home, several outbuildings including slave quarters, a kitchen, storage areas, barns, and perhaps a blacksmith area. He owned twenty-nine slaves in 1830, and the responsibilities of his wife, as mistress of the house, would have been considerable. She would have held the keys to the vital storerooms; managed the household and servants who worked with them in the garden, smokehouse, kitchen, and dairy; and supervised the livestock used for food. Households with more than thirteen slaves usually had house servants. Some slaves undoubtedly assisted Samuel in attending patients.

As a backcountry doctor, Samuel would have dispensed medicine and treated a myriad of illnesses; he would have tried to stay abreast of his profession through contact with fellow physicians and through medical school journals. The *New England Journal of Medicine and Surgery* was founded in 1812 and the *Philadelphia Journal of Medical and Physical Sciences* (later the *American Journal of Medical Sciences*) in 1820. Samuel and his brother, Reverend John Taylor Pressly, had similar roles in the community, tending to body and soul and sharing a certain intimacy across class lines. His practice as a medical doctor was extensive, and he is said to have traveled long distances to treat his patients "from Liberty Hill in Edgefield County to Calhoun's Mill in Abbeville County. The twelve-mile area was sickly with fevers during the summers and fall. The people were easy prey to pleurisy and consumption in the winter. Dr. Pressly's practice was so extensive he could seldom visit his patients oftener than every other day."[3] He was a trusted neighbor, serving as a witness for wills including his wealthy neighbor, Samuel Perrin, in 1828, and as an executor or administrator for numerous estates, sometimes with his cousin, JSP, or his brother, George, an indication of their status and respect in the community. He was also deeply involved in the Cedar Spring ARP Church, where his brother served as pastor until 1831 (see pp. 138–139) and where he was an elder; he was also actively involved in politics as was his cousin, JSP, and later his brother, George. For over two decades, Samuel was very much a part of the Hearst family and the upcountry planters' circle which included the nearby Chiles and Perrin families.

The calm of this relatively homogenous community in the late 1820s and early 1830s was shattered by two major and not unrelated occurrences: the migration of many individuals to Alabama, Mississippi, Tennessee, and the West, and the Nullification Crisis. Between 1828 and 1832, the South Carolina upcountry and especially Abbeville District, the home of John C. Calhoun, who was one of the most vocal proponents of Nullification, was rocked by the Nullification debate. Communities throughout the area were enmeshed in a spirited and frequently contentious debate, initially sparked by the passing of the Tariff Act in 1828, which increased duties on foreign imports to protect domestic industries. This Act hurt the agrarian South, which relied heavily on foreign imports. Nullification was essentially the concept that a state could ignore or refuse to apply Federal Law. In 1832, a special session of the South Carolina State Legislature adopted an Ordinance of Nullification, and John C. Calhoun and the Free Trade Party took the position that Nullification was the peaceful medium between submission to tyranny and outright revolution. The state elections in 1832 were charged with tension and violence, and political debates were said to have sometimes ended up in frontier brawls. The crisis was contentious enough to divide communities and congregations. The *Whig and Southern Nullifier* was published in Abbeville from 1831 to 1833 at the height of the debate. Most members of the Pressly family were staunch, if not outspoken, supporters of the anti-nullification position. John S. Pressly was a member of the state legislature from 1826 until 1833, when he was defeated as a Union Party candidate for Congress by the Nullification candidate, George McDuffie, who in 1834 became Governor. JSP left politics and soon joined his cousin, Reverend E. E. Pressly, in Due West. He also led attacks, as did another cousin, Reverend Samuel P. Pressly, in Newberry, against Thomas Cooper, a states' rights advocate whose deism offended the Associate Reformed Presbyterian Church, and he was instrumental in Cooper's dismissal as President of South Carolina College.

Community sentiments and divisions were sufficiently high and disruptive in the Hard Labor Section that in 1834, Dr. Samuel Pressly decided to leave Abbeville District and move to Wilcox County, Alabama. J. I. Bonner stated that Samuel "practiced his profession successfully, accumulated a considerable fortune, became discouraged on account of the political discussion and want of a settled pastor . . . and sold out and moved to Wilcox, Alabama"[4] Another revealing commentary indicates what a devastating effect the Nullification Crisis had on this close-knit community: "In 1832 the Doctrine of Nullification rage in South Carolina causing friends to be separated and families divided. The Pressly's neighborhood was equally divided, and at one time all friendships were broken. Being a man of peace, Dr. Pressly became discouraged with the conditions and in 1834 sold his possessions and moved with his family to Wilcox County, Alabama where he joined his brother, Reverend James Pressly (married to Col. Hearst's daughter, Jane), in Wilcox County, Alabama."[5] These are immensely revealing comments about the neighborhood and how the political landscape affected the Pressly family, which was in the minority both in terms of rejecting ideas of nullification and in their support of a master's right to teach slaves to read and write.

Should we be in any doubt as to the mood of the immediate neighborhood at the time, 107 men of military age in the Hard Labor Section including John Cothran, Leonard Wideman, Major John Chiles, James Holloway, James W. Sproull, James H. Wideman, Henry Hose, Thomas C. Perrin, John Lewis Devlin, and Isaac Lassiter (George Pressly did not) signed in January 1835 a pamphlet called the *Spirit of 98*.[6] It set out fourteen principles, and its signees became the roll of the "Long Cane Minute Men." The pamphlet referred to the Principles of '98, a political position advocating state rights. It argued individual states could judge the constitutionality of central government laws and decrees, and could refuse to enforce laws deemed unconstitutional. The Principles of '98 were part of the Virginia Resolutions (or Resolves) drafted in 1798 and 1799, which argued that the states had the right and the duty to declare unconstitutional any acts of Congress that were not authorized by the Constitution.

Samuel died in 1837, a little more than two years after his move. His will was probated in Abbeville District with his brother, George, serving as the executor of his estate, with $30,000 held in bond.[7] His extensive probate records reveal a large number of outstanding notes from neighbors due him, including $945.19 from Major John Chiles, $349.13 from Samuel Mouchet, and $300 from Andrew Weed, suggesting he may have left Abbeville without all of his affairs concluded. His complicated estate was not settled until the late 1840s. George may have acquired some of his brother's land, which was part of immigrant John's original plat; a portion remained in his family until the 1930s, when Dr. George Pressly Neel, sold 131 acres to F. E. Grier. It is currently owned by John Calvin Grier, a distant Pressly relation. Samuel's wife and their children continued to live in Wilcox County after his death.

While we don't know George Pressly's thoughts on Nullification, he clearly had to be comfortable enough with his neighbors' more conservative attitudes to remain in the area. By the late 1830s, he and his family were the only Presslys of his generation to remain in the Hard Labor Section and to worship at Cedar Spring ARP Church. Born in 1803, George went to Transylvania University like his brothers before him, and then to Jefferson Medical School at the University of Pennsylvania, where he graduated in 1824. His decision to go there was a remarkable and unusual choice: remarkable because only wealthy planters' sons could afford such an education, and unusual because the majority of southern doctors in the early 1820s stayed closer to home and were mainly trained through apprenticeships with established physicians. The fact that he could have continued at Transylvania University, the first "orthodox" and highly regarded medical school in the south, but chose to go to the University of Pennsylvania, speaks to his ambition and intellectual excellence as well as access to sizeable funds.

He married Isabella Hearst and became a successful and respected physician as well as a wealthy planter, eventually owning two tracts of land near his brother-in-law, Col. Hearst. George and his wife, Isabella, who died in 1858, had four children who reached adulthood. He practiced medicine from the mid-1820s through the Civil War. Physicians' activities were often recorded in account or daybooks, detailing where a country doctor traveled, the types of medicines he dispersed, babies delivered, and so on. His notebooks from the late 1830s and early 1840s, donated by Dr. Lila Bonner Miller to the South Caroliniana Library at the University of South Carolina, contain extensive descriptions of a large number of diseases with suggested remedies.[8] They may have been used for lectures or to train young doctors. His daybook lists family names with space for multiple visits along with fees for each patient. Among neighbors treated were Col. John Hearst, Thomas White Chiles, Elijah Lyon, Matthew Shanks, William Robertson, and the Yarboroughs, Fosters, Devlins, Wardlaws, Ausleys, Creswells, and Stieffels. He was paid the large sum of thirty dollars on one occasion to attend Col. Hearst's slaves. The daybook also contained visits to his Uncle John Pressly's sons, William and John B. Pressly, both of whom died in the early 1830s. It would also appear from his daybook accounts that students may have boarded with him.

George owned a one-thousand-acre plantation located a little less than two miles north of Chiles Crossroads, on the Abbeville to Charleston road (now Cedar Springs Road). His land (some of which may have belonged to his father) may have extended as far north as the current intersection of Sumter Forest and Cedar Springs roads, placing it near where the original Cedar Creek meeting house had been located. It extended south to near where the old Mt. Pleasant Church was located, off what is today Route 10. A portion of this plantation tract is now part of the Long Cane Section of Sumter National Forest (38GN389). Remains of a large home pad, indicating it was a large farmstead, a few bricks, and a large well are still visible.[9] Masses of daffodils, always an indicator of a former homestead, still bloom on the site in February. Nora Davis described the six-room farmstead on the property as one-and-a-half stories high and neatly "ceiled," noting that the large downstairs rooms had fireplaces with large windows on each side, and a tall mantel. Two additional rooms extended the full length of the house, each divided in two.[10] George's home was most likely more a large farmstead dwelling than a "plain" I-style Carolina plantation although, as Melanie A. Cabak and Mark D. Groover suggest in their interesting study, *Plantations without Columns,* these lines could blur among some "frugal" upcountry planters.[11] Remnants of agricultural terraces are clearly visible above the old road bed for the original Abbeville to Charleston Road, which passed close to his house, but at a lower elevation. Some one hundred yards from where the house stood is an old cemetery, probably a slave cemetery, with about thirty field stones carefully placed on an east to west axis. George's son, Dr. Joseph Pressly, lived on the planation beginning in the 1850s. In 1860, Joseph owned nine thousand dollars in real estate and thirty thousand in personal property (including twenty-nine slaves). When he moved to the Frazier/Pressly Octagon House in the early 1870s after his father-in-law died, Joseph's daughter, Frances, inherited a portion of the property and lived there with her husband, W. T. Bradley, until she sold the land in 1907.[12]

Living less than a mile away, further up the Abbeville to Charleston Road, was the Devlin family, many of whom like George and Samuel were also Elders in the Cedar Spring ARP church. They were close friends and also family through John Pressly's marriage to Martha Devlin. Col. James Devlin (1780–1849) was one of a number of smaller farmers in the area. Foundations for numerous small farmsteads with additional outbuildings have been found in Sumter National Forest, indicating that this was a predominant building type in the area. The remains of Devlin's good size farmstead are located off Cedar Springs Road, near the Creswell family cemetery. Identified as 38GN810 in recent Sumter National Forest archaeological records,[13] the footprint of his dwelling is still relatively intact, along with its well-preserved cellar and three chimneys; the remains of three other outbuildings and a brick-lined well also survive. By the 1830s a good size farmstead in the area would have consisted of a numbering of standing dwellings with the slave dwellings close to the main house as the majority of farmers worked alongside their slaves in the field. While the size of these farmsteads varied, Williams Place (Figure 10-1), a remarkably well-preserved large farmstead in rural Spartanburg

Figure 10-1. The two-story large house at Williams Place ca. 1850 in Glenn Springs, Spartanburg County, South Carolina.

Figures 10-2a and 2b. Dr. George W. Pressly's home site at 503 Barksdale Ferry Road near Chiles Crossroads, Bradley, South Carolina, later known as the Neel house. Photographs courtesy of author.

County, may give us some idea of what these self-sustaining farmsteads looked like. Dating from the late 1840s, with little alterations, Williams Place consists of fourteen standing structures, including a two-story large house, a stable, a one-story gable-roofed log kitchen, a chicken house, a smoke house, a smithy, a corn crib, and slave dwellings which were relatively close to the main house.[14]

By the 1850s, George also owned an elegant eight-room plantation house nearby (Figures 10-2a and 2b), which survives in good condition and is located at 503 Barksdale Ferry Road, less than two miles from his plantation tract and from Chiles Crossroads. This good sized frame dwelling with a simple classical pediment and a four column, two-story portico with a porch on each level was most recently in the possession of Glen and Kathey Rawson. It was built by George's close friend, Reverend James Madison Chiles, in the mid-1830s, around the time he married. He was the son of Major John Chiles and a playmate of George's brother, James, and his cousin, Ebenezer Erskine Pressly, who were fellow students at Union Academy in the 1820s. Chiles studied theology under Reverend John T. Pressly before he was ordained a Baptist minister. George probably purchased the property in 1853, when Chiles advertised in the *Abbeville Banner* the sale of his plantation "containing 850 acres upon the head waters of Rocky Creek," shortly before he left the area. The home, later known as the "Neel" house, was located very close to where his brother JTP had lived. George lived at the Barksdale Ferry home until sometime after 1860 when he gave the home to his daughter, Margaret, and her new husband, Dr. James A. Neel (who, like George, received his medical degree in 1859 from Jefferson Medical College in Philadelphia) after their marriage in 1860. At the time of George's death, the tract of land included eight hundred acres and most likely extended south and west from Barksdale Ferry Road near where John Pressly's (imm 1772) original plat was located.

George was a wealthy planter who, according to the 1860 census, owned $24,500 worth of land and $95,000 in personal property, including sixty-five slaves, for a total of $119,500, or roughly $3,200,000 in today's dollars. Medicine as a profession began to enjoy more esteem, and George continued to hold a respected position in the community, frequently serving as an estate executor, administrator, or witness to wills, as well as an appraiser of estates, where he was joined on several occasions by his brother-in-law, Col. John Hearst. He was very much part of this community of ambitious and entrepreneurial (and probably also conservative) planters like Major Chiles, Thomas White Chiles, Thomas Chiles Perrin, James H. Wideman, and John Cothran, and physician planters like himself, including John Wardlaw Hearst, Samuel S. Marshall, and John Livingston. Like many of them, he was actively involved in political and community affairs and was elected to the South Carolina House of Representatives for four terms from 1842 to 1849. He was one of five representatives from Abbeville District serving in the thirty-fifth General Assembly 1842–43, along with Joseph Dickson, John Burnette Black, his neighbor the planter and lawyer, Thomas Chiles Perrin, and the wealthy merchant and planter, Joel Smith of Stoney Point. George also served as a member of various county-related committees, including one for an insane asylum. Like his friend and relative, Dr. Hearst, he was also a member of the Board of Trustees for Erskine College, beginning in the 1840s, and was actively involved in the Cedar Spring Church, where he served as an elder for thirty-three years. When Reverend Hemphill, who studied theology under Reverend John Taylor Pressly in Alleghany, accepted the call to become minister at Cedar Spring Church, he was received on June 28, 1837, at George's home.

The Hearst Family

Col. John "Hard Labour" Hearst, so name to distinguish him from his cousin John "Whitehall" Hearst, was a prominent figure and an ambitious planter, who consolidated and added to his land holdings over a fifteen-year period. In addition

Figures 10-3a and 3b. Front façade and rear view of Sylvania built by Col. John Hearst, circa 1825. Bradley, South Carolina. Photographs courtesy of author.

to the 2,020 acres that included Sylvania (Figures 10-3a and 3b), and where Eden Hall was later to be built, he also owned several additional tracts, including land he inherited from his wife's brother, William Wardlaw. He married Sarah Wardlaw sometime before 1811, when their daughter, Jane (who was to marry Reverend James Pressly), was born. They had four children before Sarah died, in 1823, but

Figures 10-4a and 4b. Details of Sylvania interior with stenciled grapevine design in central hall and woodwork that is carved, grained, and marbleized, first floor interior. Photographs courtesy of author.

only one child, Dr. John Wardlaw Hearst, survived their father. Presumably Hearst's beautiful plantation Sylvania, built circa 1825, was planned before his wife's death. Modest in scale and in the Federal style with a rectangular plan, four rooms on each floor, and a central hall, Sylvania survives today in excellent condition. It has a surprisingly sophisticated and highly refined interior with a stenciled grapevine design in the central hall and carved, grained, and marbleized woodwork on the first floor, including two beautifully carved fireplaces (Figures 10-4a and 10-4b and 10-5). The plantation was centrally located less than a mile from where the old Barksdale Ferry Road crossed what is today Route 221, above Calabash Road before it angled northeast, intersecting the Abbeville to Charleston Road at Chiles Crossroads.

Figure 10-5. Detail of fireplace carving in the dining room of Sylvania. Photograph courtesy of author.

Sylvania was a place that the Pressly family knew well. It was part of their world as neighbors and through marriage to three of Col. Hearst's sisters and to his daughter, Jane (died 1832). Today, Sylvania is situated in an idyllic rural farm setting, half-hidden by trees, and surrounded by pastures and woodlands and is accessed via Calabash Road, a dirt road that crosses Calabash Branch and connects with Route 221. Set back from Millway Road, which probably follows fairly closely the late eighteenth-century road from Abbeville to Charleston, the home and surrounding farmland, evoke an earlier period of hardworking planters who aspired to some of the refinement of their low-country counterparts but who lived more unassuming lives. There are still several nineteenth-century outbuildings on the property, including a brick smokehouse (Figure 10-6), a clapboard well house, a carriage house, and barn. The front façade has an arcaded veranda with six graceful columns, above which is a dormer, embellished with a Palladian window. In the 1970s, two wings were discreetly added, flanking and set back from the original plantation home with its original interior untouched (except for plumbing and electrical upgrades).

Figure 10-6. Original brick smokehouse ca. 1825, Sylvania. Photograph courtesy of author.

Col. Hearst's name appears frequently as an executor or administrator in legal documents including for Isaac Lassiter and Patrick Gibson in 1834 and for Francis Irwin in 1828 and Elizabeth Irwin in 1835. It was on his plantation that the school house for Union Academy was built in 1820, and in 1842 "Inhabitants of Abbeville District" petitioned to establish a "Box of Election" on his property. He may have also owned a store: included in his estate papers was a "shop book" that included notes held for many customers. At the time of Col. Hearst's death in 1843, Sylvania was a medium sized plantation with sixty-nine slaves. We know from his estate sale that the home was furnished with fine furniture, including a secretary bookcase and books which sold for eighty dollars and a beaded bedstead that sold for forty-nine dollars, mirrors, silver, and some nineteen paintings (some family portraits), an unusual item in estate inventories from this period in this community.[15] His son, Dr. John Wardlaw Hearst, served as executor and posted a fifty thousand dollar bond. Thomas W. Chiles, who was married to Col. Hearst's sister, Mary, appraised the estate, and its entire contents, real and personal, were sold at a large estate sale soon after his death. The estate documents tell us much about life on this plantation. In addition to the home furnishings and several pieces of fine furniture, the sale included a large number of farm animals, wagons and farm equipment, as well as the availability to rent of several tracks of land including the home tract, which his son rented, and a plantation tract on Long Cane. Dr. Hearst purchased the majority of the furnishings, which were presumably later placed in Eden Hall; other buyers included his neighbors, Leonard Wideman, Samuel Perrin, Jr. and Major John Chiles. There were a number of books in the sale suggesting Col. Hearst was well educated. Two of Reverend Dr. Proudit's *Theological Works* from the sale are in our possession; one contains the inscription "John Hearst's Book March 28, 1831" (Figure 10-7).[16] The estate sale totaled $32,133, not including rent for tracts of land, notes due, or real estate. Some sixty slaves were sold for between $500 and $700 each. A large number of outstanding notes, many dating back to the 1820s and 1830s, totalled a significant sum and deemed "doubtful" or "desperate," were listed in the estate inventory, presumably a casualty of the 1837 Panic and drop in cotton prices. Hearst was buried next to his wife in Cedar Springs Cemetery. His gravestone, carved by the well-known Charleston gravestone maker, W. T. White, contains the simple inscription, "An impartial man an honest friend and a humble Christian."

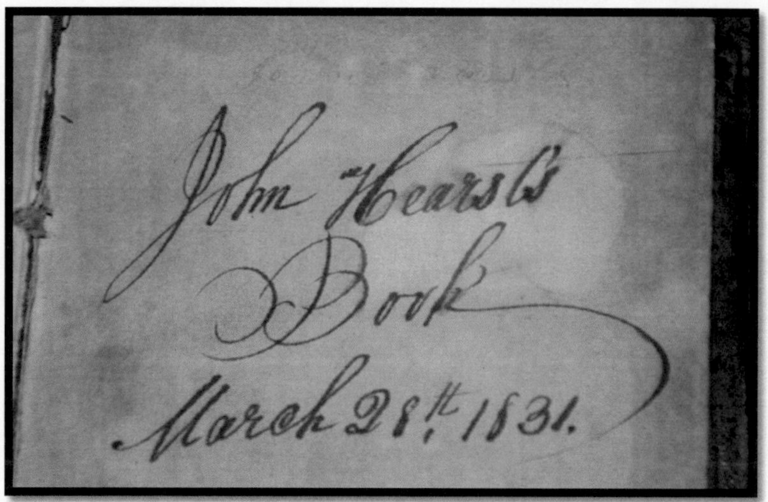

Figure 10-7. Col. Hearst's signature. Book in possession of Nancy and William Pressly.

Dr. John Wardlaw Hearst studied medicine at Miami University and married, in 1835, Ann Chiles (Figure 10-8a and 8b), the daughter of his neighbor, Major John Chiles, a wealthy planter and inn keeper who owned Chiles Crossroads. They lived initially with his parents at Sylvania, and around the time Sylvania was sold in 1847, moved to a site near where they built Eden Hall, completed circa 1854–5 (Figures 10-9a and 9b). Eden Hall is located at the northwest intersection of US 221 and Eden Hall Road (Country Road 24). It was an elite landowner plantation, partially a showpiece and more than a "plain plantation." A beautiful Greek-revival-style home designed by Henry Jones, an architect from Atlanta, it contains Egyptian influences in its interior decoration and is still a large working plantation on thousands of acres owned by the Davis family. Hearst was a well-regarded doctor and surgeon, whose kitchen is said to have also served as an operating room. His land holdings were extensive and at one time included the Peak Hill tract where William Dorn discovered gold. He presumably maintained ongoing contacts with colleagues in the area which would have included Dr. Samuel Steen Marshall's sons,

Dr. John Wardlaw Hearst.

Mrs. Ann Hearst.

Figures 10-8a and 8b. Dr. John Wardlaw Hearst and his wife Ann Chiles Hearst. Scanned from Harvey Toliver Cook's *The Hard Labor Section*, 1924. Greenville, South Carolina. Privately published. Courtesy of Wade C. Harrison.

Dr. Samuel Sproull Marshall and Dr. Joseph Warren Waldo Marshall who practiced in Whitehall where his uncle, John "Whitehall" Hearst, also resided. In the 1860 census, Dr. Hearst was the thirteenth wealthiest individual (combined real and personal assets) property holder in Abbeville District while his neighbors, Thomas Chiles Perrin and Dr. George W. Pressly, were the eleventh and seventeenth wealthiest.

Hearst took a special interest in his plantation and used progressive farming techniques, experimenting with seeds, including a variety of new vegetables, and was one of the first in the area to use fertilizers. He also bred new varieties of livestock that helped some of the smaller neighboring farmers. Beginning in the 1830s, better cultivating methods were also promoted by agricultural societies. Hearst was active in his community and known for his kindness and generosity, even after the Civil War, when he had lost most of his assets. He maintained close relations with his father's sister, Margaret, who lived with him in her later years, and her husband, John "Whitehall" Hearst, and was one of the executors of his estate in 1847.

Figures 10-9a and 9b. Eden Hall front and side facades. Davis Family, Bradley, South Carolina. Photographs courtesy of author.

Although Dr. Hearst's wife, Ann, was a Baptist who belonged to Horeb Baptist Church, where her brother Reverend James M. Chiles preached, Dr. Hearst remained closely connected to the Cedar Spring ARP Church, and he and his wife are buried there. They had no children, and when he died he left two-thirds of his estate to Erskine College, where he served as one of the original Trustees under Reverend E. E. Pressly.[17] It was the largest gift to the college up until that time. George Pressly's son-in-law, Dr. James D. Neel, was one of the executors of his estate.

In 1847, Dr. Hearst's neighbor, James H. Wideman (1823–1896), purchased Sylvania and a portion of Col. Hearst's land. He was a successful planter and a friend of Dr. Hearst over the next several decades. A graduate of South Carolina College (now the University of South Carolina), James was a devout Baptist who served for many years as deacon of Horeb Baptist Church, where he is buried; he was also a Trustee of Furman College and Moderator for the Edgefield and Abbeville Baptist associations. Two of his sons, Charles and Arthur, became physicians and lived on adjacent property in the latter part of the nineteenth century. Sylvania and its beautifully maintained outbuildings and farm land are still owned by his descendants, Mr. and Mrs. Frank J. Wideman III, who live there. James was the son of Leonard Wideman Jr. (1798–1847), a very wealthy planter who owned Oak Grove plantation which included some 1,600 acres off Barksdale Ferry Road between Troy and Indian Branch, a tributary of Rocky Creek east of Troy. He also owned several other tracts of land, which he seemed to have systematically acquired in the 1820s and 1830s, including the "Pressly Track," and tracts from Abner Perrin, Jr. Many of the legal documents related to these purchases are in the Wideman Family Papers. Leonard was married to Sarah Carson Patterson, a daughter of his neighbor, Josiah C. Patterson, and his wife Martha Carson (a sister of Major John Hearst's wife). According to local tradition, Leonard was a cruel master, and in December 1847, he was murdered by several of his slaves. He is buried in the Patterson-Wideman cemetery, near Ivy Gates, where his wife, Sarah, her father, Josiah, who died in 1835, and their daughter, Margaret Wideman, and her husband, Thomas Jefferson Lyons, are also buried. Dr. George Pressly served as one of Wideman's executors. His estate sale, which included some 109 slaves, reveals he was an immensely wealthy man, and a sum of eighty thousand dollars was placed in bond. His wife, Sarah, managed the plantation until her death in 1863; her estate sale included 1,648 acres.[18]

Chapter 11

Entrepreneurial Planters, Bonds of Kinship, and the Cyclical Economy

Bonds of Kinship

Numerous marriages took place among the wealthy and mostly very large families in this neighborhood, who, for the most part, married mainly in their peer group. If we look just at the Hearst family, in addition to the numerous marriages among the Presslys previously mentioned (three of Col. Hearst's sisters married David Pressly's sons and his daughter, Jane, a fourth), the Hearst connections included Col. Hearst's marriage to Sarah Wardlaw, that of his brother Joseph, Jr. (b. 1789) to Mary Perrin, daughter of Abner Perrin, and that of his sister, Margaret, who married her first cousin, John "Whitehall" Hearst (son of Major John Hearst, Jr.). Another son of Major Hearst, Lewis, married his first cousin, Martha, daughter of his uncle, George Hearst (and his wife Jane Pressly). Col. Hearst's sister, Mary, married Thomas White Chiles (1793–1865), son of another neighbor, Abner Chiles, and his son, John Wardlaw Hearst (1783–1847), married, as we have seen, Ann Chiles, daughter of Major John Chiles (and brother of Abner). There were also numerous marriages among the Chileses, Perrin, and Cothran families, including a number among cousins, and also among the Cothrans, Perrins, Sproulls, and Marshalls. These marriages created a complicated and interconnected grid of kinship among and between groups of families of the same social class, which very much defined this neighborhood (Figure 11-1).

A woman's choice of a husband was one of the most important decisions she would make. Preserving family wealth was particularly important, and in the South, there were more frequent marriages among cousins, with the added benefit for women being they could remain near their family. Women tended to marry very young and were often only teenagers when they found themselves running a household. At this time, women could not yet vote, and an inherited estate generally became the possession of her husband's. Most women living in this upcountry, patriarchal society between 1800 and 1840 would have lived circumscribed lives that were, apart from regular church and communal occasions, mainly centered on their household. For the most part, their lives would not have been easy. Married to men who lived busy lives as clergymen, physicians, lawyers, and politicians, as well as farmers, and who traveled frequently, or to farmers and planters who worked long days

Figure 11-1. ACME Google map showing location of key local roads, sites, and planation homes in what was a portion of the Hard Labor Section, 1820–50.

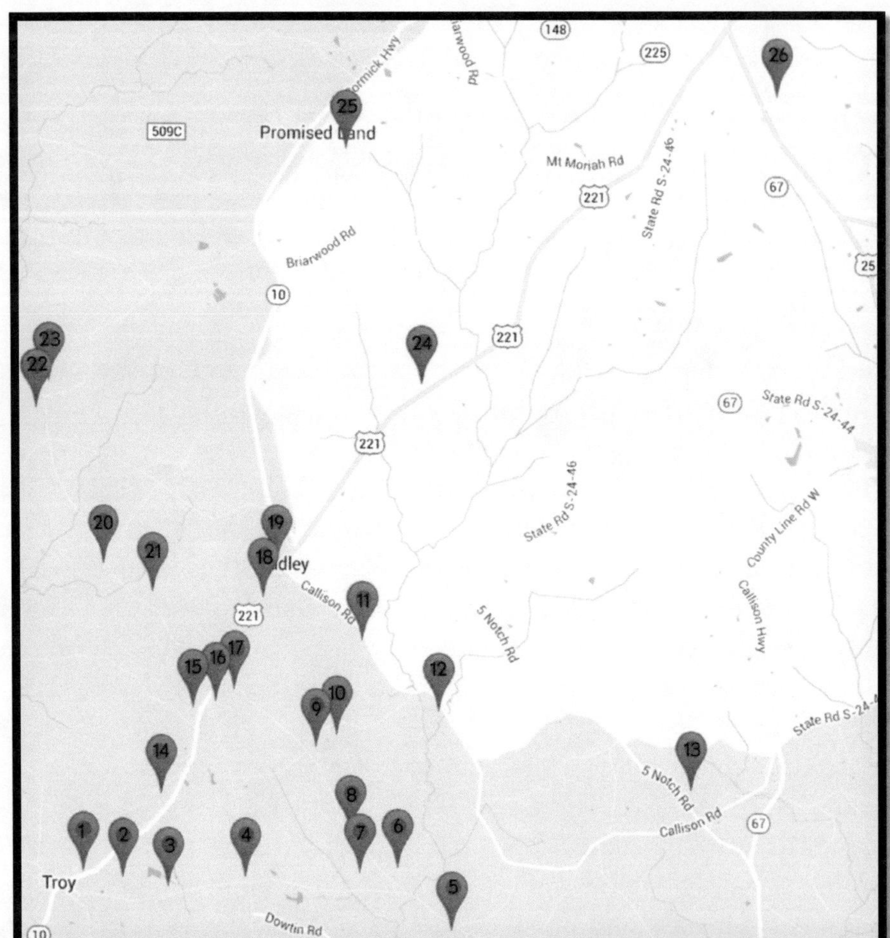

1. Approximate location of Leonard Wideman's plantation
2. Approximate location of Abner Perrin's Post Office and home
3. Dr. Samuel Pressly
4. Eden Hall (Dr. John Wardlaw Hearst)
5. Winterseat (Wade Samuel Cothran)
6. Cotton Level (Thomas Chiles Perrin)
7. Samuel Perrin's Plantation
8. Perrin Place
9. Sylvania (Col. John Hearst)
10. Millway Plantation (John Cothran)
11. William Chiles's Cabin
12. Chiles's Mill and later Cothran's Bridge
13. Mount Vernon (James Sproull)
14. George Pressly's home on Barksdale Ferry Road
15. Horeb Baptist Church
16. James Madison Chiles (and later J. H. Chiles, Jr.)
17. Chiles Crossroads (Major John Chiles)
18. Peach Lawn (Thomas White Chiles)
19. Bradley
20. Col. James Devlin Farmstead
21. George Pressly's Plantation on the Abbeville to Charleston Road
22. Cedar Springs ARP Church
23. Frazier/Pressly Octagon House
24. White Hall Place (Joel Lipscomb and later Dr. Samuel Sproull Marshall)
25. Dr. Samuel Steen Marshall (later Promised Land)
26. Scotch Cross (J. Wesley Brooks)

in the field, they had little leisure time. They played important and often arduous roles, running the domestic operations of the household including supervising livestock used for food. Households with more than thirteen slaves usually had house servants who would have helped make candles, soap, and clothes for the entire household, including slaves. Looms and spinning wheels were a ubiquitous item in estate inventories. They would also tend herb and vegetable gardens which would have contained plants that could have been used to dye fabric as well as for medicinal purposes.

Figure 11-2. William Chiles's eighteenth-century cabin on Route 10, Bradley, South Carolina. Photograph courtesy of author.

In addition, women would have borne numerous children, nursing them through many illnesses. Women's diaries and letters from the period attest to the melancholy, exhaustion, and heartbreak that so many experienced as they suffered through difficult pregnancies with little medical care. Many died in childbirth or lost young children. Elite planters' wives were not spared, and there is a real poignancy to some of their letters as they despaired over their constant illnesses and exhaustion, cared for children and the household, and apologized to their husbands over the loss of their good looks from frequent pregnancies. Many women died in childbirth and new wives of the widowers, often still in their teens, had to assume responsibility for their husbands' children. If we look at some of the women in this discrete community, many bore eleven or more children: Thomas Chiles Perrin and his wife had eleven children with three dying young; Dr. Joseph Lowry Pressly had three sons and eight daughters with only six surviving; Sarah Elizabeth Chiles, married to Wade Elephare Cothran, had twelve children with one dying in infancy; and John "Whitehall Hearst" and his wife Margaret had twelve children, only seven of whom survived.

Wives would have also played a significant role in ensuring the health and hygiene of a plantation or large farmstead population. The scrapbook became the medium for recording and passing on information on diseases and health remedies, as well as recipes and housekeeping and gardening advice. An unmarried sister, such as Martha Pressly and Esther Pressly, was a welcomed source of labor in the household. Wives would have also been responsible for the spiritual and physical well-being of their children and the entire household. They frequently led morning and evening prayer sessions in the household, which for most Associate Reformed Presbyterians included their slaves. As there is a dearth of primary material related to the family, the main accounts that we have of Pressly women are the generic descriptions of them in church histories, where they are described as "indispensable helpmates" to their husbands and "pious and good Christian women" who played important roles in their congregations. It is significant that so many Pressly daughters married established, middle-class professionals; several also married ministers in the Associate Reformed Presbyterian Church, sharing with many of their brothers and cousins a life devoted to the ministry. Longevity is a distinct trait in the family, and many Pressly daughters lived unusually long lives for the time, which is all the more exceptional because many of them bore as many as eight to ten children.

Women in the backcountry and particularly in the Hard Labor Creek area, probably did not suffer the loneliness experienced by many low country plantation mistresses, who lived isolated lives on big plantations, bereft of female companionship except for family. They were part of a thriving community situated at the crossroads of several major traveling routes between Augusta, Abbeville, and Charleston. This was a close-knit neighborhood of extended family members who were in easy walking distance or a short horseback ride away, providing opportunities to socialize or seek support. Footpaths and bridle paths would have crisscrossed this area. And being so close to nearby taverns and stores, the gathering point for community exchanges, they probably had an opportunity to share local news, if only second hand.

One also begins to see a change in the 1840s, as widows assumed more authority over their husbands' estates and wives over managing their husbands' business affairs. Sarah Wideman, Leonard's widow, and Elizabeth Chiles, Major John Chiles's widow, were both wealthy women in the 1850 and 1860 census. After his death in 1860, John Cothran's daughter, Elizabeth

Figure 11-3. Major John Chiles, owner of Chiles Crossroads.

Perrin Cothran, managed Millway Plantation with over one hundred slaves, while her brother was away in the Civil War. Cothran also made it specifically clear in his will that the estate and property given to his son and daughter "shall be to and for their sole and separate use and behalf." Many wives aggressively pursued the best education possible for their children.

The Chileses and Perrins

Col. John Hearst's closest neighbor in the 1820s was Major John Chiles, one of the founders of Union Academy and a member of one of the most important families in the area. Major Chiles's father, William Chiles (1736–1804), arrived from Virginia with his wife, Agnes White Chiles, and settled in the community immediately after the end of the Revolutionary War. He acquired four hundred acres from the estate of Andrew Williamson and built a log cabin home on what is today Callison Road. He continued to acquire land, and at the time of his death in 1804, William was wealthy enough to be one of the few planters in the immediate neighborhood to own as many as eighteen slaves. Like the Hearsts, his sons also continued to enhance their holdings during the first decades of the nineteenth century, becoming large property owners who, according to Margaret Watson, in her *Greenwood Sketches*, owned by the mid-nineteenth century, over five miles of property extending from Troy to Bradley on both sides of the Barksdale Ferry Road.[1] William bequeathed land to his sons, Rueben and Major John Chiles, and left his home tract to another son, William Chiles. Rueben acquired significant additional acreage in his own right, building a mill on Hard Labor Creek in 1802, and by the time he died circa 1808, he owned some 1918 acres. (John Pressly, Samuel Perrin, and Philip Stieffle made the inventory of Reuben's estate).[2] The Chiles family cemetery, where numerous members of the family are buried, including William and his sons, Reuben and Major John Chiles, is located off Callison Road near William's home site. His log cabin home was later dismantled and rebuilt on Highway 10, where it still stands today (Figure 11-2).[3]

Major John Chiles (Figure 11-3) was a wealthy planter who may have had some merchant-related dealings, as he was involved in 1808 in a lawsuit with William Pressly, immigrant David Pressly's son and a Charleston factor merchant, which he eventually lost. He built, circa 1815–20, Chiles Crossroads, one of the most important homes in the neighborhood, which was located about a mile and a half away from Sylvania, at the intersection of Barksdale Ferry Road and the Abbeville to Charleston Road. It is clearly marked with the word *Ent.* on Robert Mills's map (Figure 9-1). Chiles Crossroads was a place where stagecoach drivers changed horses and found food and lodging. It was a large, three-story house, much bigger than Sylvania, with fourteen rooms, some decorated with hand-carved woodwork and painted ceilings and wainscoting. Its third floor had a sleeping space for slaves,

Figure 11-4a and 4b. Scotch Cross, built by J. Wesley Brooks circa 1815–20. Greenwood, South Carolina. Photographs courtesy of author.

and may have had a ballroom. The house was elevated off the ground on brick piers and a porch extended around it.[4] It may have been similar to White Hall Place, another stage coach inn and home built by John Lipscomb circa 1815 and also shown on Mills's map. It was located a few miles away at the northeast corner of the intersection of Barksdale Ferry Road and Five Notch Road in the general vicinity of General Williamson's White Hall Plantation. Allen Glover had a store near this intersection and was first postmaster of Whitehall Post Office established in 1817. John Lipscomb served as postmaster beginning in 1820. Major Chiles would have known White Hall Place as his sister, Elizabeth, was married to Joel Lipscomb (1760–1836), John Lipscomb's uncle.[5] (The Lipscombs, like John Chiles, were Baptists and members of the Siloam Baptist Church). White Hall Place burnt down in the 1930s, but the nearby, remarkably preserved Scotch Cross, a large wood framed two-story home with a double portico, is said to have been built on the same design as White Hall Place and around the same time. It may give us a good idea of what Chiles Crossroads may have looked like (Figures 11-4a and 4-b and 11-5). Although not of the scale and elegance of Mulberry Plantation built 1820 near Camden, South Carolina, and later the home of James Chestnut and wife, Mary, Scotch Cross was considered elaborate for its day. Its eight twenty-by-twelve-foot rooms were decorated with mantels, molding, carved bannisters, stair railings, and panel wainscoting hauled in from Charleston. Located on Barksdale Ferry Road, near its junction with Matthew Road, it was built by John Lipscomb's brother-in-law, J. Wesley Brooks, for his wife, Ann Lipscomb and is privately owned today.

Figure 11-5. Original out buildings from Scotch Cross. Greenwood, South Carolina. Photo courtesy of author.

Shortly after he finished building Chiles Crossroads, Major Chiles purchased in 1821 an additional 782 acres that bordered, among others, John Pressly. He was an acquaintance of Dr. Samuel Pressly and when Samuel's cousin, Robert Pressly, died in 1831, Chiles joined him in making the inventory of his estate. Chiles was not only a wealthy planter and tavern owner, but also a sheriff of the district, a member of the state legislature, and for many years a deacon, first at Bethany Church in Edgefield County, where he was a founding member, and then at nearby Horeb Baptist Church where several generations of Chiles, Cothrans, and Harrisons are buried. After his first wife died, Major Chiles married his cousin, Elizabeth Chiles Sullivan (the daughter of Benjamin Chiles) in 1836 and they had five children together. (Their youngest son, Benjamin, later married James H. Wideman's daughter, Sarah). Chiles died in 1846, and Thomas Chiles Perrin (the son of his sister, Eunice Chiles Perrin) served as executor; his neighbor, John Cothran, and nephew, Thomas W. Chiles, witnessed his will. After his death, the plantation was maintained by his wife and children and remained in family hands until the 1870s, when Wade Elephare Cothran, who was married to Major Chiles's daughter, Sarah Elizabeth, (with his second wife) purchased the plantation at a sale in 1872 (Figures 11-6a and 6b).[6] His family continued to live there until his death in 1901, when the site was leased to a neighboring farmer; Chiles Crossroads burned to the ground in 1910. A 1939 aerial survey shows numerous buildings still on the site which was still a working farm. The original house pad and remains of brick chimneys are still visible on the home site, owned by a descendent, John Harrison.

Figures 11-6a and 6b. Wade Elephare Cothran and his wife Sarah Elizabeth Chiles.

Major Chiles's son (with his first wife), Reverend James Madison Chiles (Figure 11-7), was also a wealthy planter, who owned fifty-one slaves in 1850, once again underscoring the profile of this generation both as professionals and planters. Reverend Chiles helped organize the Horeb Baptist Church in 1841, although it was functioning earlier as an arm of the Bethany Church (Figure 11-8). It was located less than a mile from his home on Barksdale Ferry Road, and among the first applicants to the church were his neighbors, Samuel Perrin, Jr., James Frazier, John Gaston [Ghaston], Eunice Chiles, Ann Chiles Hearst (Dr. Hearst's wife), and

Figure 11-7. Reverend James Madison Chiles.

several black slaves. It is of interest that four of Alexander Pressly's children (David Pressly, Jr.'s son) are recorded in the Bethany and Horeb Baptist Church records: William joining in 1839, John Thompson, and Sarah Ann in 1841, and James in 1843.[7] Several other churches were organized nearby during this period, including the Damascus Baptist Church in 1831, the Mt. Lebanon Baptist Church in Edgefield District in 1832, Mt. Lebanon Methodist Church circa 1830, Walnut Grove Baptist in 1826, and Ashbury Methodist, near Verdery, circa 1821. Reverend Chiles also helped to create the Hopkins School for boys in 1846 in nearby Greenwood, where he eventually moved. He continued to preach from time to time at Horeb and was buried there in 1862 with his friend, Dr. George Pressly, reading a prayer at his interment. (Sometime later Reverend Richard Furman led a more formal service).

Figure 11-8. Horeb Baptist Church, Bradley, South Carolina. Photograph courtesy of author.

Thomas White Chiles (1793–1865), Major Chiles's nephew and married to Col. Hearst's sister, Mary, was another wealthy property owner in this close-knit community. Little is known about his business dealings but he is said to have owned several plantations and stores and had forty-nine slaves in 1860. He inherited much of his father's (Rueben Chiles) land, including the Mill at Hard Labor Creek. He owned forty-nine slaves in 1860 and lived at Peach Lawn, a large plantation located north of Chiles Crossroads but below Bradley on what is today Route 10. The "weather-boarded house made of heart pine" burned down sometime after he died in 1865. It may have been located near where Cedar Ridge Hunting Lodge is today. Thomas gave his daughter, Jane Hearst Chiles, a plantation near Bradley (she married General Patrick Henry Bradley, for whom the town is named), and his daughter, Mary Isabella, who married Robert Lites, a plantation on Barksdale Ferry Road in an area known as Indian Hills, where a portion of the town of Troy was later built. The Indian Hills Post Office opened in 1854, most likely in one of Chiles's stores, with Thomas Jefferson Lyons (son-in-law of Leonard Wideman) serving as postmaster. The remainder of Thomas White Chiles's holdings were divided among his heirs after his death in 1865, with his son, George Pressly Chiles (1842–1871), named after Dr. George Pressly, receiving some 1,300 acres of land bordering his brother, John Hearst Chiles, Major Chiles's estate, and Wade E. Cothran.[8] According to Paul Grier's map of 1894, John Hearst Chiles lived on the east side of the Abbeville to Charleston Road near Chiles Crossroads. Although many of his relatives were Baptists, Thomas Chiles was actively involved with the Cedar Spring ARP Church, where he and his wife are buried, as are their daughters Mary Isabella and her husband, Robert Lites, and Jane and her husband, General Patrick Bradley, an elder in the Church. His sons, George Pressly Chiles and John Hearst Chiles (1825–1903), the latter for many years an elder at the Church, are also buried at Cedar Springs.

Living along the Abbeville to Charleston Road, near the Chileses, Presslys, and Hearsts, was another major land owner, the Perrin family. William Perrin (1712–87) migrated with his large family from Virginia in 1772, and settled in the in the Edgefield District near Winterseat not far from John Pressly (imm 1772). He and his eldest son, Abner, were Patriots in the Revolutionary War, the latter was a Quarter Master for the lower Ninety Six Regiment of the South Carolina Militia, and after the war was over, they quickly acquired significant acreage, some of which belonged to German Lutheran Loyalists who fled to Halifax. By the time William Perrin died in 1787, he was a man of some wealth with land, several feather beds—a symbol of status at the time—and at least nine slaves.[9] His sons, William, Abner, and Samuel, also became major land owners, purchasing land on both sides of Hard Labor Creek and the Abbeville to Charleston Road, as well as land in Edgefield District. Abner, who married Sarah Foster, purchased over two thousand acres between 1785 and 1800. After he died in 1799, his wife married his first cousin, Robert Perrin, an established merchant who owner land near Winterseat. Abner's daughter,

Mary Perrin, married Col. Hearst's brother, Joseph Hearst, Jr. and his son, Abner Perrin, Jr. (1798–1877), married Mary Carson Patterson, daughter of Josiah Patterson and sister of Leonard Wideman's wife Sarah. Abner Jr. continued to acquire land between Troy and Winterseat, near Dr. Samuel Pressly, Alexander Pressly, Leonard Wideman, Josiah Patterson, and Col. Hearst, and several deeds relating to his land acquisitions and sales are among the Wideman Family Papers.[10] He served as postmaster at Perrin's Post Office which opened at his home in 1832. His home was located at the intersection of Barksdale Ferry Road and Mill Road, near the current town of Troy and the Indian Branch of Rocky Creek and is shown on a survey of his land in the Wideman Family Papers (Figure 11-9). In the 1830s, Abner sold some of his holdings to Leonard Wideman.

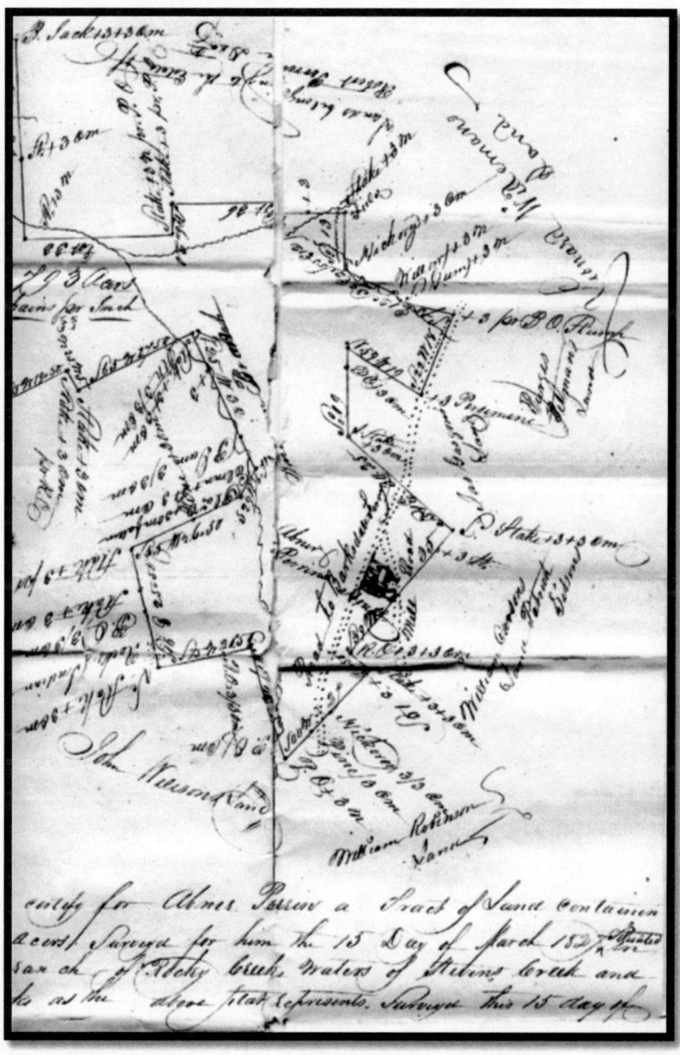

Figure 11-9. Detail of 1830 survey of Abner Perrin's track of land showing Indian Branch, a tributary of Rocky Creek, and his home at the intersection of Mill and Barksdale Ferry Roads. Courtesy of Wideman Family Papers. Bradley, South Carolina.

William Perrin's younger son, Samuel Perrin, married in 1795 Eunice Chiles (sister of Reuben Chiles and Major John Chiles) and became a wealthy planter, eventually owning over two thousand acres, which included the land he inherited from his father and the 742-acre plantation he purchased in 1818. His home was on the west side of the Abbeville to Charleston Road, about one-and-a-half miles above where it crossed the Long Cane Road and was set back from the road and close to Calabash Branch. His immediate neighbors, according to his recorded plat, included James Adamson, Camp, Henry Gable, Mrs. Haney, Hose, Joseph Hearst, John Holloway, Samuel Mouchet, and James and Philip Stieffle. Patrick Gibson's 1826 survey for Col. Hearst indicates a portion of Perrin's land was adjacent to Samuel Pressly.

Figure 11-10. Thomas Chiles Perrin. Courtesy of Thomas Perrin Harrison.

Figure 11-11. Marker for Thomas Chiles Perrin's home, Abbeville, South Carolina. Photograph courtesy of author.

Samuel died in 1828 and his estate sale reveals that he lived in a well-furnished home with some fine pieces of furniture, including a mahogany side board which sold for sixty dollars, an unusually fine piece of furniture among estate inventories in this area at the time. The sale also contained a large number of livestock (over 175), a carriage and harness, other luxury items like watches and clocks, silverware, glass decanters, five feather beds, books, blacksmith tools, and an unusually-well-fitted kitchen. He also owned forty-one slaves.[11.] It is interesting to compare his extensive estate inventory with that of his neighbor, John Pressly (William's son), who died two years earlier. John's modest sale represents the contents of a small farming household with subsistence food, like bushels of dried fruit, and basic household furniture and kitchen implements. It included a number of books, a spinning wheel, gardening and farming tools, and a vegetable garden and a potato patch as well as ten guns, several bushels of corn and cotton and a small number of farm animals.

Samuel Perrin's wife, Eunice, continued to live on the plantation until her death in 1846. She died intestate and on December 16, 1846 the *Abbeville Banner* printed an advertisement for her estate sale noting that the "remainder" of her estate and "a valuable track of land sold in two pieces" were to be sold on December 30.[12] The land was almost certainly bought by her sons, Samuel Perrin, Jr. (1818–1880) and Thomas Chiles Perrin (1805–1878). Samuel, Jr. also purchased the majority of the household furnishings and implements and soon after built a large, two-story frame home known as the "Perrin Place" on his portion of the land. The house, which had four square brick pillars supporting the porch roof across the front, was built closer to the Abbeville to Charleston Road than that of his father's and was probably grander, more like Eden Hall. It burned down in the 1920s, and today numerous piles of bricks mark where the house was located. The family cemetery, where Samuel and his wife, Eunice Chiles, and two of Samuel, Jr.'s wives (he was married three times) were buried near the first home site. It was inadvertently destroyed, probably through logging, and nothing remains to mark the graves.

Samuel Perrin was among the group of farmers who founded Union Academy in 1820 on Col. Hearst's property. His son, Thomas Chiles Perrin, along with Ebenezer Erskine Pressly, James Pressly, and James Madison Chiles, were in the first class. Thomas, a graduate from South Carolina College in Columbia in 1826, was admitted to the Bar in 1827 and practiced in Abbeville, where he married Jane Eliza Wardlaw (daughter of James Wardlaw). He became a nationally known politician and prominent legislator who was the first signer of the Ordinance of Succession in Columbia, South Carolina. Elected President of the Greenville and Columbia Railroad in 1853, he served consecutive annual terms until 1861 (Figure 11-10). In 1844, Thomas Perrin purchased 765 acres from the estate of Henry Hose, near his father's plantation on the Abbeville to Charleston Road, about one-mile north of where it intersected the Long Cane Road. Original grants for this land included the Palatine settlers Conrad Merk, Christian Zang, Abraham Flick, and Johannes Zwilling. His Hard Labor plantation became known as Cotton Level plantation and according to his 1853 tax records, he owned some 1,200 acres at Cotton Level where he had thirty-eight slaves. The Perrin Family papers in the Wilson Library at the University of North Carolina indicate that, in addition to Cotton Level, he also had a plantation called Fourville, consisting in 1853 of some 1,500 acres and located west of Abbeville with forty-four slaves, and some 2,500 acres of land in the village of Abbeville with twenty-four slaves.[13]

Cotton Level became one of the camping sites along the way for farmers, merchants, and wagoners hauling goods from Abbeville to Augusta.[14] Perrin is said to have put out large iron pots and cooking utensils for travelers' use, along with places to care for livestock. Cotton Level also became a neighborhood meeting spot to gather news. There is some confusion as to whether there was ever a plantation home or large farmstead on the east side of the Abbeville to Charleston Road, where Cotton Level plantation was located; the semi-ruined building on the property today is thought to have been an overseer's house (date unknown) and would have been too small to have housed Perrin's large family. It is possible Thomas and his family continued to live in his father's house after his mother's death which would have been on the plat of land he bought at her estate sale and which later became associated with Cotton Level. His family sometimes referred to the home where they lived as Hard Labor and the plantation as Cotton Level.

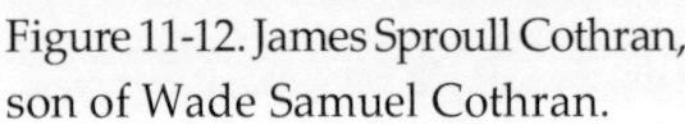

Figure 11-12. James Sproull Cothran, son of Wade Samuel Cothran.

Figure 11-13. Emma Perrin, daughter of Thomas Chiles Perrin (on left) and wife of James Sproull Cothran, and her sister, Mary Eunice Perrin, first wife of Francis Eugene Harrison. Samuel Alexander Cothran and Frank Harrison Cothran, *Chiles-Cothran Notes and an update after more than a half-century*, 1992 (*Chiles-Cothran Notes* published 1936).

Agriculture Production records of 1860 indicate that in addition to short staple cotton, Perrin also grew wheat, corn, peas, rye, oats, and sweet potatoes and produced wool, beeswax, molasses, and honey, giving us an insight into the variety of farm production at the time. According to the 1860 census, he owned over 120 slaves and twenty-five slave houses on his three Abbeville District properties and his total worth in personal property and land in today's dollars would have been $5,264,400. In the late 1850s, Thomas built a large Greek Revival home in the village of Abbeville which had seven rooms on each of its three floors, and twenty-two fireplaces, making an important statement about his sophistication and ambitions. The Perrin Family papers also document a lavish shopping trip that he and his wife took to New York in the fall of 1858 to furnish their home. There are receipts for numerous pieces of fine furniture, services of silver, china, glasses, linens, and expensive rugs, as well as luxurious fabrics for curtains and ladies' apparel.[15] The family lived in the Abbeville mansion until it was destroyed by fire in 1877. The site is identified today by a historical marker (Figure 11-11), which notes that when it was built, it was "one of the finest and most commodious mansions in the State." When the family moved to Abbeville, Perrin's daughter, Emma, and her husband, James Sproull Cothran (son of Wade Cothran, owner of Winterseat), took over Cotton Level (Figures 11-12 and 11-13). After Thomas died in 1878, his son, James Wardlaw Perrin, lived at Cotton Level; it was subsequently sold to John Wardlaw Chiles (son of Major Chiles's brother, William). Today, some of his relatives, members of the Harrison family, have regained ownership of some of his property along Millway Road. Thomas was deeply involved in the Upper Long Cane Presbyterian Church where he served as an elder for many years and where he is buried.

The Cothrans, Sproulls, and Marshalls

John Cothran (1799–1860) was an astute and ambitious businessman and wealthy planter who owned a plantation across the street from Col. Hearst. He, along with his brother, Wade, represented a new kind of planter who, having witnessed the 1837 Panic and drop in cotton prices, diversified their interests and became players in the mercantile world. In addition to his good-size plantation and store, he operated a lumber business in Edgefield and acted as a "Factors and Commission Merchant" with his oldest son, John Rushton Cothran (who died age twenty-two in 1855), his brother, Wade, and Henry Jeffers in Charleston. He initially lived near the town of Cambridge, where he owned a plantation, Hickory Grove, and several stores. Circa 1836, he sold his holdings and purchased some one thousand acres directly across the street from Sylvania at what is today 907 Millway Road. Original grants to this property included Rueben and John Chiles, Isaac da Costa, Moses Cohen, and William Dorris, a neighbor of David Pressly (imm 1767). Cothran built Millway Plantation circa 1837–38 and around the same time also acquired an additional 1,186 acres on the east side of Hard Labor Creek, probably from Dr. Samuel Steen Marshall, whose holdings extended from Whitehall to what was later known as the Promised Land. Cothran later referred to this purchase as

Quarter Place. In 1840, he married Samuel Perrin's daughter, Elizabeth Lee Perrin (1803–1874), his fourth wife. Millway was a large, two-story Carolina I-style Piedmont farmhouse elevated on brick piers with four large rooms and central hallway on each floor. An early twentieth-century photo shows it was a good size home, similar to a rural "plain-style" plantation home, with five large windows across the front. Two large exterior chimneys located on the gable ends, a one-story gallery in the front, and a shed appended to the rear of the dwelling. We know from Cothran's estate inventory that the first floor consisted of a drawing room, sitting room, dining room, family chamber, and shed room.[16] Millway was more modest in size and style than Chiles Crossroads or Scotch Cross and, while larger, was less refined and sophisticated than Sylvania. Associated outbuildings would have included a kitchen, well, outhouses, corn cribs, barns, and a smoke house. Millpond Road went from the Abbeville to Charleston Road across the Millway property, along the south side of the house, to Chiles's mill and then across Hard Labor Creek (later known as Cothran's bridge) to Callison Road. The current antebellum style home on the site reflects a 1913 renovation and addition by Cothran's grandson, Wade Cothran Harrison which left the integrity of the interior rooms of the older nineteenth-century structure relatively intact. At the same time Millpond Road was moved north of the house. Millway is still in Harrison family hands (Figure 11-14).

Figure 11-14. Millway Plantation, Millway Road, Bradley, South Carolina. Photograph courtesy of the author.

In addition to his factor merchant business, Jeffers & Cothrans, Cothran was also a Director of Farmers and Exchange Bank in Charleston, which opened in 1853 and was one of several important banks in South Carolina from this period publishing their own currency (Figure 11-15). He was involved in local affairs, helping to organize one of the area's primary schools, Mt. Pleasant School, in January 1852 and was appointed its Chairman. He had a store on his property where, beginning in 1854, the Millway Post Office was located and he served as postmaster. He may have also had a second store, Cothrans & Stephens. He owned seventy-six slaves in 1850, and close to one hundred in 1860 when he had nineteen slave houses. Cothran was close to his neighbor, William Chiles, Jr. (1779–1849), who we know from the Perrin Family Papers made frequent purchases at his stores, and he served as executor of Chiles's estate after he died in 1849.

Figure 11-15. Banknote from Farmers & Exchange Bank, Charleston, South Carolina, with portraits of Franklin Harper Elmore and John C. Calhoun. Photograph courtesy of author. From the collection of William L. Pressly, Atlanta, Georgia.

When Cothran died in 1860, his wife, Elizabeth, purchased almost all of the household items and furniture at his estate sale (it would appear to have been a modestly furnished home) as well as a new carriage and harness, which sold for four hundred dollars. He left his wife the home tract of eight hundred acres and divided another piece of land known as the quarter tract between his son, Wade Elephare Cothran (b. 1837) with his third wife, and his daughter, Elizabeth (who he had with his fourth wife, Elizabeth Perrin). Elizabeth attended Reverend Ferdinand Jacob's Seminary for Young Ladies in Charleston where at least one of Thomas Chiles Perrin's daughters also went. Elizabeth managed the plantation while her brother was away during the Civil War and later became Francis Eugene Harrison's third wife in 1878, which is how the Harrison connection became part of the family (Harrison's second wife was Thomas Chiles Perrin's daughter Mary

Eunice). Wade E. Cothran married in 1861, Sarah Elizabeth Chiles, Major Chiles's daughter from his second marriage, adding to the remarkably complex intermarriages among these neighboring families).

Figure 11-16. Wade Samuel Cothran, oil on canvas by unknown artist, possibly Dr. Charles Kingsmore, in the late 1840s or early 1850s. Thomas Perrin Cothran, *The Perrin Family: with Particular Reference to Samuel Perrin 1770–1828 son of William, son of John, and his descendants*, 1924.

John Cothran's brother, Wade Samuel Cothran (1804–1877) (Figure 11-16), purchased land not far from Cotton Level, but in Edgefield District in 1831, including acreage originally owned by William Perrin. His one-thousand-acre plantation, known as Winterseat, was located further down the Abbeville to Charleston Road on the far side of the Winterseat Bridge after it crossed over Hard Labor Creek. He married Frances Elizabeth Sproull, daughter of the planter and merchant James Sproull and his wife Rebecca Caldwell in 1828. A post office opened at Winterseat in 1832, with Wade Cothran as postmaster, and he and his brother, John, also ran a store there from 1832 until 1847. Winterseat became a regular stagecoach stop and inn between Abbeville and Edgefield. His home according to his daughter, Mary Cothran Mitchell, was called Red Top and she later recalled in her *Chronicles* that one of the rooms was papered with a hunting scene.[17] Wade also purchased in the 1830s ten and a half acres of land from Joseph Hearst, Jr. to build a summer place, known as Summerseat, located on higher ground about three miles east. Wade sold the Winterseat property in 1847, and the post office closed in 1854 and was replaced by Millway Post Office. Wade later became a large plantation owner in Rome, Georgia and continued business enterprises with Henry Jeffers. His son, James Sproull Cothran, married Thomas Chiles Perrin's daughter, Emma Chiles Perrin and later served in the US House of Representatives from 1887–1891.

Figures 11-17a and 17b. James Sproull's home Mount Vernon, later known as Green Pastures. Greenwood, South Carolina. Photograph 11-17a courtesy of James Hodges Harrison.

James Sproull (1782–1825) lived some two miles away from Sylvania and Winterseat on Five Notch Road near Cunning Creek, having moved there circa 1820 from Newberry. "Sproulls" is identified on Mills's 1820 map. James, or his family after his death, built a beautiful plantation home known as Mount Vernon on Five Notch Road (Figures 11-17a and 11-17b) where he also had his store.[18] The house was probably completed after his death for Sproull requested in his 1825 will that his executors "have a comfortable dwelling built for the use of my family, to be 50 feet long, 22 feet wide, 12 feet passage in the middle . . . two shed rooms in the back part and open piazza in front . . . to cost between 2500 and 3000 dollars."[19] Sited near the road on a slight elevation, the home would have provided an expansive view of his plantation. It was elegantly designed with wainscoting, cabinets, doors, and paneling said to have been made in Orangeburg, and had a terraced garden, a summer kitchen, barns and slave quarters. Sproull operated a merchant business in Hamburg and headed the mercantile firm of Sproull and Pinchback in Augusta. Five Notch Road, where his home and store were located, passed by Stoney Point and White Hall Place plantations and provided a direct route to Augusta. James Sproull died in 1825 but his family continued to run a very successful planation until the 1860s, when the house began to fall into disrepair and was sold.

Mary Cothran Mitchell, in her *Chronicles*, gives us an illuminating account of what life was like at Mount Vernon in the 1830s and 1840s and by extension at other large, self-sustaining plantations in the Hard Labor area. She described Mount Vernon as "a social settlement with its surroundings of everything necessary for use, convenience, and comfort for a large family. It appeared more like a village than a private home, embracing every imaginable building from the stately old dwelling to the two-story pigeon house (with its ornamental verandas) . . . .to say nothing of what had been a flourishing country store."[20] James Sproull and his wife and other members of their family are buried in the family cemetery clearly visible on the property, sited not far from the house (Figure 11-18). Harry Maxon carefully restored Mount Vernon in the 1930s and renamed it Green Pastures. It burned down in the 1970s when it was struck by lightning after coming into the possession of the Harrison family.

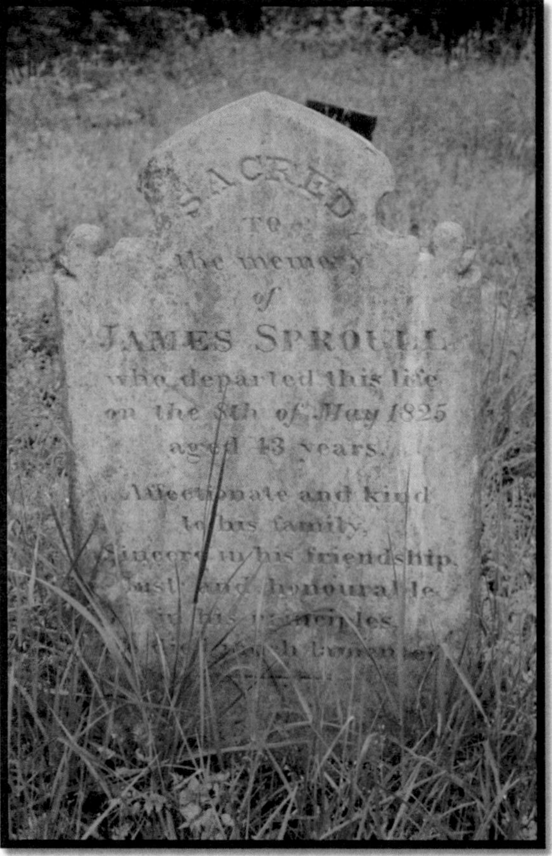

Figure 11-18. Gravestone of James Sproull. Sproull Family Cemetery, Five Notch Road, Greenwood County, South Carolina. Photograph courtesy of author.

Figure 11-19. Portrait of Dr. Samuel Steen Marshall by William James Hubbard, whereabouts unknown.

The Sproull connection is interesting in several respects underscoring once again the intricate kinship patterns that defined this neighborhood. Rebecca Caldwell Sproull's niece, Martha Caldwell, was John Cothran's second wife; James and Rebecca's Sproull's son, James Caldwell Sproull (died 1868), married Margaret Elizabeth (Eliza) Marshall, the daughter of the wealthy planter and physician, Dr. Samuel Steen Marshall (1787–1861), who lived nearby. Mitchell in her *Chronicles* describes James Caldwell Sproull as having a "well-regulated well-disciplined plantation . . . [with] well selected orchards, vineyards, a beautiful flower garden" and an abundance of livestock. His father-in-law, Dr. Samuel Steen Marshall, (Figure 11-19) studied medicine in Charleston under Dr. Warren Waldo around 1810, the same time Samuel Pressly was studying medicine, and returned to Whitehall to take up his practice and marry in 1815 Elizabeth Clopton Foster (1797–1870), whose mother was Margaret Perrin, Samuel Perrin's sister. A very successful and respected physician, Marshall gave up his medical career around 1830, and devoted his time to farming. He became widely known as a progressive planter who developed the model of a self-sufficient plantation, where he grew almost all the food for people and livestock and had cotton and woolen clothes and even shoes made on his plantation. He built what was said to have been an elegant home called Cedar Grove, at the south corner of the intersection of highway 221 and state highway 156 (Whitehall Road), and by 1860 owned 147 slaves and sufficient assets to make him the fifth wealthiest person in Abbeville District. After his death in 1861 and the conclusion of the Civil War, his estate sold between three thousand and five thousand acres, including his plantation home, to the South Carolina Land Commission to create fifty-acre home tracks for blacks. It became known as the Promised Land.

Dr. Marshall's son, Jedu Foster Marshall, was an attorney, and two other sons were physicians, both practicing for a time in Whitehall. One son, Dr. Samuel Sproull Marshall, graduated from Charleston Medical School in 1839 and married Anne E. Barratt, daughter of Dr. John Perkins Barratt (Figures 11-20a and 11-20b). He purchased White Hall Place circa 1845 from the Lipscombs and lived there until 1860, when he moved from the area. His brother, Dr. Joseph Warren Waldo Marshall, had connections with the Presslys, having studied under John S. Pressly at the Academy in Due West and then at Erskine College where he graduated in 1843. After practicing in Whitehall, he moved his medical practice to the village of Abbeville and was killed in the Civil War. The Marshalls were among the wealthiest families in Abbeville District in 1860. Samuel Steen Marshall was the sixth wealthiest and his sons Joseph Warren Marshall were respectively the fourth and fifth, a reminder of the wealth concentrated in this small area of Abbeville District.

Figures 11-20a and 20b. Dr. Samuel Sproull Marshall and his wife Anne Barrett.

Also living in the Whitehall neighborhood was John "Whitehall" Hearst who knew the Marshalls; George Marshall (1779–1852), was a witness to his will. Joel Smith, the wealthy planter, merchant, postmaster, and politician who lived at Stoney Point, also off Five Notch Road but several miles further north, was also part of this circle. He was in the South Carolina House of Representatives from 1840–1848 during the same period as Dr. George W. Pressly. He was married to George Marshall's daughter, Isabella Elizabeth, and we know from the Perrin Family Papers that he had extensive business contacts with Thomas Chiles Perrin. Smith died in 1855. According to the 1860 census, his son, Austus M. Smith, was the second-wealthiest man in Abbeville District after John C. Calhoun, owning 138 slaves and twenty-five slave houses. After his death in 1862, a casualty of the Civil War, his sister and her husband, D. Wyatt Aiken, took over Stoney Point, where he too was an advocate of progressive farming methods.

The Cyclical Economy, the Small Farmer, and the Country Store

There was a close interaction among these wealthy planters and neighboring smaller farmers. Many of these families had known one another over several generations; they attended the same churches, their children were playmates and went to the same primary schools. We know from census data that tradespeople, overseers, and "hirelings" also lived in close proximity. In the immediate area near the Abbeville to Charleston Road, these farmers included the Robinsons, Dowtins, Stieffles, Devlins, Pattersons, Mouchets, Gastins, Hendersons, Adamsons, Cables, Lassiters, and Hollways, to name but a few.

By the 1820s, the spread of cotton as a cash crop tied smaller farmers to a larger local and regional economic network in Abbeville and Edgefield districts. Because small farmers could grow cotton as effectively as large planters, they increased in number, and as a result, there was a greater demand for the country store. The general store, always a crucial element in backcountry rural life, became especially important for the smaller and midsized farmer. Cash from cotton sales or from subsistence crops sold to their planter neighbors or storekeepers allowed them to purchase luxury goods. Whereas the larger plantation owner was more likely to deal directly with the coastal cotton factor merchant and, as we have seen, also be partners in mercantile businesses, the small farmer was dependent on local shopkeepers for food stuff and dry goods and the sale of his cotton. Given its central location, it is not surprising that there were several country stores in the Hard Labor area, including stores run by planters, which added to the social dynamics of the community.

General stores played an important social role and function for the yeoman farmer and rich planter. Located either on the ground level of a framed house or in a separate framed or brick building, they were places to gather and to exchange news and conversation for both men and women and served as one of the few social centers in rural areas. Taverns and stores were also places for political gatherings. The country store merchant became a critical player in community economics. Crops yielded income once a year, and the merchant provided the credit for the rest of the year for purchasing dry goods, groceries, farm equipment, etc. Borrowing on future crops was common place. The cyclical nature of the farmer's world necessitated a credit or bartering system. Lewis Atherton in his book, *The Southern Country Store,* estimated that 60 percent to 75 percent of all merchandise purchased by farmers was obtained on credit, for which storekeepers would collect payment once a year in goods or cash, generally in early January. Merchants in turn often had creditors in the wholesale markets on the coast. Given the complexity of these exchanges, merchants were generally well educated. The country store merchant also acted as the intermediator—taking in crops and selling them to city merchants, especially for the smaller farmers in rural areas, and sometimes opening saw mills and grist mills to process bartered crops. A country store owner might barter a sufficient amount of cotton from small farmers to retain his own cotton factor merchant. In rural areas like the Hard Labor Section, the store owner was likely to be regarded as a friend and neighbor, but many still had to deal with the stereotype of the greedy and cunning merchant and the fact that the independent small farmer resented his dependence on the country store.

Figure 11-21. Henderson's Store, Verdery, South Carolina. Photograph courtesy of author.

The remains of Henderson's store on Highway 10 in Verdery (Figure 11-21), as well as the well-preserved 1815 Sompayrac General Store in Society Hill, Darlington County, give us some idea of what an old nineteenth-century store in the area might have looked like. They offered everything from basic dry goods, like coffee and sugar, to whiskey and farming tools and supplies and a variety of household items, clothing and luxury items, and even medicines. Bartered goods from farmers included cotton, wheat, flax seed, tallow, brandy, deerskins, beeswax, etc. As the century progressed, stores offered increasingly more sophisticated food supplies and a greater variety of items, including luxury goods such as fabrics, silk, silverware, and china. An 1841 store ledger from an Abbeville District store includes the sale of champagne and white satin, powder puffs, pearl buttons, gingham and calico, and a wide variety of cookware.[21]

While the large plantation owner frequented or ran the country store, they relied mainly on the cotton factor merchant to serve as their personal representative in the market place. Factor merchants were generally given discretion in terms of the timing of cotton sales which allowed the planter to receive the best price in a variety of markets. The factor merchant also purchased plantation goods and personal items for the planter, making a commission on each sale or purchase. The factor merchant served almost as a personal banker, advancing credit in goods and cash on future crops and even paying bills for goods bought from other merchants. Merchants were not the only ones to extend credit and notes. Many planters, including the Hearsts, Chileses, Perrins, and George and Samuel Pressly, made loans to neighbors, both to gain good will and strengthen political and social connections. This was a risky enterprise and many notes found in estate records were deemed doubtful.

What it interesting and perhaps unusual in the Hard Labor community is the fact, as we have seen, that several neighborhood stores were run by wealthy planters which for many may have enhanced their political and commercial aspirations. Some were also players in urban circles like Charleston and Augusta. Some of their stores were the equivalent of a plantation commissary, intended to meet plantation and slave needs, and where subsistence crops from neighboring small farmers could be bartered for store goods. David Pressly (died 1818) was a merchant probably by the 1790s, and, as noted earlier, Robert Perrin had a store in the same area as early as 1800 and Thomas Chiles is said to have had several stores. James Sproull had a store on Five Notch Road as early as 1821 and Wade Cothran, who had extensive plantation holdings, opened a general store at Winterseat in 1832, which he ran with his brother, John. By the 1850s, Cothran had a store at Millway plantation across the street from Sylvania, which opened after the one at Winterseat closed. He also had his cotton factor business in Charleston. Joel Smith served as postmaster from 1824 to 1844 at the post office, located at his plantation and store, Stoney Point, near where his father had opened a store as early as 1800.

A Wealthy Planter Class and Slavery

The planters and professionals highlighted in this section, Part III, including George Pressly, straddled more than one generation. Samuel Perrin died in 1828, and by the 1830s and 1840s, things began to change as the first generation of prominent planters who had enjoyed the first cotton boom began to die: Col. Hearst in 1843; his cousin, John Whitehall Hearst, in 1848; Major John Chiles in 1846; Josiah Patterson in 1835, and his son Josiah, Jr, in 1850; and Leonard Wideman in 1847. As we saw, their sons (many now lawyers, physicians, and politicians), for the most part, continued to expand and consolidate their holdings, and the area continued to thrive. By the late 1840s, when the second cotton boom took hold, we see a new spurt of large plantation homes being constructed, including Samuel Perrin, Jr.'s Perrin Place, circa 1850, and in the 1850s Eden Hall and Ivy Gates (Figure 11-22), both designed by the Atlanta architect, Henry Jones, while he was working on the Lower Long Cane ARP Church. Jones also designed Bordeaux Hall for Dr. John Gibert in 1859 in McCormick, although its construction was interrupted by the Civil

War. During the same period, James Frazier built the Octagon House (Figure 11-23) where Dr. Joseph Pressly, who married Frazier's daughter, would later live. The fact that both the Lower Long Cane ARP Church (Figure 11-24) and Cedar Spring ARP Church (Figure 11-25) erected new church buildings in the 1850s also speaks to the continued prosperity the community enjoyed until the devastation of the Civil War.

Figure 11-22. Ivy Gates, Dr. Wideman's House, circa 1855, Troy, South Carolina. Photograph courtesy of author.

Figure 11-23. The Frazier/Pressly Octagon House, Cedar Springs Historic District, South Carolina. Photograph courtesy of author.

Figure 11-24. Lower Long Cane Associate Reformed Presbyterian Church, near Troy, South Carolina. Photograph courtesy of author.

Figure 11-25. Cedar Springs Associate Reformed Presbyterian Church, Cedar Springs Historic District, South Carolina. Photograph courtesy of author.

The Hard Labor area was a center of wealth and political and financial power within the larger world of antebellum South Carolina, one strengthened by the numerous marriages among wealthy planter families over several generations. In the decades before the Civil War, these planters enjoyed professional success and prospered. Many, as we have seen, also held important positions in banks and railroads, as Charleston merchants, and as leading politicians in South Carolina, as well as elders and officers in their respective churches. They also held positions of respect and trust in this small neighborhood, serving as executors of small farmers' wills and leaders in their respective churches. While they were hard-working farmers, they also shared a level of worldliness and sophistication. They increasingly prided themselves in using progressive farming methods and, as we have seen, in creating self-sustaining and beautiful plantations (Hearst, Marshall, Sproull).

Estate inventories and sales provide a snapshot view of personal property and holdings, including the number of slaves on such estates, the extent of farm equipment, wagons, and livestock, and type of crops grown. These inventories tell us a good deal about their standard of living, some revealing more frugality than others. In addition to basic household utensils, supplies, and equipment, including looms and spinning wheels, most of these plantation homes while well-furnished did not usually have expensive Charleston or Philadelphia furniture. Only occasionally does one see a chest or sideboard selling for over fifty dollars even in wealthy estates such as that of Leonard Wideman and Col. Hearst, where we have inventories detailing furnishings room by room. They do reveal, however, luxury or consumption goods like linens, glass decanters, silver, rugs, china, feather beds, clocks and gold watches, etc. These were very much working plantations and in addition to a variety of farm equipment, inventories included a large numbers of farm animals, including hogs, cows, sheep, mules, horses, geese, and ducks, recently harvested crops, and tracts of rented land. Affluence was also reflected in the number of wagons, carriages, buggies, and fine horses.

Their world was also a world of slavery, and wealth was measured, above all, in the amount of land and the number of slaves owned. Slaves were a fundamental element in the daily life of these planters and farmers, a way of life justified by their interpretation of the Bible, even to the number of lashes a master might deal out. There was a large concentration of slaves in the Hard Labor area; among the small number of planters and farmers living along/near a three-mile stretch of the Abbeville Road to Charleston, from just above where it crossed Barksdale Ferry Road to where it intersected with Long Cane Road, they owned collectively over 450 slaves. Because of this concentration of planters, slaves on plantations in the Hard Labor community probably were able to have some contact with one another; the close physical proximity allowed for Sunday visits and for separated families to have time alone. Given this was a major transportation route, they would not have had the isolation shared by many slaves on low-country plantations who were miles away from roads and other plantations. Apart from a few surviving plantation ledgers, firsthand accounts about slaves in this area are rare, although we do have a court case in which J. Johnson sued Leonard Wideman for not paying the remaining one hundred dollars on the note he held for the purchase of a slave named Charles.[22] Wideman countered that Johnson had misrepresented Charles's character, arguing that rather than humble, sober, and honest as represented, Charles was insubordinate, vicious, a drunkard, and a runaway. Johnson testified this was not the case when Charles was his slave. (Alexander Pressly served as a witness for Johnson, testifying that Wideman had told him that he knew of Charles's bad character under a previous owner, with whom Charles played cards and drank). Wideman lost this case, the judge ruling "Like Master like Man" and that Wideman, not the slave's former owner, was responsible for his behavior. Wideman went so far as to make an appeal to the State Supreme Court, which he also lost.

Census slave schedules offer a few specifics about the slave community. In 1860, George Pressly, for example, had ten slave houses and sixty-six slaves (the census notes four were "mulattos"), who were relatively youthful and therefore a productive workforce. His neighbor, John Devlin, had six slave houses, and ten of his slaves were listed as "mulatto," while Sarah Wideman, Leonard's widow, had eight slave houses with half of her slaves described as "mulattos," an unusually high percentage. Slave houses varied in size and could accommodate between one and eight people and sometimes more than one family. Slave families might have a small garden and a few farm animals like chickens and pigs and the ability to grow more than subsistence food. John Cothran, who had one hundred slaves and nineteen slave houses in 1860, had a country store that was probably as much a plantation commissary where slaves could barter or purchase a few items. Mistresses often taught slaves how to home spin cotton and woolen cloth so there could be some variety in addition to the clothing allotted annually by the master of the house. Slaves were sometimes given gifts of money.[23]

For most of the planters discussed here, religion was a central part of their lives, and they had leadership positions in their respective churches. They most likely provided access to Sunday services for their slaves or even had a special building erected where traveling missionaries could preach. Baptists were particularly active in this regard. Some slaves, with the permission of their masters, became church members, and ministers sometimes held special church services for slaves on Saturday afternoon after they finished their work week. We also know that several black slaves were admitted to the Horeb Baptist Church and its mother church, Bethany Baptist. In ARP families, slaves would have been part of the morning and evening prayer sessions. On one occasion, in 1856, Thomas Chiles Perrin bought tickets for a number of his slaves to attend a religious camp meeting.

The issue of slavery and the ARP's position came to a head in Abbeville District, beginning in the mid-1830s, when the General Assembly of the State of South Carolina passed legislation in December 1834 that declared, "If any person shall hereafter teach any slave to read or write . . . such person if a free white person, upon conviction thereof, shall . . . be fined not exceeding one hundred dollars and imprisoned not more than six months. The informer shall be entitled to one half of the fine." ARP ministers and laity from Abbeville District, including the Cedar Springs, Lower Long Cane, and Chester congregations, sent petitions to the legislature strongly denouncing the new law and proclaiming their intentions to defy it. In contrast, the Upper Long Cane Presbyterian Church sent a competing petition in 1835, asking the legislature to shut down ARP Sunday schools that were in defiance of the law. Along with Psalm singing and observing the Sabbath, one of the most important rituals in the Associate Reformed Presbyterian faith were the daily devotional services that took place for the entire household. Although the Synod accepted the institution of slavery, it strongly believed, as reflected in its meeting minutes from 1825, that it was "the duty of Masters to instruct their servants to read the word of God." Slaves were taught how to read the Bible and shorter catechisms. Many planters from the area, including George W. Pressly, signed a petition in 1838 to repeal the law prohibiting slaves to read.[24]

One of the most tragic and painful aspects of slave life was the separation of families when masters died and estates were divided, or when owners moved west, taking only some of their slaves with them. Older children were frequently separated from their mothers, and wives and husbands sold to different masters, almost certainly never seeing one another again. Occasionally, planters would suggest in their wills that certain slaves stay together, but we know from the estate sales and auctions among these planters that slaves were routinely sold to many different buyers. For the most part, slaves were simply part of the estate inventory, a commodity frequently listed on the same page as bales of cotton or mules, a fact that never ceases to remain jarring. In addition to auctions, slaves were also sold individually to new masters sometimes for a high sum if they had a needed skill. Thomas Chiles Perrin, for example, bought "a negro man named Elias a Blacksmith" from Joel Smith for the hefty sum of $1,005 in 1852. Given the number of slave owners who died or left the area in the late 1830 and 1840s, including Major Chiles, Col. Hearst, Leonard Wideman, William Chiles, Jr., and John Whitehall Hearst, this had to be a period of major disruption and anxiety for the slave community, as many were sold and extended families divided. The murder of Leonard Wideman in December 1847 by disgruntled slaves, as well as the ensuing trial and their hangings, had to add to the tension and fear in the community for slave and master alike. The death of Dr. Augustus Burt by an angry slave in the lower Horn Creek area in nearby Edgefield District, just nine months earlier, had generated intense discussions.[25]

By 1840, Dr. George Pressly was very much part of this world, but the rest of his relatives, apart from Alexander Pressly and some of his children who had not yet moved to Mississippi, had left. Clearly, conflicting political ideologies, the desire for better land, and major changes in the Associate Reformed Presbyterian Church accounted for part of this drift. Many Pressly kin had migrated west and no longer had slaves; others settled in newly formed ARP congregations in other areas in the South. The center of Pressly family life shifted to Due West, South Carolina, and to Erskine College and Seminary. "Part IV: The Learned and Sacred Conversation" tells the first part of this story.

NOTES

Chapter 9: The Hard Labor Section: A Prosperous, Rural Farming Community

1. By 1830, one half of the sixty million tons of cotton produced in South Carolina came from the lower piedmont counties of Abbeville, Fairfield, Edgefield, and Laurens.

2. Robert Mills, *Statistics of South Carolina, Including a View of Its Natural, Civil, and Military History, General and Particular,* Charleston, SC, 1826.

3. The best lands in the county were valued at twenty dollars per acre, with inferior land averaging between five and ten dollars per acre. Compared to other places in South Carolina, Mills considered living expenses in Abbeville County as "moderate, scarcely exceeding eight dollars per month." By 1836, the town of Abbeville had grown considerably with 436 inhabitants; numerous stores; five taverns; a professional class of physicians, lawyers, and clergy; and various artisans, such as shoemakers and silversmiths.

4. As suggested in a letter written by John E. Pressly, published in *ARP Magazine,* January 7, 1886; Jim Gettys shared a transcription by Lowry Ware with me.

5. John Devlin (1771–1850) served as a guardian along with Martha Devlin Pressly for her son, John E. Pressly, after her husband's death. William Chiles, John Hearst Jr., and his two brothers-in-law, John Lindsey and James Drennan, made an inventory of the estate on October 31, 1826. The estate sale totaled $622.931/4 excluding land. (See Probate Records, Abbeville County Courthouse, Box 7, Packet 831.) The estate may not have been fully settled until the late 1840s as a note in the estate files (signed by his son, John) reads: "Received from John Devlin my lawful guardian $840 and $300 while I was at Erskine from 1837 to 1847 being in full my distribution shares of my father's estate both real and personal." E. E. Pressly helped raise John's son, who lived with him and attended school in Due West after his mother married Josiah McGaw in 1836 (with whom she had four children), the son of Samuel Patterson's sister, Sarah McGaw.

6. J. I. Bonner, *Sketch of Reverend J. P. Pressly, DD. Published by the Order of the Second Associate Reformed Presbytery,* Due West, 1878 notes "Samuel settled three miles south of Cedar Spring Church at a place known as the Brick House."

7. Nora Davis, *An Historical Sketch of Cedar Spring Associate Reformed Presbyterian Church,* unpublished manuscript in McCain Library, Erskine College, Due West (ca. 1940s).

8. Robert Pressly and his brother John S. Pressly sold 148 acres, part of a tract originally granted to Robert Thompson, to Moses Thompson for the sum of $185 on July of 1819. The transaction is part of the Wideman Family Papers. Moses Thompson died in 1831 and his estate was administered by John Pressly and Dr. Samuel Pressly, Probate Records, Abbeville County Courthouse, Box 91, Pack 2252. Leonard Wideman may have acquired this land and it could have been the Pressly track listed for rent in his 1847 estate sale.

9. George was administrator of his estate; an announcement in the Edgefield Advertiser, June 3, 1841 states Court has ruled that John's widow, Elizabeth, and children Margaret, Elizabeth, David R., Nathaniel W., and George W. lived out of state.

10. The Wideman Family Papers in the possession of Frank Wideman, III, contain numerous deeds and legal documents from 1826–1829 that relate to Col. Hearst's consolidation of his land holding as he acquired his siblings' shares of their father's estate and other land. There are also documents related to Abner Perrin, a brother-in-law of Leonard Wideman, and to Wideman-related land purchases in the first half of the nineteenth century. I am most grateful to Frank Wideman and his wife, Lisa, for their gracious hospitality, their interest

in this project, and their willingness to share helpful information from family papers and other documents related to Sylvania and the Hearst family. Their assistance in making this material accessible and helpful replies to my many inquiries is greatly appreciated.

11. A survey for William Hearst in January 1805 laid out 229 acres, presumably his inherited share of his father's estate. His land was adjacent to his siblings Nancy, George, and Thomas Hearst, and to James Puckett, James Houston (?), and Abraham Russell. The survey is part of the Wideman Papers.

12. Box 42, Package 944. Probate Records, Abbeville County Courthouse. The rest of William Hearst's estate was sold off, and the proceeds (as per his will) were divided between the children of his full brothers and sisters, a total of twenty-eight children, each of whom received $92.07¾, including William's four children. His estate was not settled until December 8, 1834.

13. Neighbors adjoining Joseph Hearst 933 acres of land when he purchased in on March 16, 1802 included Samuel Crozier, John Ghaston. Elizabeth Kirkwood, Samuel McClinton, Mouchet, Mrs. Pressly and William Pressly. Plat recorded in South Carolina Department of Archives & History, Series S213192, Vol. 0038, p. 00645.

14. The land adjoined both Chiles and Hearst. The legal transfer was signed January 1829 by Chiles and an informal survey (more a sketch) was done by Patrick Gibson around the same time.

15. John S. Pressly, "Reminiscences of Union Academy," *Due-West Telescope*, February 13, 1857.

16. Reverend James Rogers was head of a classical school in Fairfield. Another school, Ebenezer Academy in York, was taken under the patronage of the Synod of the South circa 1825. Primary schools, often called common schools, could have been privately run or part of the free school system established by the State in 1811.

17. Tom Horton, *The American Eton Moses Waddel's famed Willington Academy*, Trafford Publishing, 2012.

18. J. I. Bonner, "Biographical Sketch Reverend E. E. Pressly, D. D," *Due West Telescope. V*ol. III, no. 14, April 2, 1852. He also states that J. A. Calhoun was a classmate of Thomas Chiles Perrin at Union Academy.

Chapter 10: The Presslys and Hearsts: Physicians, Planters, and the Nullification Crisis

1. Cakak and Groover (2004) examined thirteen antebellum plantation homes in the Sumter National Forest area. The average floor plan for an upcountry plantation home was approximately 1,138 square feet with houses consisting of two or three levels with four chimneys and generally built on a brick pier foundation.

2. Sworn chain bearers assisted surveyors and were generally neighbors who owned adjacent land.

3. Thomas Carpenter Read, *The Descendants of Thomas Lee of Charleston, South Carolina, 1710–1769: A Genealogical-Biographical Compilation,* Columbia, SC, 1964, R. L. Bryan Company, p. 4.

4. Bonner. *Sketch of Reverend J. P. Pressly*, 1878.

5. Read, *The Descendants of Thomas Lee of Charleston,* pp. 244–5.

6. Included in the Cothran/Harrison Family Papers, Millway Plantation, Bradley, South Carolina. The original signed pamphlet was in the possession of Wade C. Harrison in 1949.

7. Samuel's legatees included his brother, John Taylor, and his mother, Jane Pressly, who, for several years, continued to receive annual dividends in the amount of $452.60. Some of Samuel's children were educated in Due West at the Academy or Erskine College, and estate expenses, including clothing, board, and tuition for them, were being paid in 1839 and 1840. In 1847, A. M. Cook, the second husband of Samuel's daughter, Eliza, filed a claim against George Pressly, the estate's executor, for lack of payment. Eliza's stake was worth more than $6,000. Probate Records, Abbeville County Courthouse, Box 72, Pack 1771. Samuel is buried in Hamburg Cemetery in Oak Hill, Wilcox County, Alabama.

8. George W. Pressly Papers 1832–1846, Manuscript Collection, South Caroliniana Library, University of South Carolina, Columbia, SC, no. 28413893.

9. I am grateful to Jim Bates for providing material related to the USDA Park Service's purchase of this land which included an archaeological survey and deed search, and also for taking us to the site and showing us the location of the house and graveyard.

10. Davis, *Cedar Spring*, typescript, McCain Library, Erskine College, Due West.

11. See Cabak and Groover, *Plantations without Pillars, Archaeology, Wealth and Material Life at Bull Hill*, Vol. 1, Savannah River Archaeological Research Papers 11, 2004. For an interesting discussion about "plain" plantations and frugal planters focusing on the Bush Family.

12. Dr. Joseph Pressly's daughter, Frances, and her husband, Dr. Bradley, lived on the property until 1907. The site is 38GN389 in the Park report of April 16, 2013. Agricultural terraces are clearly visible. George's name appeared in a petition supporting a public road to run from "John Wideman's on Long Cane Road to G. W. Presleys [*sic*] near Mount Pleasant Church": S165029 Miscellaneous Communications to the General Assembly 1857 assessing damage to Thomas Creswell's property by this road.

13. I would like to thank Jim Bates for providing me with information on the old Devlin homestead and on the nearby Creswell Cemetery located about a hundred yards north of the site in the direction of Cedar Springs. James Devlin was married to Mary Ann Paul; whose mother was the daughter of Widow Jane Pressly. Compared to the estates of Major Chiles or Col. Hearst, Col. Devlin's estate was modest with many fewer animals, nine slaves, and a limited amount of farm tools. He did have, however, one wagon (valued at sixty-two dollars) and gin thrashers. Probate Records, Abbeville County Courthouse, Box 115, Pack 3383—died 1849.

14. Benjamin Resnick, *The Williams Place: A Scotch-Irish Farmstead in the South Carolina Piedmont*. Volumes in Historical Archaeology, Columbia, South Carolina: South Carolina Institute of Archaeology and Anthropology, University of South Carolina. 1988 (DAR ID: 137284).

15. Probate Records, Abbeville County Courthouse, Box 47, Package 1060 and Box 49, Package 1127.

16. We also have a Proudit volume owned by and with the signature of Thomas White Chiles.

17. After his wife's death in the 1880s, the entire planation was sold to John Calvin Kennedy. Hearst also owned land in Georgia. Kennedy's daughter, Malvina Grier, and her husband, Ebbie Francis Grier, who was a great-grandson of Reverend E. E. Pressly, bought

out the property from her siblings. She lived at Eden Hall until her death in 1980. The *Charleston Index Journal,* May 2, 1987, described the sale of one thousand acres, several homes, and antique furnishings. According to Stephen Davis, whose family currently owns Eden Hall, the contents of the attic were bought as a lot for two hundred dollars and included old furniture, quite possibly from Sylvania, as well as numerous boxes of letters and documents, and memorabilia. Their whereabouts, if they survive at all, are not known.

18. Leonard Wideman was a very wealthy planter and the detailed inventory of his personal assets included extensive furniture and household fineries. Among his executors were his neighbors, Dr. John Wardlaw Hearst and Dr. George W. Pressly, as well as his son, James H. Wideman; a bond of eighty thousand dollars was bound to David Lesley. An advertisement for his estate sale in the *Abbeville Banner* in January 1848 stated 109 slaves were for sale and nine tracts of land, including the "Pressly Track," were available for rent. Probate Records, Abbeville County Courthouse, Box 122, Pack 3605. His daughter, Margaret Wideman, also remained in the area and married Thomas Jefferson Lyons. After Sarah Wideman died, her son, James, advertised two estate sales in Charleston and Abbeville papers one in 1862 when the property did not sell, and the second after the War. The latter included in addition to 1648 acres "a large amount of provisions, stock, implements [*sic*] of husbandry, confederate bonds, &o."

Chapter 11: Entrepreneurial Planters, Bonds of Kinship, and the Cyclical Economy

1. Watson, *Greenwood Sketches.*

2. Rueben Chiles will, Probate Records, Abbeville County Courthouse, Box 21, Pack 468. John Pressly, Samuel Pressly and Phillip Stieffle did the estate inventory.

3. The Chiles Cemetery is located north of Millpond Road on the west side of Callison Road. There are about fifty graves marked by fieldstones or sunken places.

4. Watson, *Greenwood Sketches;* and William Benjamin Cothran and Samuel Alexander Cothran, *Cothran-Chiles Notes and an update after more than a half-century,* Aiken, South Carolina, 1992, pp. 437–39.

5. Llewellyn M. Toulon, "Brigadier General Andrew Williamson and Whitehall, Part II," *Journal of Backcountry Studies,* Vol. 7, No. 2 (Fall 2012). The wealthy planter, Dr. Samuel Sproull Marshall, later lived at White Hall Place.

6. October 9 1872 "Valuable Cotton Planation for sale . . . the Quarter Tract of land on which Major John Chiles lived . . . situated on Hard Labor Creek." Thomas C. Perrin, executor, advertised in *Abbeville Press and Banner.*

7. A transcription of the Bethany Church and Horeb Baptist Church minutes are in the Cothran-Harrison papers at Millway Plantation, Bradley, South Carolina.

8. Sale of George Pressly Chiles's estate advertised in *Abbeville Press and Banner.*

9. William Perrin receives grants in 1773/74; his son, Abner Perrin, acquired one thousand acres on Hard Labor Creek in 1792. Samuel acquires forty-two acres on Hard Labor Creek and Calabash Branch (27/11/1818, Series S213192, vol. 0045, p. 00353). Recorded plats neighboring this land were owned by James Adamson, Camp, Henry Gabel, Mrs. Haney, Joseph Hearst, Hoe, John Holloway, Samuel Mouchet, James, and Philip Stieffle (Stephel).

10. Several deeds and surveys related to land owned by Abner Perrin, Jr. are in the Wideman Family Papers. Cook in his book, the *Hard Labor Section,* p. 41 notes that Henry Cook bought 288 acres next to Abner Perrin on a ridge near Rocky Creek and built his

house (where JTP later lived) near where the "Neel House" (where George Pressly lived) was built in the mid-1830s.

11. Samuel Perrin sale, Probate Records, Abbeville County Courthouse, Box 75, Pack 1833.

12. Eunice Perrin's sale, Probate Records, Abbeville County Courthouse, Box 119, Pack 352912. See Thomas Perrin Cothran, *The Perrin Family: with particular reference to Samuel Perrin, son of William, son of John, and his descendants*, 1992 reprinted text from 1924; and Thomas Perrin Harrison, *The Honorable Thomas Chiles Perrin of Abbeville, South Carolina: Forebears and Descendants,* Greenville, SC, 1983.

13. Perrin Family Papers, Folder 3, Wilson Library, University of North Carolina, Chapel Hill.

15. Perrin Family Papers, Folder 4.

16. John Cothran estate materials included in S. A. Cothran and W. B. Cothran, *Cothran-Chiles Notes and an update after more than a half century.*1936 and 1992. This is an immensely helpful book and a remarkable testament to the Chiles-Cothran-Harrison families that have seriously researched their history for over a century. It includes much helpful information about the community.

17. "Mary Cothran Mitchells's Chronicles," published in *Cothran-Chiles Notes*, pp 443–476. Mitchell (1836–1913) wrote these Chronicles in 1889.

18. I would like to thank Frank Harrison, Jim Harrison, and Wade Harrison for their assistance in looking for photographs of Mount Vernon.

19. A typescript of Sproull's will is in the South Carolina Department of Archives and History Estate. Box 84, Pkg. 2055 Probate Record Office, Abbeville County Courthouse.

20. Chronicles.

21. Store accounts, 1841–42, #10552 (OCLC # 663127402) South Caroliniana Library, University of South Carolina, Columbia.

22. Ariela J. Gross, *Double Character Slavery and Mastery in the Antebellum Courtroom,* Athens: University of Georgia, 2006, pp. 80–83 and "Like Master, Like Man: Constructing Whiteness in the Commercial Law of Slavery, 1800–1861, *Cardozo Law Review*, 1996–97.

23. See W. J. Megginson, *African American Life in South Carolina's Upper Piedmont, 1780–1900,*Columbia: University of South Carolina Press, 2006.

24. See also, "Citizens of Abbeville District, Petition for the Repeal of an 1834 Law Prohibiting Slaves from being taught to Read the Bible," circa 1837 in the South Carolina, Department of Archives and History, series S165015, item 2822.

25. Leonard Todd, *Carolina Clay: The Life and Legen of the Slave Potter, Dave*. 2008.

PART IV

The Learned and Sacred Conversation: The Pressly Family's Destiny

Introduction

Within the context of this secular world there was, for our family and for many others in the Hard Labor community, including the Hearsts and Thomas W. Chiles, the dominant presence of the Cedar Spring congregation and the increasingly more insular Associate Reformed Presbyterian Church. Part IV discusses the Pressly family and its relationship to a different world, not one of politics, farming, and commerce, but rather of education and a spiritual life. "The Learned and Sacred Conversation" essentially parallels the time frame of the discussion of the secular world.

The initial impetus for founding Union Academy, discussed in the previous section, was probably nondenominational. However, the existence of secondary schools like Union Academy were essential to the viability and health of the Church, especially to the Associate Reformed Synod of the South, for which a classical education was a prerequisite for seminary education and the ministry. Beginning with the Union Academy in 1820, education and teaching became a central theme in the Pressly family's history. John Taylor Pressly, Samuel Patterson Pressly, and John S. Pressly all taught there in its early years, and Ebenezer Erskine Pressly and James Patterson Pressly were among its first students. They all went on to become distinguished educators and clergymen. Each of them recognized that a passion for learning and an intellectual understanding of the scriptures were essential to developing a profound and deeply pious connection with the church. They devoted their lives to being teachers, and it was as educators and theologians, as much as in the pulpit, that the Pressly family, over the next several generations, was to make its most lasting contributions.

Chapter 12

Setting the Course in Education and the Ministry: Reverend John Taylor Pressly and Reverend Samuel Patterson Pressly

Reverend John Taylor Pressly, Professor of Theology and Minister at Cedar Spring Congregation, 1816–1831

Reverend John Taylor Pressly, the son of David Pressly (died 1818), was known for the clarity of his writings and sermons, and as a gifted theologian. He set the course as early as 1812 when, after he graduated from Transylvania University in Lexington, Kentucky, he went to New York City, perhaps with the assistance of Reverend Alexander Porter, to study under Dr. John Mitchell Mason. Dr. Mason was considered one of the most accomplished pastors of his time and a man of extensive classical learning and distinguished scholarship. JTP was licensed to preach in the spring of 1815 and spent the next year, as was customary, doing missionary work, traveling horseback through several states. He was ordained on July 3, 1816, at the Cedar Spring Associate Reformed Church, where he had been baptized. As Pastor at Cedar Spring, JTP inherited a congregation severely weakened by the exodus to Preble County, Ohio, of at least half of its membership, and by the growing strength of other denominations, in particular the Baptists, in the area. Very early on, he became a leader in the Synod of the Carolinas and Georgia and as early as 1820, at its request, he wrote from Cedar Spring a "Pastoral Letter" which was intended to alert congregations without pastors to be aware of dangers "against [which] it will be your duty to guard." Published in 1822, it alerted them to the "alarming evil" of the Profanation of the Sabbath, the Profanation of God's name, and "drunkedness." These could be counteracted by the family worship of God and by religious instruction of children.[1]

In 1822, the Synod decided to separate itself from the Associate Reformed Presbyterian Church, forming an independent Synod, the Associate Reformed Synod of the South. The move to become an independent Synod was significant, the first step in protecting this branch of the denomination from what many saw as the beginnings of assimilation and liberalism from the North and the relaxing of a strict adherence to "the church of our forbearers." The new Synod created a First and Second Presbytery and remained independent of the larger Presbyterian Church through all of the changes that took place as the nineteenth century progressed. By the end of the century, it had become a distinctly regional denomination. JTP was certainly initially a leader in this new Synod, and although he never wavered from his belief in the exclusive use of the Hebrew psalms and the sanctity of the Sabbath, he may have had more liberal tendencies to which his congregation was not receptive. Many years later in 1862, JSP commented, "It is well known that the then Pastor's mind had been imbued with lax notions, broached a few years previous by Dr. Mason." They were "not so relished" by old people, and "it is well known that Dr. John T. Pressly renounced those newfangled notices, touching on Catholic communion and an enlarged Psalmody before he left the South."[2] It was not uncommon for parishioners to engage in an intense immersion in religious doctrine. JSP gives us an insight into the type of conversations that took place in an article published in the *Due West Telescope* in June 1862 about William Hearst, who during the 1820s would often ride back from Sabbath services with JTP: "Secular topics, in no form, were admitted, and we know this as the predominant principle and practice of the generality of those who, at that time, were regarded as exemplary members of Cedar Spring and Long Cane."[3]

By the 1820s, spurred on by the need for an educated ministry, denominational-specific seminaries began to increase. In 1825, the new Associate Reformed Synod of the South, recognizing the need not only to train more young men for the ministry but also to have them trained in a seminary exclusively devoted to its faith, voted to form a theological school. It appointed Reverend John Hemphill of the First Presbytery and Reverend John Taylor Pressly of the Second Presbytery to become professors of theology in addition to their duties as ministers. Hemphill was to teach didactic and polemic theology, and Pressly was to teach oriental languages, biblical criticisms, and church history. This was not a practical arrangement because the two lived one hundred miles away from one another. By 1827, this task fell to JTP alone, with his home and the Cedar Spring Church serving as the seminary classroom. In 1827, he received an honorary MA degree from Miami University in Ohio. In 1828, the Lower Long Cane and Cedar Spring congregations reconciled and joined together again after the split that had taken place in 1803, when Reverend Porter resigned, and JTP served both congregations in addition to his increased teaching demands.

One of JTP's most significant contributions during this period, in addition to stabilizing the Cedar Spring congregation weakened by westward migrations, was his important role in training the next generation of ministers. He developed a reputation early in his career as a gifted professor of theology, teaching his cousins Ebenezer Erskine Pressly, Samuel Patterson Pressly (son of his uncle John Pressly), and JSP, and his younger brother, James Patterson Pressly, as well as many others, including Reverend H. Bryson, Reverend Joseph McCrery, and his neighbor, Reverend James Madison Chiles, later a Baptist minister. In his training of these young men, JTP instilled the beliefs of his devout Scottish forbearers, including the commitment to the exclusivity of the Hebrew Psalms and the communal experience that the congregation shared in their metrical form of singing. He almost certainly also instilled in them the importance of a profound intellectual understanding of the scriptures. All of these men were deeply erudite. During this period of intense study, E. E. and his cousin, James

Pressly, were also occasional supplies for the Due West Corner congregation, where JTP and his cousin, Reverend Samuel Patterson Pressly, also preached.

As noted earlier, JTP lived near his brother, Samuel, in a modest "pioneer house of hewn logs," with a chimney at each end, typical of the I-style farmhouses of the time. It had a porch along the south that extended the full length of the house. Located off Barksdale Ferry Road on land later owned by his brother, George, his home also served as the Synod's first seminary. It was apparently destroyed in a hurricane between 1850 and 1860. JTP is listed in the 1820 census with two children under ten years old and two slaves, and in the 1830 census with five children as well as his mother living with him, and eleven slaves. This would indicate that he would have had a farmstead that produced cash crops, almost certainly cotton, and that he was not opposed to slavery, a position in keeping with the Synod of the South. He and his wife, Jane, had nine children, only four of whom survived into adulthood. Their son, Joseph, later became an ordained minister in Pennsylvania and their infant son, John Mason Pressly, was buried next to his grandfather, David Pressly, in Cedar Springs Cemetery.

A minister held a position of respect in the community, especially during this period. Samuel Leard in his historical address at Cedar Spring Church in June 1879 noted that "The Doctor and the Minister wore broadcloth and possibly a few others" while most men and women wore homespun clothes.[4] Leard also mentioned that the minister road to church in a barouche, a nineteenth-century horse drawn carriage with a high front seat for the driver and two double facing inside seats. JTP served not only his congregation but also preached at other congregations in the Second Presbytery without permanent ministers as well as attended numerous Synod meetings, and he became a leading and highly visible figure in the Synod of the South. A minister's life was not easy nor was it easy for his family. Ministers were frequently torn between the priority of family and what could be argued was the higher priority of God and the church. They undertook missionary tours—JTP took a two-month missionary trip to Tennessee in 1819—and many, like him, made it a practice to visit parishioners in their homes, often traveling long distances by horseback and spending nights away from family. In addition to preparing sermons and teaching duties, ministers were also called upon to address family and neighbor-related disputes, as well as mediate other issues. As a result, a minister's wife sometimes had to assume responsibilities normally assigned to the head of household, including managing, planting and harvesting crops, and sometimes also overseeing slaves. Wives frequently also provided devotional discipline and leadership within the household, given the frequent absence of their husbands. The entire family, including slaves, attended morning and evening devotional sessions where psalms were sung, passages from the Bible read, and children were taught the shorter catechisms. Wives married to ministers, which included many Pressly daughters, had an additional responsibility of providing counsel to their husbands, who were often challenged by a variety of parishioner disputes and family ills and they played important roles attracting women parishioners who were essential to the growth of congregations. Their assistance was compensated for by the generally close and dependent relationship that existed between husband and wife within the clerical family and the fact that their lives together were centered on piety and the strict rituals of church life.

On October 10, 1831, the Associate Reformed Synod of the West, which openly supported an antislavery position, elected Reverend John Taylor Pressly as Professor of Theology at its Theological Seminary in Allegheny, Pennsylvania. By the end of the year, he and his family had moved north to Pennsylvania. It was only after he settled in Pittsburgh that he also accepted a call, late in 1832, to become the first pastor of the First Associate Reformed Presbyterian Church of Allegheny. In the same year, Jefferson College, Washington, Pennsylvania, conferred on him an honorary Doctor of Divinity degree. He later served as a Trustee there from 1839 to 1865. It is interesting to speculate on the reasons for this move. Like his brother, Samuel, JTP was discouraged by the Nullification Crisis and the ongoing divisions and disturbances that it caused within the community and the church. Although not against slavery, he was strongly against Secession. Another reason contributing to his decision could have been his awareness of a more insular and orthodox regrouping within the new Synod of the South. As we will see, his cousin, Samuel Pressly, certainly felt this in Newberry, and, as suggested earlier, there are hints that JTP may have also pushed boundaries in Cedar Spring. There were ongoing debates and tensions in many congregations between strictly adhering to the church of our fathers and a desire for more relaxed doctrines, which, while preserving the absolute sanctity of psalm singing, loosened the strictures around closed Communion that would eventually move the denomination to a less isolationist position. The tension and bitterness between the Synod of the South and the Synods of the West and North were also over slavery. This increased sufficiently by 1834 that the Synod of the South decided to pass a resolution stating that "in their opinion it is prejudicial to the Southern Church to send our young men to the North or West, either to college or a Theological Seminary."

The move to Alleghany was a major appointment for JTP, offering him the opportunity to lead in a larger arena, the growing Synod of the West, and in a more metropolitan area across the river from Pittsburgh. He was a leader by temperament and made worldly by his travels and education in New York. He was immensely erudite and a prolific writer, defending many arcane positions. In 1842, JTP founded *The Preacher,* a semi-monthly religious paper, and in 1848 he published a lengthy rebuttal entitled *Ralston's Inquiry into the Propriety of Using an Evangelical Psalmody in the Worship of God* (Alleghany: John B. Kennedy, 1848). It is a passionate and lengthy defense of the use of Hebrew Psalms and Psalmody. One of his most satisfying achievements later in his career was to have a leading role in helping to create the United Presbyterian Church in 1858. On May 26, 1858, the Reformed and Associate Presbyterian Churches united to form the United Presbyterian Church at City Hall in Pittsburgh. The new church had 54,778 communicants, 5 Synods, 49 Presbyteries, and 419 ministers. JTP was the moderator of its first General Assembly.

JTP left a remarkable legacy. Although contemporary and posthumous descriptions of JTP reflect the flowery prose of the times, several attributes emerge that clearly defined this man. He is said to have had the demeanor of a cultured, dignified, Christian gentleman, and as preacher he was remarkable for his clearness of conception and expression; he "gave to his delivery power approaching the magisterial." He was a large man, six feet tall with keen, dark eyes and a strong and sonorous voice. He is said to have displayed a fine personal appearance and was dignified and solemn in his actions. Images of him reflect this demeanor (Figures 12-1). He died in 1870, and his wife followed in 1873; they are buried in Union Dale Cemetery, in Pittsburgh, Pennsylvania. In 1881, a memorial plaque was erected in the First United Presbyterian Church of Alleghany where he served, praising him as a "Good and Great Man."

Figure 12-1. Reverend John Taylor Pressly.
Associate Reformed Presbyterian Church, *Centennial History of the ARP Church, 1803–1903*, (Charleston: Presses of Walker, Evans, and Cogswell, 1905).

Reverend Samuel Patterson Pressly: Preacher and Professor of Belle Lettres and Moral Philosophy and History

During this same period in the 1820s, JTP's cousin, Reverend Samuel Patterson Pressly, the oldest son of John Pressly (imm John Pressly's son), had a similar task of serving as pastor for four congregations and also teaching higher classes, first at the Newberry Academy in the village of Newberry, where he made his home, and then at the Classical and English High School at Prosperity Church, which he organized in 1830. Born on September 25, 1799, little is known about Samuel's early years. The first son of John and Margaret Patterson Pressly, he probably joined his father in Preble County, Ohio, circa 1813. It is not clear where he received his secondary school education, but he graduated on July 12, 1820, from Transylvania University, the same year as his cousin, George Pressly. After he returned home, Samuel taught at Union Academy while studying theology under JTP and then went on to Princeton Theological Seminary, where he graduated in 1824. He was ordained at Cedar Spring Church on May 15, 1825, and installed the following year as preacher for the united churches of Head Springs, Kings Creek, Prosperity, and Cannon Creek, which became part of the Second Presbytery in November of that same year. He married Jane West Todd on December 22, 1825, and they had two daughters who survived into adulthood. In 1826, Samuel became treasurer of the new Theological Fund established to support the Synod's new seminary. According to documents in the Abbeville Probate Court, he was appointed in 1831 the guardian (responsible for his education, etc.) of a William P. Pressly, probably the son of his younger brother by the same name.[5] He was also the administrator of the estate of another brother, John Brown Pressly, who died in 1832 intestate and insolvent. In both instances, Samuel's cousin, Dr. George W. Pressly, was also involved. John Brown Pressly's bankruptcy proceedings were particularly complex and involved his wife, Maria Bowen, who he married in 1829, and his father, John Pressly. The last years of John's life had to be extremely difficult, with two sons with his first wife, Margaret Patterson, dying young.

Samuel was said to have been an animated minister and a man of "popular manners, fine address and able as a preacher," one who successfully added many members to all of the churches under his guidance.[6] Although a slave owner (he had three slaves in 1830), he was said to have been a very liberal man and "under his administration his church relaxed the rigor of close communion" and as a result "his churches doubled communicants." He also introduced a new custom of holding a special service for blacks on Saturday afternoons, having them sit in front pew seats. Some parishioners, however, strongly objected to his more liberal ways, and in 1833 or 1834, the Session decided to remove him. He resigned first, asking to connect himself with a sister denomination, whereby he joined the Presbyterian Church. In 1834, he received an honorary degree from Miami University and was appointed Professor of Belle Lettres and of Moral Philosophy and History at Franklin College in Athens, Georgia, which later became the University of Georgia. He taught a course in Mental Philosophy to senior AB students, a very early course in psychology. He died young and is buried in the old Jackson Street Cemetery on the University of Georgia campus in Athens (where Reverend Moses Waddel is also buried). His impressive gravestone survives in remarkably good condition. His last name is spelled incorrectly as "Pressley" (Figure 12-2). The date of his death is given as "29 September 1836" at age thirty-six; however, it is sometimes also listed as 1839. His gravestone was carved and signed by the well-known Charleston stone carver, W. T. White.

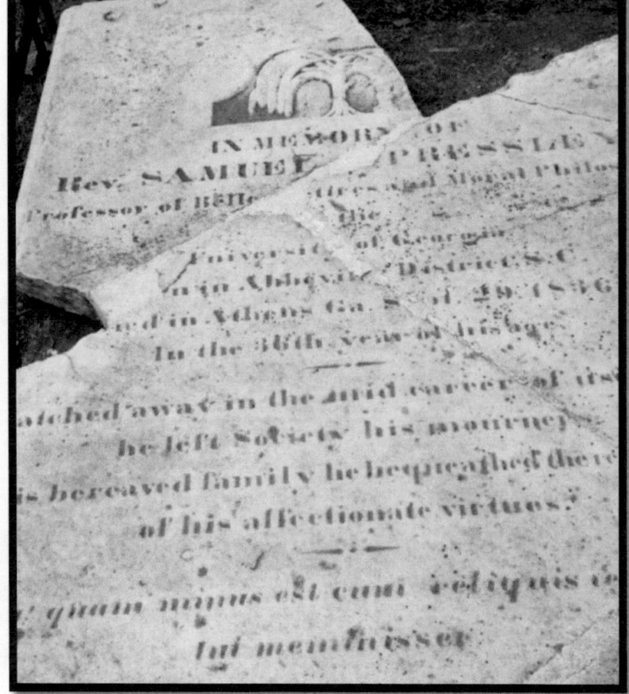

Figure 12-2. Gravestone of Rev. Samuel Patterson Pressly, Jackson Cemetery, Athens, Georgia. Photograph courtesy of author.

Chapter 13

Passing the Mantle: Erskine College and Seminary

The Academy

With JTP's departure for Alleghany, the leadership for the Synod of the South in Abbeville District began to shift to his newly ordained cousin, Reverend Ebenezer Erskine Pressly, who was installed as pastor in August 1830 for both the Due West Associate Reformed Presbyterian Church and the Generostee ARP Church in Anderson District. By the end of the decade, Due West, located some eighteen miles from Cedar Springs, was to become the home of the Synod's Erskine College and Seminary and eventually the new center of Pressly family life.

After studying four years at Union Academy, Ebenezer traveled by horseback at age sixteen with his cousin, James Patterson Pressly, to Transylvania University in Lexington, Kentucky, as his older cousins had done before him. There they connected with Robert Hamilton Bishop, a Presbyterian minister and professor of history, and joined him as he set out for Miami University in Oxford, Ohio, to become its first president. The two boys entered the first class of Miami University on November 1, 1824, and graduated in 1826.[1] There were twelve students who graduated from this first class, and nine of them went on to become ministers. E. E. stayed an extra season to take more classes, and then returned home where he studied theology, along with James, under his cousin JTP at the Synod's Seminary. Oxford was not far from Israel Township in Preble County.

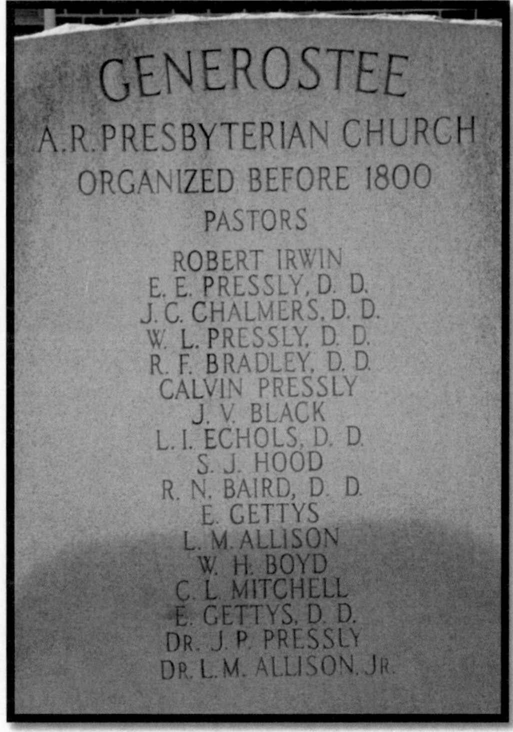

Figure 13-1. Stone marker at Generostee Church, Iva, South Carolina, where Rev. E. E. Pressly served as the Church's second pastor and where several family members were later to serve. Photograph courtesy of author.

Figure 13-2 View of Due West Associate Reformed Presbyterian Church, circa 1850s. Lithograph by P. S. Duval & Son, Philadelphia. Private Collection. Photography courtesy of author.

After completing his theological studies, Ebenezer Erskine (called "Ebbie" by his family and friends; today he is more commonly referred to as E. E.) was licensed to preach on February 21, 1829. During his missionary year, he preached in the Abbeville, Laurens, and Anderson districts in South Carolina and also throughout Georgia, Florida, and Alabama. We still have the saddlebag that he was said to have taken with him as he rode horseback to numerous small communities in the South. He was installed as pastor of Generostee ARP Church, becoming its second minister, and of Due West ARP Church on August 7, 1830, and married Elizabeth Agnew, daughter of Samuel Agnew of Due West, the following February 10, 1831 (Figure 13-1).

One cannot minimize the impact of JTP's departure for Alleghany at the end of 1831 on the young pastor, Ebenezer Erskine Pressly. It helped set the course for his life. At the age twenty-three he was catapulted into a leadership role, assuming the position (although not formally appointed until later) of Professor of Theology for the Synod of the South, formerly held by his cousin. His home became its seminary. At the same time, he also served two congregations twenty-five miles apart. Generostee was a stable congregation that had put up a new church building in 1828, whereas Due West had been severely weakened two decades earlier by the exodus of almost half its parishioners who had left to join the Hopewell Church in Preble County, Ohio. Due West had been without a steady minister since 1803, when Peter McMullan left, and E. E. seized the opportunity to revitalize the long dormant church, attracting leading families and elders from nearby Greenville, who left in part over the Nullification Crisis. Shortly after he was installed as pastor, the congregation erected its third building and first frame structure. Reverend Pressly oversaw the appointment of a new bench of elders, which included James Lindsay, John Lindsay, Andrew C. Hawthorn, James Fair, and John Sims, who were to become instrumental in helping him rejuvenate this church and help ensure that the Synod's new academy would be established in Due West. On February 18, 1834, E. E. and twenty-six members of the congregation organized "The Education Society of Due West Corner," whose purpose was to aid indigent young men in heir progress toward the Gospel ministry.[2] They anticipated by several months the Synod of the South's decision to create a new academy.

Figure 13-3. Reverend Ebenezer Erskine Pressly by Dr. C. H. Kingsmore, Eupheamian Literary Society, Erskine College, Due West, South Carolina. Photograph courtesy of author.

Figure 13-4. Reverend Ebenezer Erskine Pressly by Dr. C. H. Kingsmore, oil on canvas. From the collection of Nancy and William Pressly, Atlanta, Georgia. Photograph courtesy of author.

On November 10, 1834, the Associate Reformed Synod of the South, at its meeting at Due West Corner, voted to establish one or more schools or academies, and it charged the membership to investigate the possibility of raising funds and to present offers to support this effort at the next annual meeting. Due West was successful in raising sufficient funds—some three thousand dollars, and the Synod voted to establish "The school at Due West Corner" with John S. Pressly (JSP) as its principal and teacher. Reverend E. E. Pressly was elected as one of the five members of the school's Board of Directors. The aim was to "establish an academy for training young men to enter the junior class of a respectable college."[3] It opened on February 1, 1836, as the Mount Vernon Academy, with about twenty students enrolled. Classes were taught in a one-room structure with JSP teaching the boys at one end and E. E. teaching the girls at the other end. Within a year the congregation had built a two-room building and seven small log cabins that served as classrooms. The Academy School was incorporated in 1837 (James Foster and John Devlin, elders at Cedar Spring Church, composed the committee to secure the charter) and given an official state charter under the name, The Clark and Erskine Seminary, after Reverend Thomas Clark and Reverends Ebenezer and Ralph Erskine, two of the founders of the Seceder denomination in Scotland in 1733. The charter encompassed both the Academy, which was the scholarly part and called the "Literary Department," and the seminary, which was known as the "Theological Department." In 1838, under JSP's teaching and leadership, the Academy had thirty-three students enrolled. That same year E. E. was elected Professor of Theology.

Figure 13-5. Reverend E. E. Pressly's I-style farmhouse, Due West, South Carolina. Photograph courtesy of author.

JSP played an important role in these first years, before E. E. became president of Erskine, and his life and career at various points continued to be closely intertwined with that of his cousin. It was at Union Academy that JSP began in 1822 his "creer [*sic*] of classical teaching" a field whose "usefulness in which he labored at intervals for the balance of his life."[4] After teaching at Union Academy for two years, he went on to teach at schools in Cambridge and Beaver Dam; and then, in 1828, he headed the high school at Church Hill Academy, near Lowndesville, where he had studied a decade earlier under Reverend James Gambel. JSP, a tall slender man, was an accomplished linguist who excelled at teaching Greek and Latin, and was known for his strict and unyielding disciplinary style. As a teacher, he was described as faithful and systematic and "devoted to his work . . . with clear perception of right and wrong in conduct, he was a kindly heart and commanded the esteem and respect of his pupils." In his alumni address given on July 10, 1867, at Erskine College, Col. R. A. Fair described the difference in the approach between JSP and E. E., both of whom he described as excellent teachers: "The former [JSP] was stern, exacting, and unyielding, enforcing his rules by resort to *birch* and expulsion. The

Figure 13-6. A daguerreotype photograph showing E. E. at the deathbed of his daughter, Cypriana. Copy in possession of Nancy and William Pressly.

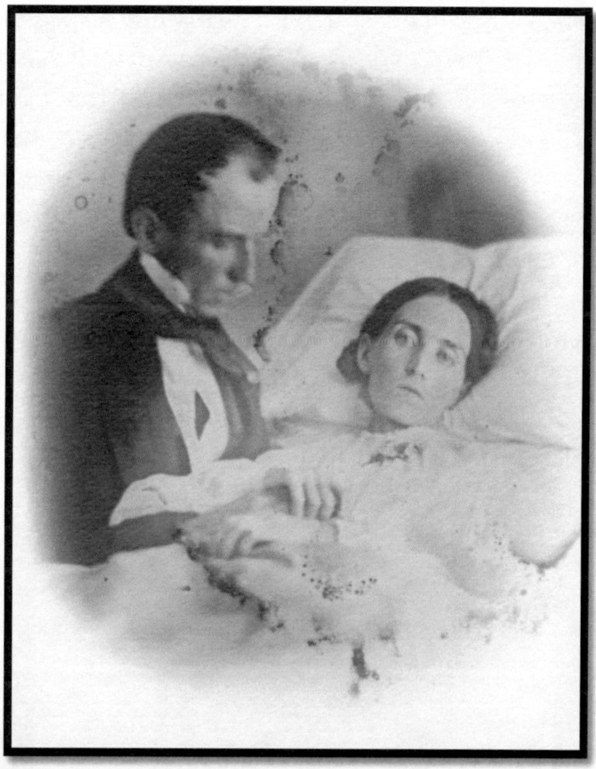

latter [E. E.] was gentle, persuasive and forgiving. . . . The one was obeyed because he was feared, the other because he was beloved."[5]

In 1839, JSP resigned as head of the Literary Department of Clark and Erskine Seminary over a conflict in his approach to discipline, in which the trustees overturned his decision. He studied theology, first at Miami University and then under his cousin, JTP, at the Allegany Seminary. He was licensed by the Second Presbytery of the Synod of the South on October 8, 1840, and ordained at Coddle Creek, North Carolina, on October 14, 1841, which was the same year that E. E. served as the moderator of the General Synod at Coddle Creek. In 1842, he accepted a call from Ebenezer and Bethel Churches in Jefferson County, Georgia, which were the same congregations headed by Reverend Joseph Lowry who was a brother-in-law and close colleague of JTP. JSP married Martha Jane Strong, daughter of Reverend Charles Strong, on October 29 of that same year. Due to ill health, he resigned five years later, in 1847, and eventually moved near Generostee Church in Anderson District

Figure 13-7. Reverend Ebenezer Erskine Pressly's tombstone, Due West ARP Church cemetery, Due West, South Carolina. Photograph courtesy of author.

where, during the last decade of his life, he wrote his invaluable history and other reminiscences about the Pressly family. He also taught at the Anderson Male Academy, where he was appointed principal in February 1850, the same year that E. E. Pressly accepted the appointment as principal of the Anderson Female Institute. JSP seems to have been a man of strong principles, known for his "ardent zeal" with respect to the doctrines of his faith. He supported unwaveringly the Westminster Confession of Faith, accepting no compromise to the early principles as practiced by the first Scotch-Irish settlers. However, despite his doctrinaire stance, he was apparently very amiable socially. He died June 1, 1863, and is buried in the Generostee ARP Church Cemetery, where his Uncle David Pressly is also buried (Figure 13-2).

Figure 13-8. Photograph of Reverend William Laurens Pressly, E. E. Pressly's son. From the collection of Nancy and William Pressly.

Figure 13-9. Photograph of Frances Wideman, wife of Reverend William Laurens Pressly. From the collection of Nancy and William Pressly.

Reverend Ebenezer Erskine Pressly, President of Erskine College, 1839–1847

Encouraged by the Seminary's success, the Synod decided to expand the institution's mandate; and in 1839, the Clark and Erskine Seminary became the first four-year denominational college in South Carolina. Reverend E. E. Pressly became its first President and from 1839 to 1847, "Dr. Ebbie," as his students called him, was also Professor of Moral Sciences and Head of the Theological Seminary. The success of the seminary was critical to building a strong Associate Reformed Synod of the South, and E. E. provided essential leadership during these early years.[6] While at Miami University, he had been a member of the Erodelphian Literary Society; and in 1839 he helped start the Eupheamian Literary Society, the first literary society at Erskine College. Today, a painting of E. E. by Dr. C. H. Kingsmore hangs in the Society's building, albeit in terrible condition (Figure 13-3). Kingsmore painted another portrait, probably circa 1851, of E. E. (Figure 13-4) around the same time he painted Leonard Wideman's wife, Sarah Patterson Wideman; the latter is still in the Wideman family's possession.

Figure 13-10. Reverend William Laurens Pressly and his family, circa 1903. Standing left to right: Samuel Agnew Pressly; Joseph Lowry Pressly; William Laurens Pressly, Jr.; James Hearst Pressly; John Bonner Pressly; Henry Erskine Pressly, holding Bertha, and his wife Mamie Moore; Paul Adam Pressly. Seated left to right: Effie Pressly Grier; Francis Wideman Pressly, holding "Ebe" Grier; William Laurens Pressly; Ebenezer Wideman Pressly; in front of them: Paul Livingston Grier and Barbara Grier. Photograph, Nancy and William Pressly.

In a very short time, Erskine College and Seminary had an established reputation, and in the 1840 census, fifty-one "students" are listed under E. E. Pressly's name. Boarding students usually lived with various families in the small town, so presumably they are listed under him because, as President, he was responsible for them. Encouraged by its early success, the Synod in 1840 requested its ministers to seek contributions from their congregations to construct a proper building for the college, which was successfully completed a few years later. A building was also erected for the Theological Seminary, and circa 1841, the college shortened its name to Erskine College. In these early years, E. E. began to expand the faculty, hiring in 1839 two professors, who, like himself, were educated at Miami University. Neil Gordon was Professor of Languages, and John N. Young was Professor of Mathematics and Natural Philosophy. The following year, he appointed his cousin and dear friend, Reverend James P. Pressly, as Professor of Languages, thus beginning the long tradition of Pressly family members appointed to the faculty of both the college and seminary. Another cousin, John Newton Pressly (also a Miami University graduate), who first studied theology under JTP in Alleghany in 1834 and then with his cousin, "Ebbie," at the Synod's Seminary, was also briefly added to the faculty. He was ordained in the late 1830s and installed as pastor of Bethesda, Shiloh, and Richland in Rush County, Indiana, where, because of his strong antislavery sentiments, he became affiliated with the Synod of the West.

Also in Due West beginning in 1837 was E. E.'s nephew, John Ebenezer Pressly, his deceased brother's son. After his mother, Martha Devlin Pressly, married her second husband, Josiah McGaw, in 1836, John Ebenezer was placed under his Uncle E. E.'s care and became a student at the Academy. He graduated from Erskine College in 1844 and from Erskine Seminary in 1847. After two years as a missionary he was ordained in 1849 and installed as pastor at Coddle Creek and New Perth in Iredell County, North Carolina, near the South Carolina border, where he preached for the rest of his life. In 1849, he married Martha Sherrard, and two of their sons, Neil Erskine Pressly and Mason Wiley Pressly, later went to Erskine and followed their father into the ministry.

E. E. Pressly was described as a practical man, brilliant but not profound, and not disposed, as some of his cousins, to be occupied with theoretical and erudite dissertations on fine points of theological interpretation. His practical skills would have been essential in organizing a new college and seminary. During his tenure, he showed diplomatic skills in protecting the still young Erskine College from political controversy. As noted earlier, the issue of slavery and the ARP's position came to a head in Abbeville District, after the General Assembly of the State of South Carolina passed legislation in December 1834 that declared, "If any person shall hereafter teach any slave to read or write. . . such person if a free white person, upon conviction thereof, shall . . . be fined not exceeding one hundred dollars and imprisoned not more than six months. The informer shall be entitled to one half of the fine." This controversy played out in a lengthy debate in speeches and newspaper articles over many years. Reverend William Hemphill, pastor at Cedar Spring and Lower Long Cane congregations, was particularly outraged by the legislation and undertook an aggressive campaign fully supported by his congregations. He promoted the position of the American Colonization Society, which was that slaves should be freed and repatriated to Liberia. He even delivered copies of the *African Repository* to the Euphemian Literary Society at Erskine. President Pressly wrote Hemphill on July 6, 1840, asking him to stop sending the paper: "In recommending this course I have felt much embarrassment. I cannot live in a tempest . . . I feel confident that you will not doubt my sincerity or the correctness of my intention, while perhaps you will pity my weakness for I am sensible that if I have any character this is its weakness—I cannot contend with the angry passions of mankind."[7] In 1848, after he became president of Erskine College, Reverend Grier appointed Reverend Hemphill as Professor of Latin, leaving no doubt about his opinion on this issue.

Figure 13-11. Reverend James Hearst Pressly. Photograph, Nancy and William Pressly.

Figure 13-12. Reverend Joseph Lowry Pressly. Photograph, Nancy and William Pressly.

E. E. resigned as President of Erskine College and Professor of Theology in 1846, just seven years after he was appointed. At the Synod's request, he remained until 1847, which was when Reverend Grier was appointed the next President. He left the college in excellent condition. By the time he retired the enrollment had increased to ninety-three students, including the college and seminary, with fifty-five of its graduates either already ordained as ministers or in the process of becoming ministers. In 1847, Washington and Lee University awarded him an honorary Doctor of Divinity. It is interesting to speculate on the reasons for E. E.'s resignation when he was still a young man, only thirty-eight years old. Undoubtedly he was exhausted by his efforts and the stress of his position as well as by his chronic intestinal illnesses, which eventually caused him to become addicted to morphine. He was also depressed about the tragedies in his personal life and the loss of several infant children. But in many ways, "Ebbie" was also ill-prepared for the politics of running a college and the leadership role that had been thrust upon him. He grew up without the presence of a father and, unlike his cousin JTP, had little worldly experience. His college years were spent in Oxford, Ohio, a small town, where he was part of the first graduating class of a very young university and seminary. He studied theology under his cousin at the Cedar Spring Church where he was baptized and grew up and was ordained at Due West Corner. Apart from his missionary activities, this was the only world he knew.

Figure 13-13a and 13b. Reverend Paul Adam Pressly and his wife, Lois Moffitt Pressly. Photographs, Nancy and William Pressly

After he resigned, E. E. recuperated for a few years on his farm and home, built by James Brownlee in 1834 and purchased by E. E. sometime after he had become president. Farming was an occupation that he clearly loved, and by the time of his death in 1860, he owned over 1,400 acres and had at least twenty-seven slaves. His home with its shed roof in front still survives and is located halfway between Donald's and Due West (Figure 13-5). E. E. and his wife, Elizabeth, had twelve children, most born at this home but only four survived into adulthood. In February 1850, he accepted a position as principal at Anderson Female Institute, a much less taxing position than President of Erskine, and the family moved to Moffitsville, South Carolina for two years,[8] with E. E. returning twice monthly to preach at the Due West ARP Church. When he returned to Due West, he continued to serve as

Professor of Theology in the seminary as well as pastor of the church. His wife, Elizabeth, died on June 20, 1853, followed by the death of their daughter, Cypriana, a year later on July 5, 1854, at age twenty-one. A daguerreotype photograph shows E. E. at Cypriana's deathbed (Figure 13-6). By temperament, "Ebbie" was described as "often very melancholy" and as someone who "loved to look on the dark side of things."[9] Reverend J. O. Lindsay described him "as a man of sorrows [i.e. Christ-like]." Whatever the reasons—a combination of circumstances, predisposition, and a painful intestinal illness—he was clearly easily overwrought and suffered from a nervous constitution. The photograph of him at his daughter's deathbed reveals the overwhelming melancholy that was said to have defined the last years of his life, when he was described as "bowed in grief and many the night he spent sighing and groaning and weeping and praying."[10] During this tragic period, Samuel Agnew, a nephew, lived with him for two years; his account of E. E.'s household during this period is contained in diaries housed at Erskine College.

Figure 13-14. Reverend James Patterson Pressly. Associate Reformed Presbyterian Church. *Centennial History of the ARP Church, 1803–1903*. Charleston: Presses of Walker, Evans, and Cogswell, 1905.

Figure 13-15. Reverend Frances Young Pressly, Professor of Languages and President of Erskine College. Associate Reformed Presbyterian Church. *Centennial History of the ARP Church, 1803–1903*. Charleston: Presses of Walker, Evans, and Cogswell, 1905.

He married Mary Taylor, eighteen years his junior, in 1854; and in late December of that year, they sold the home where he had lived with his first wife, along with six acres, to Joseph F. Lee, Jr. for $1,300. The family moved to a statelier home, Linden Hill, which is said to have had large columns decorating the façade and was located near the head waters of Long Cane Creek. His home tract consisted of five hundred acres at the time of his death; his plantation tract, consisting of nine hundred acres, was one and a half miles below it. We know from his estate sale that he grew cotton, wheat, and corn for export and had over fifty hogs as well as other livestock, including horses, mules, and cattle on his plantations. He had two more children with Mary Taylor, both of whom died in infancy. During this decade, he also lost a young daughter, Emma, as well as his daughter, Elizabeth (1835–1859), who had married Reverend James C. Boyd and with whom she had a child, Mary Frances Boyd (1858–1912).

Despite having been thrust into a leadership position as president of the first denominational college in South Carolina, he probably would have preferred to have remained a small town pastor and successful backcountry planter. Clearly reticent and private, Kingsmore's portraits reveal a sensitive, gentle, and intellectual man—the books by his side in one of the portraits signaling a range of scholarly interests. The titles reading from left to right are: "HISTO[RY] REFO[RMATION]," presumably John Knox's *The History of the Reformation of Religion in Scotland;* "HISTORY OF HUMANISM;" and "OLINS TRAVELS," which would be Reverend Stephen Olin's *Travels in Egypt, Arabia Petraea, and the Holy Land,* two volumes (New York, 1843). He appears dignified but at the same time unprepossessing. He is said to have had a face "unusually florid for a man of his habits," and apparently "in all his movements he was rather rapid."[11] E. E. had a special fondness for the Hebrew language. Reverend Lindsay in his 1889 Alumni Address relates that "if there was one branch of study which he loved more than another . . . it was the Hebrew language." Lindsay also noted, "Probably his strongest faculty was memory. It was both retentive and ready. His mind was a great store-house of facts, incidents, and anecdotes. He was an omnivorous reader." E. E. was an interesting preacher, when fully prepared, which was not always the case, whose "written discourses are models worthy of preservation."[12]

Beloved pastor of Due West ARP Church for thirty years, E.E. died on July 26, 1860, due to the consequences of a fall from a buggy several months earlier, and he was buried in Due West ARP Church cemetery (Figure 13-7). He died intestate. His estate was "possessed of considerable real and personal property." His estate appraisal, made on December 4, 1860, indicates he had a nicely furnished home with some fine pieces of furniture but by no means elegantly appointed. The most valuable household items were two clocks and two gold watches, a walnut secretary, four wagon carriages, and an extensive library of books, the latter appraised at $150. According to the 1860 census, his combined personal and real estate worth (including slaves) totaled $38,500, or $1,100,000 in today's dollars. His personal property sold at his estate sale for $5,285.47 (not including slaves) after a commission was taken.[13] E. E. was survived by his son, William Laurens Pressly (b. 1837), and one daughter, Marietta, as well as a granddaughter, Mary Frances Boyd (1858–1912), who later married John Perry Cook.

Ebenezer Erskine Pressly was a transitional figure between the world of Cedar Springs and Hard Labor Creek, where the family had first settled, and Due West, which was to become the educational center for the Associate Reformed Presbyterian Synod of the South. His son, William Laurens Pressly, graduated from Erskine in 1857 and married Frances Wideman, daughter of Adam Wideman II in 1858 while his father was still alive (Figures 13-8 and 13-9). After a brief career as a merchant, he attended Erskine Seminary and served as minister at Generostee Church from 1862 until 1871, when he moved to Due West ARP Church, following in his father's footsteps. He later taught at Erskine College and Seminary, becoming President of Erskine Theological Seminary in 1889, a position he held until 1906. He had his wife had a large family with one daughter and eight sons surviving into adulthood (Figure 13-10). His sons were highly accomplished—three carried on the Pressly family legacy as ministers, Reverend James Hearst Pressly, (Figure 13-11), Reverend Joseph Lowry Pressly (Figure 13-12), and my husband's grandfather, Reverend Paul A. Pressly (Figures 13-13a and 13b), who served for a time as pastor at the Ebenezer Church in Louisville, Georgia, which was where Reverend Joseph Lowry and JSP had served earlier in the nineteenth century. Two sons became physicians: Dr. Ebenezer Wideman Pressly and Henry Erskine Pressly (who died from diabetes at age thirty), and two, Samuel Agnew Pressly and John Bonner Pressly, were successful merchants. His daughter, Effie, married Paul Livingston Grier, a professor at Erskine. A large number of E. E.'s sermons and those of his son, William, survive and merit further study in the context of the complicated history of the Associate Reformed Synod of the South after 1840.[14]

Reverend James Patterson Pressly

The other important family member closely associated with Erskine College and Due West during this early period was Reverend James Patterson Pressly (David Pressly's son). E. E. appointed him in 1840 as Professor of Languages at Erskine College, and he also became Professor of Greek Exegesis and Systematic Theology at the Seminary, where he continued a long and distinguished career for over thirty-five years. Licensed on February 21, 1829, James was ordained as a minister at Generostee Church on March 27, 1830, and shortly after married Jane Hearst, the daughter of Col. John Hearst, whom he had known since childhood. In that same year, they moved to Wilcox County, Alabama, where he became the first pastor of the Lebanon Church/Ebenezer ARP Church and of the Prosperity Church in Dallas, some forty miles away. Both churches were formed in the late 1820s as a result of migrations from South Carolina, Ebenezer ARP Church by members of the Lower Long Cane and Cedar Spring congregations, including the Bonners, Dales, Jones, and McBrides, and Prosperity

Church by parishioners from Newbery and Fairfield districts. James's wife, Jane, died in childbirth on June 30, 1832; he was to marry two more times.

Reverend James Patterson Pressly was said to have been a very timid preacher who memorized his sermons, staring straight ahead as he preached and rarely gesturing (Figure 13-14). He enjoyed great success, however, as a professor, and is described as a man of intellectual depth and a scholar with an intense "love of books." Dr. Bonner wrote of him: "To a really great mind was added an intense love of books, so he became a great scholar." He was also "most conscientious [*sic*], a faithful teacher . . . He was exacting in his demands upon himself and likewise rigid in his requirements of others."[15] In 1849, he received an honorary Doctor of Divinity degree from Washington & Lee University in Virginia. Like Ebenezer Erskine, James also farmed and accumulated some wealth. In 1860, he had ten slaves and owned $2,500 worth of real estate and $29,200 in personal property worth $880,556 in today's dollars. He played an important role in the development of Erskine College and Seminary for the three and a half decades he served the institution, and he was also an important patriarchal figure for at least two generations of young Pressly men, descendants of both John (imm 1772) and David (imm 1767), who studied in Due West and at Erskine. Three of James's sons with his third wife, Mary E. Young, were students at Erskine College and Seminary. Frances Young Pressly continued his father's legacy, becoming an ordained ARP minister and serving as Professor of Languages at Erskine and later President of the College from 1899 to 1906 (Figure 13-15). In 1906, after his cousin, William Laurens Pressly (E. E.'s son), resigned, he became President of the Theological Seminary, a position he held until his death in 1934. Another son, David Brainard, also studied at Erskine and became a minister (Figure 13-16), and a third son, John Lowry Pressly (1852–1933), became Professor of Greek, Latin, and German languages at Erskine. The latter's son, James Patterson Pressly, named after his grandfather, became a minister, receiving his degree from Princeton Theological Seminary, while a second son, William Lowry Pressly (1886–1954), was a successful physician.

Figure 13-16. Reverend David Brainard Pressly. Associate Reformed Presbyterian Church. *Centennial History of the ARP Church, 1803–1903*. Charleston: Presses of Walker, Evans, and Cogswell, 1905.

Chapter 14

Due West: A Central Meeting Place and Spiritual Center

In many ways the grandchildren and great-grandchildren of immigrants John and David followed the complicated but relatively common patterns of migration in nineteenth-century America. "Splinter" groups would break off from the main cluster of kin, and then ten or fifteen years later another small group would break off and join them, eventually creating a new "main" cluster. The late 1820s and early 1830s saw a new wave of ARP parishioners from Abbeville and nearby areas, especially Chester and Fairfield, migrate further south and to the west. Many Pressly cousins and extended kin were among those who left Abbeville District and joined new congregations. Some were spurred on by the Nullification Crisis and antislavery sentiments, which shattered communities; others by the desire to join already departed relatives and settle on more fertile land. Family bonds remained strong, however, and extended kin with shared histories seemed to stay together creating small family clusters even in this diaspora. Some, like Alexander Pressly's sons Abner Perrin and Dr. J. Thompson Pressly left the church and became Baptists, settling respectively in Lowndes County, Mississippi, and Houston, Texas (Figure 14-1).

Through these migrations the family became divided into two groups, those who moved to the west and north and joined the Synod of the West and those who remained in the south, including Texas, and were part of the increasingly insular Associate Reformed Presbyterian Church and the Synod of the South. Among those who moved west were Reverend John Newton Pressly (Joseph Pressly's son and imm John's grandson) who was installed in the late 1830s as pastor for the congregations of Bethesda, Shiloh, and Richland in Rush County, Indiana, across the border from Preble County. Because of his strong antislavery sentiments, he became affiliated with the Synod of the West. He was soon joined by his brother, James, who moved with his wife, Elizabeth Hamilton, from Preble County. One of their sons, Israel Hamilton Pressly (Figure 14-2), later became a minister in Rush County. James's and John's father, Joseph, also moved with his second wife, Mary Ann, and their young family, to nearby Clinton County, Indiana, where Mary Ann was still living in 1850.[1] The family group was further augmented in the late 1830s, when Joseph's brother, John, and his second wife, Elizabeth Weed and their children left the Abbeville District and moved to Rush County, probably before John's death (ca. 1836/37). Elizabeth died in 1875 and was buried in the Milroy Cemetery, Milroy, Rush County, Indiana (Figure 14-3). The extended family living in Indiana also included some of the

Figure 14-1. Abner Perrin Pressly and Dr. J. Thompson Pressly, sons of Alexander Pressly. Abner settled in Mississippi and Thompson in Houston, Texas. Courtesy of Brad Wolfe, Hattiesburg, Mississippi.

Figure 14-2. Reverend Israel Hamilton Pressly, grandson of Joseph Pressly, born October 30, 1835, in Preble County, Ohio; died October 18, 1916, in Lawrence, Marion County, Indiana.

Figure 14-3. Gravestone for Elizabeth Weed Pressly, second wife of John Pressly. Milroy Cemetery, Rush County, Indiana.

children of Elizabeth's brother and his wife Nancy Pressly (JSP's sister) who had been born in Preble County.

Randolph County, Illinois, also in the west, was another area where family members gathered. Shortly after his death in 1831, Robert Pressly's wife, Elizabeth Clark, moved there with their nine children, probably because her husband's mother's family, the Thompsons, had settled there many years before, part of the first migration from Cedar Spring Church circa 1805. She was soon joined by her sister-in-law, Mary Pressly Baird (Robert's sister), from Preble County who arrived with her husband, John, and their large family. Lastly, also in Illinois, was David's (died 1818) youngest son, William Patterson Pressly, a wealthy merchant and philanthropist. He was a successful farmer in Preble County for some twenty years, where he remained close to his sister Elizabeth Pressly Brown's children, some of whom joined him when he moved to Monmouth, Illinois, in the late 1850s. He was a significant benefactor of Monmouth College and Warren County Library. He died in 1905, age ninety-five, and is buried in Monmouth Cemetery in Warren County, Illinois, with other members of his family. Like others living in the West, including Reverend John Newton Pressly, William severed ties with the Synod of the South and became a member of the United Presbyterian Church where his brother, Reverend John Taylor Pressly, was a leader in Alleghany, Pennsylvania.

Due West was mainly an educational and religious place, especially for those who remained connected with the Associate Reformed Presbyterian Church in the South. For members of the extended Pressly family in the South who continued to embrace this faith, Due West became a nucleus and central meeting place for bringing together the now widely dispersed family and for educating their children. Remarkably, many of these widely dispersed and now distantly related cousins maintained contact and continued to have a shared history through their continued connections with Erskine College and Seminary and the Associate Reformed Synod of the South. For many of these families and their descendants, Due West became a center for educating their children: they traveled from many different states and joined extended family members who still lived in the Abbeville District and Due West. Many eventually settled in Due West and taught at the college and seminary. Reverend James Patterson Pressly and Reverend William Laurens Pressly were important patriarchal figures at Erskine College and Seminary for several generations of young Pressly men, descendants of both John (imm 1772) and David (imm 1767). A large number of these graduates followed family tradition, becoming ordained ministers and educators.

Dr. Samuel Pressly's son, Joseph, followed his father, and became a physician, staying in Wilcox, Alabama, as did his daughter, Eliza, whose first husband was Reverend George Haslet. She and her second husband, A. M. Cook (a successful planter), owned a large, I-style planation farmhouse east of Camden in Wilcox County, Alabama, which still survives. Samuel's other daughter, Sarah, married Reverend John Miller and their son, Benjamin Meek Miller, became governor of Alabama. Both the Cooks and Millers are buried in Oak Hill Cemetery in Hamburg, Alabama, along with numerous other Pressly family members, including Samuel, his wife, and Reverend James Pressly's first wife, Jane Hearst. Many of Samuel's children and grandchildren who lived in Alabama were schooled in Due West and thereby able to maintain family connections with widely dispersed cousins. Likewise, children of Samuel's sister, Mary, and her husband Reverend Joseph Lowry also sent some of their children from Louisville, Georgia, to Due West for their education. Their son, William Strong Lowry (1816–92), became professor of Latin at Erskine College, and six of their grandsons became preachers, including Prof. Lowry's son, Reverend William Joseph Lowry (1838–1877).

If we look closely at these families one can appreciate the extent and intimacy of these connections and the number of marriages that took place between cousins. Samuel's son, Joseph, kept in close touch with his uncle, Reverend James Pressly, in Due West and Joseph's daughter, M. Belle Pressly, married her cousin, Francis Y. Pressly, James's son, and lived in Due West. Another of Samuel's sons, David Pressly (1820–1891), graduated from Miami University, studied at both Alleghany Seminary and Erskine Seminary, and became pastor of the Hopewell ARP Church in Union County, Mississippi. His son, Calvin, with his first wife, Lettie Ann Fair, studied at Erskine College and Seminary and became a minister, eventually settling in Texas. Calvin also married a daughter of Reverend James Pressly, N. Ellen Pressly. William Cornelius Pressly, one of David's sons with his second wife, also went to Erskine College, becoming a physician while another son, Thomas Peden Pressly, studied at Erskine and became an ARP minister in Troy, Tennessee.

Likewise, one of the sons of E. E.'s sister, Martha Pressly, and her husband, John Lindsay, who belonged to Prosperity ARP Church, in Taft, Tennessee, Ebenezer Erskine Lindsay, was educated at Erskine. As we saw, E. E. Pressly's nephew, John E. Pressly, studied at Due West and Erskine and served as pastor for thirty years of the Coddle Creek and Prosperity congregations in Iredell County, North Carolina. Two of his sons also went to Erskine College and Seminary and became ministers: Reverend Neil Erskine Pressly (1850–1920) and Reverend Mason Wiley Pressly (1859–1942), who later broke off ties with the ARP Synod of the South. Two of Neil's sons, Reverend Henry Elliot Pressly and Reverend Bonner Grier Pressly, went on to study at Erskine College and Seminary around the same time as some of Reverend William Lauren Pressly's sons, all of whom went to Erskine College. John E. Pressly maintained close ties with Erskine College, and in 1878, the school conferred on him the title of Doctor of Divinity. His home, the John E. Pressly House, which he purchased in 1851, still survives in Bethpage, North Carolina.

Connections with Erskine College and Seminary and ARP church also help keep alive links between John Pressly's (imm 1772) and David Pressly's (imm 1767) descendants who formed another important family cluster in York District, South Carolina and just over the border in Iredell County and Mecklenburg, North Carolina. The children of David's son, William, the Charleston factor merchant, followed a similar trajectory of accomplishment to his cousin David's (died 1818) children. William's son, William Adams (1813–1874), was a physician in Mecklenburg and his son, William Adams Pressly Jr. was a student at Erskine and later became a dentist in Rock Hill (he was the twentieth-century custodian of immigrant David's family papers, since lost). Another of William's sons, David Adams (1807–1841), studied at Yale and was an attorney. He died young at the family's home Hicklen Place in York District; his only son, William Adams Pressly, became a physician and remained in the area. William's daughter, Mary Adams (1812–1884), married Dr. Archibald Ingram Barron, a distinguished and wealthy physician and farmer who graduated from Transylvania University in 1829. He practiced medicine in York District and lived in Santuc in eastern York, from 1837–1854, primarily at Hicklin Place. He was a leading citizen of York who helped organize the ARP church there and was also a signer of the Ordinance of Succession. One of his sons, William Rowan Barron, became a physician. Archibald and his wife were buried at Ebenezer Presbyterian Church (ARP) cemetery in Rock Hill, South Carolina, a resting place for over sixteen Pressly kin as well as a large number of members of the extended Barron family.[2] William's two other sons, Benjamin Chapin Pressly (1815–1896), a lawyer and distinguished judge, and Samuel Adams Pressly, a physician, settled respectively in Charleston and Darlington County, South Carolina. Both became Baptists.

William's brother, John, also settled in the York District, near Rock Hill, where he was a member of the Tirzah ARP Church and most likely a subsistence farmer. He and his wife, Isabella Brown, had eight children who survived into adulthood and most remained in the area with two also marrying into the Barron Family. Their son, Richard McMillan Pressly, married Mary Barron (d. 1841), a sibling of Archibald Barron, with whom he had twelve children, and their daughter, Elizabeth Elinor Pressly, married another brother, John Barron (1812–1882), who became a wealthy plantation owner, eventually owning more than one hundred slaves in York County. A third son, was a physician but died very young. Richard McMillan Pressly's daughter, Isabella Virginia, married Reverend Robert Fleming Taylor (1822–1896), who was a member of the first boarding class at the Due West Academy in 1836, and of the first graduating class at Erskine College in 1842, and who boarded with E. E. Pressly. Taylor became a pastor at Neely's Creek, ARP in the York District. Isabella's brother, Reverend William Barron Pressly (1828–83) (Figure 14-4), also attended Erskine, graduating in 1849; he later attended Erskine Seminary. He was ordained as pastor in 1855 at New Stirling and Amity where he also founded Elk Shoal Academy; later his son, Reverend Leon Taylor Pressly (1822–1896), also attended Erskine College and Seminary.

The deep connection with the ARP church and Erskine College and Seminary helped sustain family connections between David and John's descendants. It is interesting to note that Mary Pressly, the daughter immigrant David's son, John, married late in life, Reverend James Cicero Boyd, an 1855 Erskine graduate whose first wife was Reverend E. E. Pressly's daughter, Elizabeth, who had died in 1859. When Reverend William Barron Pressly (imm David's great-grandson died in

1881, his cousin and close colleague, Reverend John E. Pressly (imm John's great-grandson) conducted the funeral service.[3]

For over one hundred years, Due West was a place of deep family connections and a center for the spiritual life of the Pressly family from all over the country. Dozens of cousins and several generations of family members, descended from both David (imm 1767) and John (imm 1772), were educated at Erskine College and Seminary or at Due West's Women's College, going on to make contributions to the Associate Reformed Presbyterian Church and to the intellectual and professional life in communities where they lived, many as clergy, missionaries, educators and scholars, others as physicians, wives, and mothers. Over seventy-five Pressly family members, mainly descendants of John (imm 1772) and extended kin who married into the family, including the Kennedy, Bonner, and Grier families, are buried in the Due West ARP Church cemetery, and some, including my father-in-law and mother-in-law, Dr. William Laurens Pressly and Alice McCallie Pressly, were buried there in the twenty-first century.[4]

However, as we have seen, this was also an increasingly insular world: alumni descendants returned to Erskine and clergy families continued to marry one another. The denominational world that created Erskine College could not be sustained: the faith embraced so fervently by the first generations became increasingly isolated from modern life and a broader intellectual engagement. Erskine College and Seminary became more and more a home for political conservatism, and, as the Associate Reformed Presbyterian church became an increasingly regional and more isolated denomination, Due West was no longer a central meeting place for the Pressly family. Many Pressly descendants turned to United Presbyterian Church, where they continued to distinguish themselves as elders. The Pressly kin left an extraordinary legacy of professional commitment as pastors and teachers at Erskine College and Seminary and at Due West.

Rev. William Barron Pressly

Figure 14-4. Reverend William Barron Pressly, son of Richard McMillan Pressly and great-grandson of Immigrant (67) David Pressly. Associate Reformed Presbyterian Church. *Centennial History of the ARP Church, 1803–1903*. Charleston: Presses of Walker, Evans, and Cogswell, 1905.

Chapter 15

Epilogue: Cedar Springs—
a Story of Place and the End of an Era

This history of the first ninety years of the Pressly Family in America is very much a story about a physical place—a small portion of the lower Ninety Six District from colonial times to a few decades before the Civil War. It is a story about the land and farming and the interconnectedness of neighbors and families over several generations. It is also the story of a small group of Scotch-Irish Seceder and Covenanter immigrants who settled in the backcountry of South Carolina and formed the nucleus of so many of the ARP churches later established throughout the Midwest, Texas, and the South. As they moved west, they created expanding and overlapping circles of extended kin and enduring friendships, part of the larger saga of settling new frontiers.

Figure 15-1. Cedar Springs ARP Church Cemetery, Cedar Springs Historic District, Bradley, South Carolina. Photograph courtesy of author.

This history concludes with the ending of an era for the Pressly Family living in the lower Long Cane, Cedar Springs, and Hard Labor Creek communities. These communities continued to thrive up until the Civil War. As we have seen, new churches were built in the 1850s at Lower Long Cane and at Cedar Springs, along with many plantation homes including Ivy Gates, Eden Hall, and the large Octagon House across from the Cedar Springs ARP Church (Figure 15-1). Dr. Joseph Pressly was a Major and Surgeon of the Confederate Army (27th South Carolina Infantry), and after the Civil War, he maintained a successful medical and dental practice in his home, the Octagon House, which he and his wife inherited from her father, James Frazier. Many medical students interned under him. When Joseph died intestate in 1899, his daughter, Francis (Fannie) (1856–1942), who had married W. T. Bradley in a joint ceremony with her sister Elizabeth (Lizzie), inherited a portion of the Cedar Springs Road plantation tract which remained in her hands until 1907. Lizzie married John F. Wideman, the grandson of Adam Wideman and a nephew of William Laurens Pressly—both the Bradleys and Widemans were long-time families in the area. Joseph's son, Harlan (1858–1907) also remained in the area, becoming an elder at Cedar Springs. George's daughter, Margaret Elizabeth (1839–1911), lived (as noted earlier) with husband, Dr. James A. Neel (1837–1913), in her father's home on Barksdale Ferry Road, later known as the Neel House, and they are buried in Troy Cemetery; two of their daughters, Lavinia Neel and Dr. Katherine Neel Dale, became foreign missionaries for the ARP Church. Another of George's daughters, Mary Lavinia (1834–1870), married John Pressly Kennedy (his father was an elder in the Cedar Spring Church) who later became president of Due West's Female College. Mary Lavinia died some six months before her father, in 1870. Samuel Leard poignantly described George's later years in his 1879 Centennial address at Cedar Springs. He noted that after the Civil War he saw "the good doctor" in the train station in Chester, South Carolina. According to Leard, George told him that "he had lost all-wife dead, property swallowed up in useless bonds and that that he had recently returned from Illinois whither he had gone to visit a younger brother [William]; that he had a large sum of money on his person, money sent by persons in Illinois to their friends in Chester to help them in distress." He also described himself as "a self-appointed colporteur. I am going again into the great West to distribute religious books."[1]

The devastation of the Civil War and its aftermath brought an end to the cotton plantation world. The railroads opened up new towns and opportunities in the 1880s in the area that was once the old Ninety Six District; but by the 1930s, many (such as Troy, Bradley, and Cedar Springs) were being abandoned. Founded in 1881, Troy had fourteen stores, three physicians, and a bank in 1911. Today all that remains of the old town center of Troy are the railroad tracks, a post office, a store and café, and a few abandoned buildings. The town of Troy still has a number of small farms, homes, and several churches formed after the Civil War, which remain active. The nineteenth-century rural town of Cedar Springs is today a historic site with only the 1825 log cabin Stage Coach Inn, the Frazier/Pressly Octagon House, and Cedar Springs ARP Church and its cemetery remaining. Scattered throughout the area and nearby Bradley are, as we have seen, some well-maintained antebellum homes, small farms, and occasional modern homes, along with the ruins of late eighteenth- and nineteenth-century cemeteries, small farmsteads, and decaying sharecropper homes from the early 1900s, all of which are reminders of earlier times. Much of the area is now part of Sumter National Forest, with some land leased and regularly logged. Remarkably, there are still descendants of several eighteenth and nineteenth-century families living in a three-square-mile area around Millway Road, including the Davis, Wideman, Harrison, Perrin, Cothran, Chiles, and Robinson families, some of whom are consolidating once again their ancestors' holdings.

The well-kept Cedar Springs Church and Cemetery, so central to the Pressly family history, is today a solitary place. Relatively isolated and surrounded by abandoned farmland and wooded forests, it is a moving testimony to the once vital community that lived there. The cemetery includes more than five hundred graves, some of founding members and early church elders. Many tombstones, some engraved by well-known carvers, stand intact after almost two centuries. Walking through the cemetery, one sees the names of eighteenth- and nineteenth-century families linked over generations with the Presslys and their close neighbors and friends, including Reverend Thomas Clark, the Hearsts, Devlins, Thomas White Chiles, his wife, and several members of his family, James Foster and James Morrow Foster, Samuel McClinton (who died in 1807), and members of the Kennedy and Lowry families. At least thirteen members of the Hearst family are buried here, close to David (died 1818) and William, including Joseph Hearst, Col. John Hearst, John Wardlaw Hearst, and John Whitehall Hearst and their wives. In addition to David and William and John Taylor's infant son, John Mason Pressly, other Pressly family members who are buried here include David's son, George W. Pressly; his wife, Isabella, their son, Joseph Lowry Pressly, and his wife; and at least two of their children, Antoinette Pressly and Charles Payson Pressly.

The Cedar Springs Church still has a small congregation, and members travel some considerable distance to attend church service—much as the early settlers did some 225 years ago. It is very peaceful to stand by the brick wall surrounding the churchyard and travel back in time, absorbing a sense of place. The old, late eighteenth-century road from Abbeville to Charleston is pretty much the route followed by Cedar Springs Road today, which still passes by the Frazier/Pressly Octagon House, the 1825 Stage Coach Inn, and Cedar Springs ARP Church Cemetery. Dirt roads, once major transportation routes where homes and churches stood, branch off the road on either side as it winds its way south passing Col. James Devlin's farmstead and George Pressly's plantation and crossing over current day Route 221/10 before becoming Millway Road. The road passes by Sylvania and Millway

Plantation, along a route once lined with cotton fields and plantation homes, including Chiles Crossroads, Cotton Level, and Perrin's Place, and small farms and larger farmsteads, before joining the old Long Cane to Charleston Road (now Eden Hall Road) and crossing over Hard Labor Creek, where the Winterseat Bridge stood in the mid-nineteenth century. Many early Presslys once traveled on horseback down this now forested road. This was their world and our history.

As someone who has married into this family, it is deeply moving and extraordinary to think about the legacy left by the two patriarchs, David Pressly (imm 1767) and, especially, John Pressly (imm 1772). Their children and grandchildren set a course that was to influence profoundly several generations of Presslys to come. Education and teaching became a central theme in the Pressly family's history and the learned and sacred conversation part of its destiny to this day. They left a legacy of deep piety, dignity, a love of learning and an intellectual understanding of the scriptures, and a sense of their own specialness that still defines the family.

NOTES

Chapter 12: Setting the Course in Education and the Ministry: Reverend John Taylor Pressly and Reverend Samuel Patterson Pressly

1. John Taylor Pressly, *A Pastoral Letter addressed to the Churches both settled and vacant under the care of the Second Presbytery of the Carolinas and Georgia*, Augusta, 1822.

2. JSP, "Letter of Reminiscences," published in *Due-West Telescope*, June 24, 1862. Found by Lowry Ware and provided to me by Jim Gettys.

3. JSP, "Letter of Reminiscences."

4. Samuel Leard, "Historical Address at Cedar Spring Church," June 1879, published in *Associate Reformed Presbyterian*, vol. LXXIV, January 18, 1933.

5. In 1831, Reverend Samuel Pressly became the guardian of William P. Pressly, almost certainly his nephew, after William P. Pressly (Package 3062, Box 109) died. Another brother, John Brown Pressly, was also involved. John Brown Pressly died soon after and bankrupt. See material related to his estate and foreclosure of mortgage Box 68, Package 3459, Abbeville County Probate Court. Several outstanding notes were backed by mortgage securities including one for two thousand acres. His father, John Pressly, was one of the administrators and his last child, John Brown Pressly (named after his deceased son), was born in 1834, when John would have been nearly sixty years old.

6. John Belton O'Neill and John Abney Chapman, *The Annals of Newberry: in Two Parts*, Newberry, SC, 1892, AUI.I. & HOUSEAT, p. 76; and John Brown Carwile, *Reminiscences of Newberry: Embracing Important Occurrences*, Newberry, 1890, p. 258.

Chapter 13: Passing the Mantle: Erskine College and Seminary

1. Founded in 1809, Miami University began its first year in 1824 with twenty-eight students, two faculty members, and Reverend Bishop as president. By 1839, it had 250 students from thirteen states and soon became known as the "Yale of the West."

2. Lowry Ware, *A Place Called Due West: The Home of Erskine College*, Columbia, SC, 1997, R.L. Bryan Company. Ware provides a helpful account of Due West during this period, the founding of the Due West Academy, and of E. E. Pressly; this is one of the few modern accounts of him that exists. Ware's extensive research and publications on Abbeville County and Due West are important contribution. See also, Latham, *History*.

3. Unknown. "Memoir of the Reverend John S. Pressly," *Associate Reformed Presbyterian*, n.d., found in Samuel Agnew Scrapbook, McCain Library, Erskine College. Found by Lowry Ware and shared with me by James Gettys.

4. Unknown, "Memoir."

5. Col. R. A. Fair in a *Historical Sketch*, published in the *Abbeville Press*, July 19, 1867. James Gettys kindly gave me a copy of this sketch.

6. See Joab Maudlin Lesesne, Jr., A Hundred Years of Erskine College, unpublished Ph.D. dissertation (University of South Carolina, 1967).

7. Letter to William Hemphill dated July 6, 1840, in the Hemphill Papers, Duke University.

8. Reported in *Laurensville Herald*, February 2, 1850. This is presumably different than the Johnson Female Seminary, which opened in the village of Anderson in 1848 and was begun by the Baptist minister, Reverend William B. Johnson.

9. Joseph M. Wilson, *The Presbyterian Historical Almanac and Annual Remembrance of the* published in Harvey Toliver Cook, *The Hard Labor Section*, 1924, Greenville, SC, privately published *Church*, 1861.

10. Samuel Agnew Diaries, McCain Library, Erskine College. Due West, SC.

11. *Due-West Telescope*, Dec. 20, 1861.

12. Reverend J. O. Lindsay, D.D., "Administration of Reverend E. E. Pressly, D. D." in *Semi-Annual Address*, Erskine College Delivered Due West, SC June 26, 1889, pp. 30–44, Charleston, South Carolina.

13. Box 61, pack 8, Probate Records, Abbeville County Courthouse. Twenty-seven slaves were dispersed to his heirs with the specific request from his son, William Laurens Pressly, for families to stay together. E. E.'s widow died soon after him.

14. Nancy and William Pressly have in their possession numerous handwritten sermons by E. E. Pressly and his son, William Laurens Pressly, and also typed sermons by the latter's son, Paul A. Pressly. The have been digitally archived.

15. J. I. Bonner. "A Sketch of the Life of the Reverend James. P. Pressly, D. D.," Published by the Order of the Second Associate Reformed Presbytery, Due West, SC, 1878.

Chapter 14 Due West: A Central Meeting Place and Spiritual Center

1. The 1850 census lists a "Mary A. Pressley age 45 living with a Joseph Pressley age 67 and one child, John Harris, who would have been a grandchild." This could mean immigrant John's son was still alive and his age given incorrectly. He would have been circa seventy-five.

2. I am grateful to Paul Getty for providing me with information on where members of the Barron and Pressly families were buried in Rock Hill and York County, SC.

3. Rubenstein Library at Duke University has some manuscript material consisting of forty-one items related to Reverend John E. Pressly including a copybook of sermons. RUB Bay 0035 items 1–41 c.1.

4. The family of Alice McCallie Pressly (1914–2010) has a similar history to that of the Pressly family, having been part of the same Scotch-Irish migration. Three brothers, children of Alexander McCallie, left Wigtown in the lowlands of Scotland, close to the English border in 1775 and eventually landed in Philadelphia. One of the brothers settled in Pennsylvania, the other in Kentucky, and Alice's ancestor, John, eventually settled in East Tennessee. One of the children from his second marriage, Thomas McCallie (1795–1859), moved with his family to Chattanooga in 1841 and his son, Thomas Hooke McCallie, became a minister in the Presbyterian Church. Spencer J. McCallie, one of Thomas Hooke McCallie's sons, was the father of Alice and five other children. The McCallie family also placed a high premium on education, having been instrumental in the founding of McCallie School and GPS (The Girls Preparatory School). For the family's origins and history, see *THM (Thomas Hooke McCallie): A Memoir*, edited by David McCallie (Bloomington, IN: WestBow Press, 2011).

Chapter 15 Epilogue: Cedar Springs: A Story of Place and the End of an Era

1. Samuel Leard, Historical Address at Cedar Spring Church, June 1879, published in *Associate Reformed Presbyterian*, vol. LXXIV, January 18, 1933.

Appendix A

The Pressly Surname Base in Eighteenth-Century America

In addition to our family and the Williamsburg "Pressleys," there are at least four other major Pressly surname lines, each with distinct DNA mapping, as well as several other smaller branches which migrated to America in the mid-to-late seventeenth century and eighteenth century. They came from England, the lowlands of Scotland, and from Ulster and settled mainly in Maryland, Virginia, and North and South Carolina. One branch migrated from Germany, settling first in New York and then moving to Cecil County, Maryland, and eventually to North Carolina and South Carolina. As a result, the surname base in America is extensive. During the eighteenth and nineteenth centuries it was located mainly in the South and Midwest and Texas with several unrelated Pressly families living in South Carolina during the last quarter of the eighteenth century, all of whom had ties to Virginia. There were also small clusters in upstate New York and Canada. This Appendix references some of these eighteenth- and nineteenth-century families.

James Presley and three William Presley/Priestleys in eighteenth-century Virginia

As noted in the text, my husband, Bill Pressly, joined a Presley/Pressly surname project which currently has ninety-three members and is a subgroup within Family Tree DNA. Test results within this surname project were initially sorted into four distinct DNA subgroups (A-D) with a fifth grouping members with insufficient representation to form a distinct line. While this project is no longer current, new Family Tree DNA tests results are still added if an individual joins this list. DNA results for my husband, Bill Pressly, clearly placed him in subgroup C. In addition to the exact thirty-seven marker match with Dale Presley, there was also one thirty-seven-marker match, one genetic distance removed, with Brad Thomas Presley and a thirty-seven-marker match, two genetic markers removed, the latter in sequences where mutations frequently occur, with William Cameron Presley. All three individuals identify James Presley, born in 1783, as the father of their most distantly known direct ancestor.

James father was William "Presly" who married "Easther" Cowan in 1780.[1] We don't know when William died but an "Easther Presley" appeared in the 1801 Russell County personal property tax lists and, in 1802, in the upper district of Russell County tax lists where she is listed as "Easter Prestley" with one tithe, which means James was sixteen.[2] James married Lydia Bridget "Biddy" Hatfield in 1809 and appeared in the 1810 tax lists with one tithe; his mother, "Hester Presley," is listed with no tithes, indicating they were living in different dwellings. James is listed in the 1820 Russell County census with five sons, two daughters, and one female over forty, presumably his mother. By that date he was living near the Forks of Indian Creek and Hurricane Creek, where the family remained into the twentieth century. The large and extended family of James Presley and his numerous descendants is relatively well documented, especially for his first son, William (1809–1895), and they represent a major ancestral line for the Pressly surname in America.[3]

The identity of James's father, William, is less clear, and descendants of James's children share different stories about his origins.[4] Norma Jean Crabtree in her book *Leaving a Trail: Crabtree, Bales, Jackson, Presley* notes that the family came from Yorkshire and landed in Eastern Virginia near Richmond and then moved to Winchester and Hurricane Creek. She supplies no documentary evidence to support this statement. The citation is interesting, however, because John Gotea Pressley, in his nineteenth-century history of the Williamsburg Pressleys, relates that members of the family who fought in the Civil War: claimed they had a "relationship with the South

---

[1] DNA testing results where the surname is different are less relevant. Another thirty-seven match one genetic distance removed was found with Joel J. Kane, probably the result of an unusual convergence of mutations, although ancestors on his mother's side lived in Virginia and then Abbeville—an eighteenth-century ancestor, William Henry Pickens, born in Augusta County, Virginia, October 5, 1749, son of Gabriel Pickens (b. Northern Ireland ca. 1715; died Abbeville 1775) and Zerubiah Smith. The DNA testing is on the paternal side and his family has been in the Ukraine for a few centuries.

[2] Members of the Cowan family were also living there at the time.

[3] William married Mary Runyons and secondly Sarah Stitner. He and many family members are buried in the Presley/Turner Cemetery in Hurricane Creek, Virginia, near Dickinson City and Grundy, Virginia, where Dale Presley's family lived. This is near West Virginia and not far from the North Carolina border. The Cemetery is off 81, near Route 18. Early records in the Buchanan County Courthouse were destroyed in a fire. Crabtree states that a daughter was buried near a store on Coney Fork of Indian Creek and afterwards the family went to Hurricane Creek.

[4] The Mountain Kin family tree proposes that a "James Presley," father or grandfather of the James Presley born in 1783, was born in Yorkshire and came to America with two brothers. He went first to Richmond, then to Winchester, before settling in Russell County at Forks of Indian Creek. The Turner/Farber/Horton Tree suggests that William Presley, father of James Presley, was born in Yorkshire in ca. 1765 and died in 1835 and that he was the son of Andrew Presley. This is not substantiated by Yorkshire birth records. The fact that both link their ancestor William, the father of James, to Yorkshire is of particular interest in terms of tracking our own family roots. What is also interesting here is that once again we have the story of three brothers.

Carolina branch while they were Northern prisoners . . . The Pressleys sprang from a brother of the Williamsburg brothers who settled first on the James River in VA and then went West."[5]

There were at least three individuals named William Presley or Priestley living in Fairfax, Fauquier, Loudon, and Augusta/Rockbridge counties between 1750 and 1800 who could possibly be linked with James's father and hence with our family. The first is William "Presley," originally from Prince William County, Maryland, who died in 1752 in Fairfax County, Virginia, naming three children in his will: William, Charles Stewart, and Margaret.[6] By 1765, Charles Stewart Presley was living in Cameron Parish, Loudon County, Virginia, and was last listed in Loudon County tax records in 1784. His son, Charles Presley, born circa 1764, eventually migrated to Union County, South Carolina in the 1780s where he married Mary Elizabeth Jenkins, also from Loudon County. He was listed for the first time in the Union County in the 1790 census. He is one of several Virginia families with a variation of the Pressly surname living in the South Carolina backcountry in the late eighteenth century.[7] There are no known references to Charles Stewart's brother, William, after 1765 although it is possible that he or his son was the William Pressly from Farquier County who purchased two hundred acres on branch of Camp Creek in the Camden District, South Carolina, in 1785.

The second potentially relevant person living in Rockbridge in the 1770s is a William "Presley" or "Priestley," both names are used interchangeably in legal documents, who was living in Rockbridge/Augusta County, Virginia, with his wife Mary by 1774 or earlier. They were married before 1758 when their first child, Eleanor, was born and had several other children, including William, Jr., who married Sarah Beach in 1786. James, their oldest son, was taken into the home of Reverend William Graham in order to receive a better education. He later distinguished himself as an important educator and classical scholar, settling first in Lexington, Kentucky, and then in Nashville, Tennessee, where he became President of Cumberland College in 1809.[8] William and his son William Jr. appeared in court martial records for 1777 and in Augusta County tax records in 1778 as William

---

[5] John Gotea Pressly, Pressley Family History, written circa 1889 and reprinted in *Three Rivers Historical Society*.

[6] He is presumably the same William mentioned in 1743 when a John Hepburn sold to Richard Lanham and William Thomas rights to personal estates and slaves that Thomas Tyssick had assigned to his daughter Margaret Presley, wife of William Presley; Prince George's County Maryland Records December 1, 1743. His will is recorded in Fairfax County 21 July 1752, Deed Book C. pp. 347–8.

[7] Marlene Webb, *Pressley Presley*, discuses Charles Presley and his descendants.

[8] James was a member of the first graduating class in 1785 of Liberty Hall Academy, later Washington & Lee. He married Sarah McBride on 19 April 1788 and they had six children.

"Pressley."[9] In 1779, William Sr. acquired 115 acres at Todd Springs Run on the Forks of James River on Buffalo Creek located near Hall's Meeting House, later Old Monmouth Presbyterian Church. Reverend William Graham lived on an adjoining property. At the same time William bought a lot in Lexington which he deeded to his son William Jr. in 1786 shortly before his marriage to Sarah Beach. He and his son are listed in 1787 tax roll as William "Presley" and William, Jr. His children and their marriages are well documented, and all, except, Mary, are noted in his will dated 1793 and probated 22 September 1800.[10]

Lastly, there was a third William "Presley" living in the same area as William Presley Sr. and his son, William Jr. As noted in the text, he is most likely to be our close relative and the "William Presley" who married "Esther Cowan" in 1780 and fathered James Presley. He first appeared on Rockbridge County Personal Property Tax Lists in 1787 where he is charged with tax "for self," and listed as a weaver, not a farmer, which suggests he might be a recent Irish or Scottish immigrant. He appeared on a different day in the collector's journals than William Pressly, Sr. and his son William Jr. so presumably he wasn't living adjacent to them. Despite extensive research, nothing more is known about this William except for the important finding that immigrants John and David Pressly shared a closely related ancestor with him.

Johann Valentine Preslar/Pressler/Presley

Johann Valentine Preslar/Pressler/Presley was the patriarch of another large and widely dispersed family base located mainly in the South and particularly in North Carolina, but also in New York. He was born in Germany circa 1669 and arrived in New York with his wife, Anna Christina and family, circa 1709–10. Some accounts of this family state they first stopped in New Glasgow before going to England and then sailing to New York. The family settled in Cecil County, Maryland by 1720 and several of Johannes's grandchildren were baptized at St. Stephen's Parish with the surname "Prisley." By the late 1740s, Johannes's sons John, Andrew, and Peter had moved from Cecil County to Anson County, North

[9] After his father's death, William, Jr. and other members of the family lived at Todd Springs until they sold the property to his sister and her husband. His father's will, written in 1793, was probated September 22, 1800 in Rockbridge, Virginia – Will Book # 2. See Oren F. Morton, *A History of Rockbridge County*, 1920.

[10] An undocumented family tree on Ancestry.com proposes William senior was born in Priestleyville, England or in Yorkshire and that he married Mary Hall, daughter of William Hall. Others suggest it was William Pressly Sr. who married Esther Cowan in 1781. This is unlikely since James Presley, born in 1783, is not mentioned in his will dated 1793 and probated in 1800.

Carolina. Andrew, Jr., the son of Johannes's son Andrew Presley, eventually moved his family to western North Carolina/eastern Tennessee. He and his sons Charles, Andrew II, John, and Peter "Presley" also lived for a period of time in the Charleston area and the South Carolina backcountry districts of Kershaw, Abbeville, and Union during the last quarter of the eighteenth century. Andrew Presley Jr.'s youngest son, John, is said to be the ancestor of Elvis Presley through his son Dunning (Duncan) Presley (1780–1850). Descendants of Johannes have a distinct DNA mapping, and are one of four distinct DNA lines in the Presley surname group.

John Pursley/Presley of Edgefield County

John Pursley's family, including Moses born circa 1755, John Jr., William, and Andrew Pursley, and their widowed mother Sarah, came down from Virginia sometime before the Revolutionary War and settled in Edgefield County, South Carolina.[11] Sarah Pursley subsequently married John Clackler, with whom she had at least two more children. In his Revolutionary War petition, prepared in Henry County, Georgia, and signed 18 December, 1832, John "Presley," Sarah's son, says he was born in Virginia (doesn't know what year), that he was illiterate, and that he went into service as early as July 1776 (5?) when "he marched to Ninety Six to meet the Tories" while still a "mere" boy and served on a Cherokee expedition.[12] The family name in South Carolina was Pursley, but Moses and John appear to have changed it to "Presley" when they moved to Henry County, Georgia, sometime after 1800. The Pursley line is another of the four distinct lines in the DNA Pressly surname project. The Pursley name appeared in nineteenth-century Virginia census data and family descendants can be traced to Georgia, South Carolina, Tennessee, and other Southern states. The Pursley name is found in census and militia records from 1790 onwards in Abbeville, Edgefield, and York counties, South Carolina.

---

[11] Presumably Sarah's first husband was named John since her son is identified as John Pursley Junior in her second husband's will proved in 1790. In one family tree, this John Pursley, Sr. is thought to have been born in New Glasgow, Scotland and his father identified as Hans Jurie "John" Presley who died in North Carolina in 1777. This would link him to Johannes Valentine's line. DNA testing does not support this link. Clackler died March 15, 1790.

[12] Pension application S7338. He died July 27, 1837. His name was also spelled in legal documents as Pusley, Pursley, Presley, Presly and Pursel. Nineteenth-century family members lived in South Carolina, Georgia, Arkansas, and Tennessee. John Pursley died 27 July 1837.

Other Virginia Presslys

Robert Pressley, born circa 1736–40, and his wife, Mary Elizabeth, born circa 1742. He is listed in the *Historical Register of Virginians in the Revolution . . . 1775–1783.*[13] He is of particular interest because his daughter, Catherine "Pressley," married William McCord and lived in Abbeville, South Carolina. William's brother was married to one of Widow Jane Pressly's daughters, and it is a possibility that Jane Pressly's husband and Robert Pressly's family are related.

William Presley, baptized January 17, 1766 at Episcopal Church, Kingston Parish, Gloucester, Virginia. His birth date was given as December 5, 1765. His father's given name was John and mother was Mary Jarvis; they were married on June 12, 1765 at the same church.

John Pressly, who was born in Wiltshire, England, and came to the colonies in 1746 as an indentured/bonded servant. He may have lived in Virginia.

John Presley, born in Canada circa 1765, is listed in the militia in upper Canada on February 10, 1789. His descendant, Keith Presley, is part of the same DNA group as our family.

William Presley arrived in Virginia in 1647, probably from Dorset. His wife, Jane Newman, and their children came two years later. Their large estate—he was granted 1,150 acres—was Northumberland House in Northern Neck. William died in 1656, and the family line ended a century later when Peter Presley died in 1750 without issue and left his estate to his grandson, Col. Presley Thornton.

Elizabeth Presley, born in 1739 in Fauquier, Virginia, and her half-sister **Agnes Allen Presley**. She married ca. 1767 Joseph Carter of Prince William, Virginia, and moved to Rye Cove, Virginia, ca. 1783, and Agnes married her husband's brother, Norris Carter.

---

[13] John H. Gwathmey, *Historical Register of Virginians in the Revolution, Soldiers, Sailors, Marines, 1775–1793.* Richmond, 1938, p. 637

Appendix B

Table of the Generations

This appendix is a family chart created with Legacy 8 software. It shows the descendants of John Pressly and David Pressly through six generations. It is a work in progress and by no means definitive. Not all of the dates have been thoroughly vetted. It is, however, a significant step toward creating a family genealogical tree.

Descendants of Pressly

1-Pressly
+Unknown
2-John Pressly d. 1778, Ninety Six District, SC
+Elizabeth
3-Mary Patterson Pressly b. Bef 1756
+Robert Martin
3-David Pressly b. Cir 1756, d. 24 Sep 1818, Bradley, Greenwood SC, bur. Cedar Springs ARP Church Cemetery
+Jane Patterson b. 9 Oct 1769, County Down, Ireland, m. The marriage may have been in 1789, d. 25 Feb 1856, Pittsburgh
4-Elizabeth (Jane) Pressly b. 1789-1790 ?, d. Cir 1855, Preble County, Ohio
+Dr. George Brown d. 1845, Preble County, Ohio
5-George R Brown b. 1811, d. Cir 1873
5-Jane P. Brown b. 1813, d. 1888
+William Willson
5-Grizella Brown b. 1816, d. 1870
+William Johnson
5-Sarah P. Brown b. 1818, d. 1875, Iowa
+Alexander Appleby
6-5 Children Appleby
5-Mary L Brown b. 1821
+James Glenn
5-Nancy Young Brown b. 1825, d. 1897
+James Andrew Strain d. Warren County, Illinois
4-Dr. Samuel Patterson Pressly b. 12 Sep 1792, Cedar Springs. SC, d. Oct 1837, Wilcox County, Alabama, bur. Hamburg Cemetery
+Elizabeth Knox Hearst b. 25 Feb 1791, m. 1811, d. 1875, bur. Hamburg Cemetery, Wilcox County, Alabama
5-Eliza Pressly b. 26 Mar 1812, d. 21 Nov 1870, bur. Hamburg Cemetery, Oak Hill, Alabama
+Rev. George N. Hazlett
+Abraham Mastin Cook b. 1812, d. 1868
6-Albert Cook b. 1847-1930
6-Elizabeth Knox Cook b. 1848, d. 1938
6-Tabitha Jane Cook b. 1851, d. 1895
6-Mary Caroline Cook b. 1858, d. 1932
5-Jane Hearst Pressly b. 1813, d. 1903
+Rev. Warren Flenniken b. 1805, d. 1851, Chester County, SC
6-Samuel Flenniken
6-John Calvin Flenniken
6-Warren Harvey Flenniken
6-David Reid Flenniken
6-Mary Flenniken
6-Sarah Flenniken
+Thomas Torbit
5-Dr. Joseph Hearst Pressly b. 1820-1822, d. 1872, bur. Hamburg Cemetery
+Martha Bell b. 20 Apr 1836, d. 29 May 1861, bur. Hamburg Cemetery, Oak Hill, Alabama

Produced by Legacy

Descendants of Pressly

6-Eliza (Betty) Pressly b. 1859, d. 1911
+Jennie Dale (see Dr. Joseph Hearst Pressly on page 1)
6-Minnie Pressly bur. Oak Hill, Alabama
5-Rev David Pressly b. 8 Jan 1820, d. 29 Jul 1891, bur. Salem Church Cemetery
+Letha (Lettie) Ann Fair b. 13 Jan 1825, d. 10 Oct 1849, bur. ARP Church Starkville, Miss.
6-Anna Pressly b. 1844, d. 1912
6-Rev. Calvin Pressly b. 19 Mar 1847, d. 1919, bur. Marlow Cemetery, Cameron, TX
+Sarah Brown Peden b. 13 Aug 1827, d. 13 Jan 1883, bur. ARP Church Starkville, Miss.
6-Lizzie Pressly
6-Rev. Thomas Peden Pressly b. 15 Jan 1853, d. 1923, Obion County, Tenn.
6-Dr. William Cornelius Pressly b. 1857, d. 1935
6-Sunie Pressly b. 1869, d. 1923
5-Cornelius Pressly b. 1824, d. 1847, bur. Hamburg Cemetery, Wilcox County, Alabama
5-Sarah Pressly b. 1827, d. 1886
+Rev. John Miller b. 1825, d. 1878
6-Elizabeth Miller d. Age 13
6-Samuel Patterson Miller d. At Age One
6-Nancy Barnette Miller
6-Sally (Twin of John Hearst) Miller
6-James Patterson Miller
6-Joseph Neely Miller b. 1849, d. 1910
6-John Hearst Miller (an attorney) b. 1858, d. 1919, Birmingham, Alabama
6-Gov. Benjamin Meek Miller b. 1864, d. 1944, bur. Camden Cemetery, Camden, Alabama
4-Rev. John Taylor Pressly b. 28 Mar 1795, Abbeville Co, SC, d. 1870, bur. Union Dale Cemetery, Pittsburgh, PA
+Jane Hearst b. 10 Jun 1793, Abbeville Co, SC, m. 22 Sep 1816, d. 4 Apr 1873
5-Rev. Joseph Hearst Pressly, DD b. 1817, d. 3 Nov 1874
+Anna Eliza Smith
6-John Taylor Pressly b. 5 Mar 1848, d. 22 Mar 1922
6-Joseph Hearst Pressly b. 15 Nov 1851
5-Louisa J. Pressly b. 13 Oct 1818, d. 4 Mar 1890, Missouri
+Rev. John C. Steele
6-Eight Children Steele
5-John Mason Pressly b. 1821, d. 1821, bur. Cedar Springs ARP Cemetery
5-Mary M. Pressly b. 1 Aug 1828, d. 6 Apr 1906
+Thomas McCance b. 1817, d. 1901
5-David Adgar Patterson Pressly b. Apr 1831, d. 28 February1865
5-Malinda Margaret Pressly c. 1837, d. 1921
4-Mary Patterson Pressly b. 10 Jul 1797, Cedar Springs, SC, d. 17 Nov 1875, bur. Ebenezer Churchyard near Louisville, Jefferson County, GA
+Rev Joseph Lowry b. 1777, Ebenezer, York County, SC, m. 13 Feb 1813, d. 23 Jul 1840, bur. Ebenezer Churchyard, Jefferson County, GA

Produced by Legacy

Descendants of Pressly

5-Rev. William Strong Lowry b. 10 Mar 1816, Louisville, GA, d. 28 Feb 1892, Due West, SC, bur. Due West ARP Church Cemetery
+Eliza Stevens/Stephens m. 2 Aug 1837
6-Rev. William Joseph Lowry b. 1838, d. 1877, bur. Live Oak Cemetery, Dallas County. Alabama
+Harriet Jennings O'Bannon b. 1818, d. 1851
6-Rev Jennings O'Bannon Lowry b. 1851 ?, d. 1908 ?
5-Jane Pressly Lowry b. 1818, d. 1896
+Tarleton Darley
+Robert Boyd
5-Agnes A. Lowry b. 1821
+Franklin G. Lewis
5-Sarah E. Lowry b. 20 Aug 1822, d. 1898
+Robert Jackson Patterson b. 1806, d. 1883
5-David Pressly Lowry b. 1824, d. 1868
5-Susannah Mary Lowry b. 1827, d. 1895
+James Trimble b. 1827, d. 1852
5-Julia Lowry b. 1836, d. 1888
5-Rev. James Robert Alexander Lowry b. 1838, d. 1898, bur. Prosperity Cemetery, Dallas County, Alabama
+Unknown
6-Lowry
4-Dr. George William Pressly b. 9 Feb 1803, Abbeville District, SC, c. 6 Mar 1803, d. 29 Dec 1870, bur. Cedar Springs ARP Church cemetery, Bradley, SC
+Isabella Hearst b. 28 Mar 1806, m. 1820, d. 1858, Cedar Springs, bur. Cedar Springs ARP Church
5-Dr. Joseph Lowry Pressly b. 1829, d. 1900, bur. Cedar Springs ARP Church Cemetery
+Tallulah Hazeltine Frazier b. 1832, d. 1919, Cedar Springs, par. Unknown and Unknown
6-Elizabeth (Lizzie) Pressly b. 1855, d. 1898
6-Frances (Fanny) Pressly b. 1856, d. 1942
6-Harlan David Pressly b. 1858, d. 1907
6-Charles Payson Pressly b. 1860, d. 1945, bur. Cedar Springs ARP Church
6-Antoinette Pressly b. 1862, d. 1938
6-Dr. George William Pressly b. 1870, d. 1940
5-Mary Lavinia Pressly b. Cir 1834, d. 1870
+John Pressly Kennedy b. 1827, d. 1897
6-Jane Isabel Kennedy b. 1855, d. 1943
6-Archibald Selden Kennedy b. 1857, d. 1924
6-Dr. John Payson Kennedy b. 1864, d. 1944
6-Julia Kennedy b. 1867, d. 1890
5-Margaret Elizabeth Pressly b. 1839, d. 1911-1913, Troy, Greenwood SC
+Dr. James A. Neel b. 1837, d. 1913
6-Emma Neel b. 1861, d. 1937
6-Dr. George Pressly Neel b. 1866, d. 1939
6-Belle Hearst Neel b. 1868, d. 1901

Produced by Legacy

Descendants of Pressly

6-Mary Lavinia Neel b. 1870, d. 1930
6-Dr. Katherine Neel b. 1872, d. 1941
4-Rev. James Patterson Pressly b. 25 Nov 1808, Abbeville Co, SC, d. 30 Mar 1877, bur. Due West ARP Church Cemetery
+Mary E. Young
5-Nancy E. Pressly b. 1846, d. 1913
+Rev. Calvin Pressly b. 19 Mar 1847, d. 1919, bur. Marlow Cemetery, Cameron, TX, par. Rev David Pressly and Letha (Lettie) Ann Fair
5-Rev. David Brainard Pressly b. 28 Oct 1848, d. 24 Sep 1888
+Martha Lois Grier
6-Mary Pressly
6-James Grier Pressly
5-Rev. Francis Young Pressly b. 18 Jan 1853, Due West, d. Dec 1934, bur. Due West ARP Church Cemetery
+Louise M. Reid d. 25 Sep 1905
6-Paul Ayres Pressly
+M. Belle Pressly d. 16 Nov 1942
5-Prof. John Lowry Pressly b. 1857, d. 1933
+Josephine LeGal b. 1858, d. 1910
6-Rev. James Patterson Pressly b. 1882, d. After 1978
6-Jean LeGal Pressly b. 1885, d. 1969
6-Dr. William Lowry Pressly b. 1886, d. 1954
6-Eleanor Louise Pressly b. 1894, d. 1955
+Eliza Bonner Young b. 1813, d. 1841, bur. Due West Cemetery
5-Jane Patterson Pressly b. 1835, d. 1872
+Samuel Watson Reid b. 1831, d. Feb 1900
6-Rev. Samuel Watson Reid b. 1867, d. 1945
5-Samuel P. Pressly b. 1839, d. 1918, Due West
+Jane Hearst (wife 1) b. 1811, d. 1832, Hamburg Cemetery, Oak Hill, Alabama
4-William Patterson Pressly b. 17 Mar 1811, Abbeville District, d. 1905, Monmouth, Warren County, Ill
+Mary Gilmore m. 1833, d. 1836
+Martha Miller b. 1806, d. 1885
3-William Pressly b. Cir 1757, d. Cir 1809-1810
+Elizabeth (Betsy) Hearst
4-John Pressly b. circ 1794, Abbeville District, d. 1826
+Martha Devlin b. 1800, m. 1823, d. 1870
5-Rev. and DD John Ebenezer Pressly b. 3 Nov 1826, d. 16 May 1897, bur. Coddle Creek Church, Iredell County, North Carolina
+Martha Sara Sherard b. 1825, m. 1849, d. 1908, bur. Coddle Creek Church, Iredell County, North Carolina
6-Rev. DD Neil Erskine Pressly b. 11 Sep 1850, d. 1920
6-William Sherard Pressly b. 1852, d. 1872, bur. Coddle Creek Church, Iredell County, North Carolina
6-Barron Wright Pressly b. 1857, d. 1934
6-Rev. Mason Wiley Pressly b. 1859, d. 1942, bur. Coddle Creek Church, Iredell County, North Carolina
6-Samuel J. Pressly b. 1863, d. 1915, bur. Coddle Creek Church, Iredell County, North Carolina

Produced by Legacy

Descendants of Pressly

6-Palmer Alexander Pressly b. 1866, d. 1871, bur. Coddle Creek Church, Iredell County, North Carolina

4-Martha "Patsy" Pressly b. 1801, Abbeville Disrtrict, c. 29 Nov 1801, Cedar Springs ARP Church, d. 2 Apr 1882, bur. Prosperity Cemetery, Dallas County, Alabama

+John Lindsey b. 28 Jun 1800, m. 23 Dec 1824, d. 14 Jan 1884, bur. Prosperity Cemetery, Yukon, Lincoln County, Tennessee

5-William Pressly Lindsay b. 6 Oct 1825, Abbeville Co, SC, d. 1 Oc 1901

5-Mary Ann Lindsay b. 14 Sep 1828

+William J. Galloway m. 1845

5-Joseph b. 7 Jan 1831, Abbeville Co, SC, d. 10 Dec 1860, Chattanooga, Tenn

5-Elizabeth Jane Lindsay b. 27 Oct 1833

+James Spence m. 1864

5-Rev. Ebenezer Erskine Lindsay b. 23 May 1836, d. 16 Feb 1899, Ora, Laurens County, SC

5-Lisa Lindsay b. 30 Jul 1840

+John Stuart m. 1860

5-John Lindsay b. 4 Aug 1843, bur. 9 Jun 1917

+Mary Frances Sloan

6-Rev. Archibald Thompson Lindsay b. 1877, d. 1949

6-Rev. Ebenezer Erskine Lindsay b. 1877, d. 1922

4-Jane Pressly b. ca. 1806, Cedar Springs, Abbeville

+Unknown

4-Rev. Ebenezer Erskine Pressly b. 23 Dec 1808, Cedar Springs, Abbeville, d. 26 Jul 1860, Due West, bur. Due West ARP Church Cemetery

+Elizabeth Agnew m. 10 Feb 1831, d. 20 June 1853

5-Cyprianna Pressly b. Cir 1833 possibly 19 November 1832, d. 5 Jul 1854

+Isben Rice

5-Elizabeth (Lizzie) Pressly b. Cir 26 Oct 1834-1835, d. 4 June 1859 (bible), bur. Cedar Springs ARP Church

+Unknown

6-Mary Frances Boyd b. 1858, d. 1912, Newberry Counry, SC

5-Rev. William Laurens Pressly b. 1837, d. 8 Jun 1906, Due West, SC, bur. Due West ARP Church Cemetery

+Frances Elizabeth Wideman b. 23 Dec 1838 or (39), Abbeville Co, SC, m. 23 Dec 1858, d. 23 Mar 1914, Due West, SC

6-Dr. Ebenezer Wideman Pressly b. 20 Nov 1863, d. 1930

6-Rev. James Hearst Pressly b. 8 Mar 1866, d. 1955, bur. Oakwood Cemetery, Statesville, Iredell County, NC

6-Rev. Joseph Lowry Pressly b. 1868

6-William Laurens Pressly Jr b. 1870, d. 1940

6-Samuel Agnew Pressly b. 1872

6-Dr. Henry Erskine Pressly b. 1874, d. 1909 (of diabetes)

6-David Lindsay Pressly b. 1876, d. 1901

6-Rev. Paul Adam Pressly b. 30 Sep 1878, Due West, SC, d. 22 Apr 1936, Chester, SC

6-John Bonner Pressly b. 1880

6-Effie Lillian Pressly b. 5 Nov 1861, d. 21 Feb 1927, Due West

5-Emma Pressly b. 1843, d. 1850

5-Marietta (Etta) Pressly b. 1 Feb 1844, Greenwood, County SC, d. 1890

Produced by Legacy

Descendants of Pressly

+Dr. Patton (see Marietta (Etta) Pressly on page 5)

6-Mary Patton

+Mary Ann Taylor d. 20 August 1860 age 34 (see Rev. Ebenezer Erskine Pressly on page 5)

3-Martha Pressly

+Archibald Hamilton m. 6 May 1815, Preble County, Ohio

3-John Pressly b. Cir 1774-1776, d. Cir 1836-1837, Boone City, Indianna??

+Margaret Patterson b. 25 Dec 1780 ?, m. 15 Nov 1798, Cedar Springs Associate Reform Presbyterian Church, d. 10 Feb 1814 ?, Not Documented??

4-Rev. Samuel Patterson Pressly b. 25 Sep 1799, Cedar Springs, d. Cir 1836, bur. Athens, Georgia, Jackson Street Cemetery

+Jane West Todd b. Cir 1789, m. 22 Dec 1825, d. 1875

5-Eliza Antoinnete Pressly

+Dr. William E. Black

5-Corinna Myrtise Pressly b. 1836, d. 1920

+William C. Harris

4-John Brown Pressly b. 1805, d. 1832

+Maria Bowen m. 12 Dec 1828

4-William P. Pressly d. 1831

+Elizabeth Weed b. Cir 1793, Abbeville Co, SC, m. 4 Apr 1816, Preble County, Ohio, d. 1875, bur. Milroy Cemetery, Rush County, Indiana

4-Margaret P. Pressly b. 1818

4-Nathaniel Weed Pressly b. Cir 1819, d. 1883

+Nancy A. Foster m. 1845

5-Robert Theodore Pressly b. 1848, d. 1897

4-David Knox Pressly b. 1821, Abbeville Co, SC, d. 1881, Salem Cemetery, Boone County, Indiana

+Mary Ann Maze b. 1828, m. 16 Sep 1845, Rush County, Indianna, d. 1862, bur. Salem Cemetery, Boone County, Indiana

5-John Thomas Pressly

5-Isabel F. Pressly

5-Rebecca F. Pressly

5-Samuel Maze Pressly b. 1856-1898, d. Iowa, bur. Sidney Cemetery, Fremont County, Iowa

4-Elizabeth A. Pressly b. Cir 1825

4-Joseph L. Pressly b. Cir 1827

4-George William Pressly b. Cir 1830

4-John Brown Pressly b. 1834, d. 1879

3-Joseph Pressly b. 1774-1776, d. Cir 1855, bur. Union Chapel Cemetary, Clifton County??

+Rebecca Dyson??

4-James Pressly b. circ 1799, d. 1849, bur. Fall Creek Union Cemetery, Marion County, Indiana

+Elizabeth Hamilton m. 23 Jan 1823

5-John T. Pressly b. 1831

5-Rev. Israel Hamilton Pressly b. 1835, d. 1916, Fall Creek Union Cemetery

+Lucinda C. Ringer b. 1835, d. 1867

5-James Andrew Pressly b. 1840, d. 1902

4-Deborah Pressly b. Cir 1809

Produced by Legacy

Descendants of Pressly

+James Shirley? (see Deborah Pressly on page 6)
4-Mary Pressly
+Michael Harris m. 1825
4-Rev. John Newton Pressly b. 1813, Preble County, Ohio, d. 1866 ?
+Mary Dorcas m. 1839
+Mary Ann Stuart b. 1805 ?, m. 5 Apr 1825 (see Joseph Pressly on page 6)
4-Joseph Taylor Pressly b. Aug 1830, d. 1894, bur. Crown Hill Cemetery, Marion County, Indiana
4-Robert Pressly b. 1835 ?, d. 1902 ?
4-Margaret Pressly b. 1835 ?
2-David (Imm 1767) Pressly b. Cir 1730, d. Jan 1785, Charleston, SC
+Ester Brown
3-Samuel Pressly b. Ayr, Scotland near Glasgow (day Christened, c. 1756, d. Bef 1810
+Elizabeth Thompson b. 13 Aug 1758, Ireland, d. Cir 1798
4-Robert Pressly b. Cir 1784, d. 1830-1831
+Elizabeth Clark m. 14 Dec 1809 ?, Abbeville Co, SC, d. Randolph County, Illinois
5-David Pressly b. Cir Nov 1810, d. 1880, Iowa City
+Mary Polly Jane Cook
6-Dr. Joseph Pressly d. Iowa?
6-Margaret Pressly b. 1843, d. 1930, Iowa?
5-Nancy Pressly b. 1815, d. 1849
5-Banjamin Pressly b. Cir 1816, d. 1847
5-Robert Pressly b. 1817-1818, d. 1890
5-Samuel Pressly b. Cir 1818, d. 1870, Illinois
+Nancy Jane Huey b. 1821, d. 1907
6-Elizabeth Pressly b. 1841
6-Rev. Harry M. Pressly b. 1845
6-Cephas J. Pressly b. 1849, d. 1911
6-Samuel A. Pressly d. 1856
6-John Bryson Pressly b. 1851, d. 1916, Randolph County, Illinois
6-Sidney R. Pressly b. 1859
5-Jane Pressly b. Cir 1823
5-Joseph Pressly b. 1827
4-Mary Pressly b. 1790 ?, d. 20 Mar 1854 ?, Randolph County, Illinois
+John Baird b. 1783-1788, m. 1810, d. 1851
5-Had 12 children Baird
4-Nancy (Agnes) Jane Pressly b. Cir 1790, d. Cir 1839, Rush County, Indiana
+Andrew Reuben Weed b. 1790 ?, d. 1825, Preble County, Ohio, bur. Hopewell Church
5-Samuel Weed b. 1810, d. 1844, New Castle, Henry County, Indiana
5-Elizabeth Clark Weed b. 1813, d. 1855, Preble County, Ohio
5-Nathaniel Weed b. 1816, d. 1862, Boone County, Indianna
+Jane Turner m. 1838
5-John Pressly Weed b. 1818
5-Martha Gray Weed b. 1820
5-Andrew Gray Weed b. 1822, d. 1872, Boone County, Indiana
+Isabella Maze m. 1842

Produced by Legacy

Descendants of Pressly

4-Rev. John S. Pressly b. 11 Nov 1793, d. 1 Jun 1863, Iva, Anderson County, SC, bur. Generostee ARP Church

+Mary Jane Strong b. 18 Jan 1820, m. 29 Sep 1842 (see Rev. John S. Pressly on page 7)

3-David Pressly b. Christened 21 Sept 1760, Lochwinnoch, Renfrewshire, Scotland, d. 1834, bur. Generostee Cemetery, Anderson County, SC

+Ann Edmiston (Edmonston) b. 1763, m. 16 Nov 1784, d. 17 Nov 1848, bur. Generosteee Cemetery, Anderson County, SC

4-James Pressly b. 1787, d. Cir 1850

+Eleanor Hinds

+Elizabeth Ardrey b. 1790, d. 1868

5-David A. Pressly b. 1791, d. Jul 1865

+Elizabeth Todd m. Cir 1837

6-Rev. Ebenezer Erskine Pressly

5-Mary Ann Pressly b. 1810, d. 1882

+William Underwood

5-William Ardrey Pressly b. 1816, d. 1865

+Arabella G. Harden

6-Ralph Alexander Pressly b. 1839, d. 1912

6-Rosa Rebecca Pressly b. 1845, d. 1915, Atlanta, GA, bur. Casey's Cemetery, Atlanta, Fulton County, GA

6-William Calvin Pressly b. 1847, d. 1930, Florida

6-James W. Pressly b. 1850

5-Matilda Pressly b. 1813, d. 1849, Abbeville Co, SC

+Lewis McAllister

5-Jane Pressly b. Cir 1820, d. 1877

+Samuel Lindsey

5-Elvira Pressly b. Cir 1823, d. Cir 1843, Lowndesville, Abbeville Co. SC

5-Eliza Pressly b. 1823, d. 1843

+Israel McAllister

4-David Pressly b. 26 Mar 1791

+Elizabeth Gaway?

4-Alexander Edmiston Pressly b. 1793, d. 1863, bur. Beersheba Cemetery. Lowndes, Miss.

+Tabitha Thompson

5-William Pressly

5-Dr. John Thompson Pressly b. 1818, d. 1908, Houston, Texas

+Clarissa Arnold m. 24 Dec 1848

5-Sarah Ann Pressly b. 1822 ?

5-David W. Pressly

5-Abner Perrin Pressly b. 1833, d. 1912, bur. Woodlawn Cemetery, Caledonia, Lowndes County, Miss.

+Sarah Gates

4-Ester Brown Pressly b. 1 May 1795

+Charles Porter

4-Jean Pressly b. 8 Dec 1796, d. 8 Oct 1797

4-Jane Miller Pressly b. 15 Mar 1798

+William O'Bryant

4-Elizabeth Pressly b. 3 Apr 1800, bur. 1882

+Richard E. Porter

Descendants of Pressly

4-Agnes (Nancy) Pressly b. 17 Mar 1802
+Elijah Willbanks
4-Mary Ann Pressly b. 1789
+Sochin Johnson
4-Rachel Miller Pressly b. 10 Dec 1803, d. 1839
3-John Pressly b. Cir 1772-1773, Abbeville Co, SC, d. don't know when he died yet
+Isabella Brown b. 1778, m. 15 Nov 1798, Abbeville Co, SC, d. Cir 1850, bur. Ebenezer Church, Rock HIll, York County, SC
4-William Pressly
4-John Pressly
4-Halum Pressly
4-Richard M. Pressly b. 1800, d. 18 Nov 1871 ?, York County, SC, bur. Ebenezer Church, Rock HIll, York County, SC
+Mary H Barron b. 1809, d. 1841
5-Isabella Virginia Pressly b. 1826, d. After 1910, Atlanta, GA
+Rev. Robert Fleming Taylor d. Atlanta, GA
6-Mary Elizabeth Taylor b. 1847, d. 1926
5-Rev William Barron Pressly b. 2 Mar 1828, York County, SC, d. 25 Nov 1883, Statesville, NC, bur. New Stirling Cemetery, Cool Springs, Iredell County, NC
+Lorena Evelina Harris b. 1840, d. 1909, bur. New Stirling
6-Rev. Leon Taylor Pressly
6-Dr. John McMillan Pressly b. 1859, d. 1891
6-William Francis Pressly
5-Jane E. Pressly b. 19 Oct 1829, d. 1869
5-Dr Samuel M. Pressly b. 31 Dec 1830, York County, SC, d. 9 Nov 1851, bur. Ebenezer Church, Rock HIll, York County, SC
5-Mary Lavenia "Minnie" Pressly b. 1832-1839, d. After 1902
+Rev. James Ciscero Boyd b. 1833, d. 1902
5-Ann Eliza Barron Pressly b. 1834, York County, SC, d. 15 Jul 1893, York County, SC
5-Margaret M. Pressly b. 1837, d. 13 Mar 1878, bur. Ebenezer Church, Rock HIll, York County, SC
+Stephen Johnson
5-Nancy Rebecca Pressly b. 20 Oct 1840, d. 26 Apr 1930
5-Benjamin E. Pressly b. 1836, York County, SC, d. 15 Jul 1891, York County, SC
4-Nancy Pressly b. Cir 1808, d. 1889
4-Eliza Pressly b. 1812, d. 1881-1884, bur. Ebenezer Church, Rock HIll, York County, SC
+John Barron d. 1887
5-10 Children Barron
4-Harriet Pressly b. 1818, d. Cir 1842, bur. Ebenezer Church, Rock HIll, York County, SC
3-Mary Ann Pressly b. 1766 ?
+Stephen Thomas
3-Ester Pressly b. Cir 1768, d. Nov 1848
3-Agnes Pressly b. Cir 1762
+Henry Wyly
4-Elizabeth Wyly

Produced by Legacy

Descendants of Pressly

3-William Pressly b. (not certain ca. 1772-1778), York, South Carolina, d. 5 Apr 1820, Charleston, SC

+Eliza Eleanor Adams b. 1784, m. 13 Dec 1804, Charleston, SC, d. 24 Jul 1818, York County, SC, bur. Ebenezer Church, Rock HIll, York County, SC

4-David Adams Pressly b. 10 Apr 1807 ?, d. 1841, at summer house Hicklin Place, York District, bur. Ebenezer Church, Rock HIll, York County, SC

+Elizabeth Todd m. Cir 1837

5-Dr. William Adams Pressly d. 1874

4-Mary Adams Pressly b. 10 May 1812, Summerville, York, SC, d. 1884, bur. Rose Hill Cemetery, York County, SC

+Dr. Archibald Ingram Barron b. 1807, d. 1887

5-Dr. William Rowan Barron b. 1836, d. 1917

4-Dr. William Adams Pressly b. 26 Aug 1813, d. 1874, bur. Steele Creek Cemetery

+Lavina Elizabeth Steele b. 1829, d. 1902

5-Mary Steele Pressly b. 1851, d. 1923

5-Ann Eleanor Pressly b. 1853, d. 1943

5-Rosa Jane Pressly b. 1855, d. 1939

+William McKinley

5-Margaret Wilhelmina Pressly b. 1858, d. 1911, bur. Laurel Wood Cemetery

5-Dr. William Adams Pressly b. 1866, d. 1944, bur. Laurelwood

+Unknown

6-Five Children Pressly

+Addie Jenkins

4-Ann Esther Pressly b. 16 Jan 1809 ?, Charleston, SC, d. 1878

+Prof George Anderson

5-George Pressly Anderson

4-Benjamin Chaplin Pressly b. 14 Feb 1815, Long Cane Settlement, Abbeville or Hicklin Place, d. 1896

+Louisa Wheeler

+Mary Burckmeyer

4-Dr. Samuel Henry Pressly b. 1817, Charleston, SC, d. 1885, bur. Society Hill, Darlington County, SC

+Jane Edwards

+Sarah McIver

Bibliography

"Abbeville District Colonial Plats Map." Mapping Colonial Abbeville. Accessed March 28, 2016. http://www.bfthompson.com/abbeville_colonial_plats/abbeville_colonial plat _map.htm.

Ancestry.com. "Major John Chiles." Rootsweb. Accessed March 28, 2016. http://freepages.genealogy.rootsweb.ancestry.com/~janiceksmith/chiles/John%20Chiles/johnchiles1773.jpg.

Anderson, William L. "Cherokee Clay from Duche to Wedgewood: The Journal of Thomas Griffiths, 1767," *North Carolina Historical Review.* Vol. LXIII, no. 4, October 1986.

Associate Reformed Presbyterian Church. *Centennial History of the ARP Church, 1803–1903*. Charleston: Presses of Walker, Evans, and Cogswell, 1905.

Atherton, Lewis Eldon. *The Southern Country Store 1800–1860.* New York: Greenwood Press, 1968 reprint.

Benson, Robert W. *Historical and Archaeological Report: Cultural Resources Overview of the Sumter National Forest,* April 2006, Southeastern Archaeological Services, Inc.

Billingsley, Carolyn Earl. *Communities of Kinship Antebellum Families and the Settlement of the Cotton Frontier.* Athens: University of Georgia Press, 2004.

Birdsong Family Genealogy. "Beattie – Marshall Ancestors." Samuel Steen Marshall – Anne E. Barratt. Accessed March 28, 2016. http://www.birdsongfamily.com/genealogy/set7_Beattie-Marshall/2SS_Marshall-Anne_Barratt.htm.

Bonner, J. I. "Biographical Sketch of Reverend E. E. Pressly, D. D." *Due-West Telescope,* August 1, 1852.

Bonner, J. I. "Biographical Sketch of Dr. E. E. Pressly." *Due-West Telescope,* December 20, 1861.

Bonner, J. I. *A Sketch of the Life of James Patterson Pressly.* Due West: Second Associate Reformed Presbytery, 1878.

Bowen, Ann Heard. *Greenwood County: A History.* Greenwood: Sandlapper Publishing Company, 1992.

Bullock, W. P, and Paul L Grier. "Official topographical map of Abbeville Co., South Carolina." Library of Congress. (S.l.: P.L. Grier, c. 1895). Accessed March 28, 2016. https://www.loc.gov/item/2012586235.

Byrne, Frank. *Becoming Bourgeois Merchant Culture in the South, 1820–1865*: University of Kentucky, 2006.

Cabak, Melanie, and Mark D. Groover. *Plantation without Pillars: Archaeology, Wealth, and Material Life at Bush Hill.* Savannah River Archaeological Research Papers 11. Columbia: University of South Carolina, 2004.

The Cahans Project. "History." Accessed March 28, 2016. http://www.cahans.ie/history/.

Carlisle, H. A. *The History of Lowndesville, South Carolina,* Danielsville: Heritage Papers, 1987.

"Catawba Trail." Family Search. Accessed March 28, 2016. https://familysearch.org/learn/wiki/en/Catawba_Trail.

Chepesiuk, Ron, *The Scotch-Irish from the North of Ireland to the Making of America.* Jefferson, NC: McFarland & Co., 2005.

Clark, Murtie June. *Loyalists in the Southern Campaign of the Revolutionary War.* Baltimore: Genealogical Publishing Co., 1981.

Clinton, Catherine. *The Plantation Mistress: Woman's World in the Old South.* New York: Pantheon Books, 1982.

Cook, H. C. *Hard Labour Section,* 1923.

Cothran, Samuel Alexander and Frank Harrison Cothran. *Chiles-Cothran Notes and an update after more than a half century.*1992 (*Chiles-Cothran Notes* published 1936)

Cothran, Thomas Perrin. *The Perrin Family: with Particular Reference to Samuel Perrin 1770–1828 son of William, son of John, and his descendants* with index added by Joel Ives Townsend. Jr. Greenville: 1992 written circa 1924.

Crabtree, Norma Jean. *Leaving a Trail: Crabtree, Bates, Jackson, Presley.* Prinit Press, Dublin, Indiana. 1987.

Davis, Katherine. "The Featherbed Aristocracy: Abbeville District in the 1790s," *The South Carolina Historical Magazine,* vol. 80, no.2, April 1979, pp. 136–144.

Davis, Nora. *An Historical Sketch of Cedar Spring Associate Reformed Presbyterian Church* unpublished manuscript in Erskine College.

Davis, Nora. A*n Historical Sketch of the Long Cane Associate Reformed Presbyterian Church.* Available online http://www.longcanearp.org/noradavis.html..

Dickson, R. J. *Ulster Emigration to Colonial America 1718–1775.* Belfast: Ulster Historical Foundation, 1966.

Downey, Tom. *Planting a Capitalist South, Masters, Merchants, and Manufacturers in the Southern Interior, 1790–1860.* Baton Rouge: LSU Press, 2006.

Edmonds, Bobby F. *The Making of McCormick County.* McCormick: Cedar Hill, UNLTD, 1999.

Edmonds, Bobby F. *Destiny of the Scots-Irish: A Family Saga.* McCormick: Cedar Hill, UNLTD, 2004.

Galloway, J. C., et al., *The Centennial History of the Associate Reformed Presbyterian Church: 1803–1903,* Charleston: Presses of Walker, Evans & Cogswell Co., 1905.

Graham, A. A. *History of Preble County, Ohio.* Cleveland: Williams & Bros, 1881.

"Great Indian Warpath." Family Search. Accessed March 28, 2016. http://familysearch.org/learn/wiki/en/Great_Indian_Warpath.

Griffin, Patrick. *The People with No Name: Ireland's Ulster Scots, America's Scots Irish, and the Creation of a British Atlantic World:* Princeton, 2001.

Hamilton, Bufort Lindsay. *James Hearst Pressly, D.D 1866–1955: The Spirit of* 212, Stoney Point: 1966.

Harrison, Thomas Perrin. *The Honorable Thomas Chiles Perrin of Abbeville, South Carolina: Forbears and Descendants.* Greenville: A. Press, 1983.

Hofstra, Warren R., edited by. *Ulster to America The Scots-Irish Migration Experience 1689–1830.* Knoxville: University of Tennessee Pres, 2012.

"Hopewell Church – Israel Township." Destination Preble. Accessed March 28, 2016. http://www.destinationpreble.com/historic-churches/hopewell-church-israel-township/.

Horton, Tom. *The American Eton Moses Waddel's famed Willington Academy*, Trafford Publishing, 2012.

Hofstra, Warren R. editor. *Ulster to America: The Scots-Irish Migration Experience, 1680–1830.* Knoxville: University of Tennessee 2011.

Howe, George. *History of the Presbyterian Church in South Carolina.* Duffie and Chapman, 1883.

Ives, Larry. *Colonial Forts of South Carolina, 1670–1775*. Columbia: USC Press, 1970.

"James Sproull Cothran." Find a Grave. Accessed March 28, 2016. http://www.findagrave.com/cgi-bin/fg.cgi?page=gr&GRid=7187952.

Klein, Rachel N. *Unification of a Slave State: The Rise of the Planter Class in the South Carolina Backcountry 1760–1808*. Columbia: University of South Carolina Press, 1990.

Latham, Reverend Robert. *History of the Associate Reformed Synod of the South to which is prefixed A History of the Associate Reformed and Reformed Presbyterian Churches*, Harrisburg: 1881.

Leard, Samuel. "Historical Address at Cedar Springs Church, June 1879." *Associate Reformed Presbyterian,* Vol. LXXIV, January 18, 1933.

Lesesne, Joab Mauldin. *A Hundred Years of Erskine College, 1839–1939*. Ph.D. Dissertation, University of South Carolina, 1967.

Library of Congress Online. "A New and Accurate Map of the Province of South Carolina in North America." London: J. Hinton, 1779. Accessed March 28, 2016. https://www.loc.gov/item/2013593294.

Library of Congress Online. "Plan of the city of New York; an exact prospect of Charlestown: the metropolis of the province of South Carolina." (London: s.n., to 1776, 1762). Accessed March 28, 2016. https://www.loc.gov/item/2002625451.

Library of Congress Online. No title. Last modified April 11, 2001. http://memory.loc.gov/pnp/habshaer/sc/sc0700/sc0762/color/571763cv.jpg.

Reverend J. O. Lindsay. D. D., "Administration of Reverend E. E. Pressly, D. D." in *Semi-Annual Address, Erskine College Delivered Due West, S.C. June 26, 1889,* pp. 30–44, Charleston, South Carolina, 1890.

Little Mountain Yesterday. "Little Mountain in the 1600s and 1700s." Accessed March 28, 2016.
http://www.littlemountainsc.com/images/history/fullsize/f011.jpg.

"Lochwinnoch." Wikiwand. Accessed March 28, 2016.
www.wikiwand.com/en/lochwinnoch.

Logan, John H. *History of the Upper Country of South Carolina,* 1859, vol. 1, Winsborough: Southern Historical Press, reprinted.

Loose Colonial Plats. Records of the South Carolina Secretary of State, 1731–1775. Box 13, Folder 1539, Plat 10. South Carolina Department of Archives and History.

Loose Colonial Plats. Records of the South Carolina Secretary of State, 1731–1775. Box 13, Folder 1539, Plat 12. South Carolina Department of Archives and History.

Lossing, Benson J. "Scene at the Cowpens." *Pictorial Field book of the Revolution in the Carolinas and Georgia,* vol II, New York: Harper & Brothers (1851–52).

Lowry, R. E. *History of Preble County, Ohio.* Indianapolis: B. F. Bowen & Company, Inc., 1915.

McClinton, Arthur T. *McClinton Families of the Old Ninety Six and Abbeville Districts, South Carolina and their Westward Movement in the Colonial and Early Years of America.* Madison: University of Wisconsin, 2007.

McCough, Hugh. Presbyterian Emigration from Ulster to South Carolina; the Cahan Exodus from Ballybay to Abbeville in 1764.
Magoo.co,/Hugh/Cahans.html.

Megginson, W. J. *African American Life in South Carolina's Upper Piedmont, 1780–1900.* Columbia: University of South Carolina Press, 2006.

Mills, Robert. *Statistics of South Carolina, Including a View of its Natural, Civil, and Military History, General and Particular*. Charleston: Hurlbut and Lloyd, 1826.

Mills, Robert. *Atlas of the State of South Carolina,* 1825. All maps were surveyed by others approximately. . . A new facsimile edition of the original published in 1825. With an introduction by Francis Marion Hutson Columbia, SC, Lucy Hampton Bostick and Fant H. Thornley, 1938.

Moore, Peter N. *World of Toil and Strife: Community Transformation in Backcountry South Carolina,* 1750–1805 Columbia: University of South Carolina Press, 2007.

Moore, Joseph S. *Irish Radicals, Southern Conservatives: Slavery, religious liberty, and the Presbyterian fringe in the Atlantic World*. Greensborough: University of North Carolina Dissertation.

Moore, Peter N. *World of Toil and Strife, Community Transformations in Backcountry South Carolina,* 1750–1805. Columbia: The University of South Carolina Press, 2007.

Moss, Bobby Gilmer. *Roster of South Carolina Patriot in the American Revolution.* Baltimore: Genealogical Publishing, Inc.,1983.

"Northern Ireland Map." Discover North Ireland. Accessed March 28, 2016. https://www.discovernorthernireland.com/accomfinder/images/locationMap08.gif.

"Old Brick Church." The Associate Reformed Presbyterian Church. Accessed March 28, 2016. http://arpchurch.org/old-brick-church/.

Orr, Brian J. *As God is my Witness: The Presbyterian Kirk, Covenanters & the Ulster Scots.* Bowie: Heritage Books, 2002.

Patterson, Carroll Ruffin. *From County Down to South Carolina, Samuel Patterson and his Descendants in Upper South Carolina and Beyond*. Decatur, 1964.

Patterson, Daniel W. "Background Legends of a Minister's Death." *Southern Spaces*. Published October 30, 2012.
http://southernspaces.org/2012/backcountry-legends-ministers-death.

Patterson, Daniel W. *The True Image: Gravestone Art and the Culture of Scotch Irish Settlers in the Pennsylvania and Carolina Backcountry.* Chapel Hill: The University of North Carolina Press, 2012.

Phillips, John Renning, *The Good Intent The story and Heritage of a Fresno Family.* New York: Magnolia Group Press, 2007.

Porter, H. Leonard III. *Destiny of the Scotch-Irish*, 1990. Winter Haven: The Porter Company.

Pressley, John Gotea. *Pressley Family History.* Three Rivers Historical Society, Hemingway, South Carolina.

Pressly, John S. "Letter of Reminiscences," published in *Due-West Telescope,* June 24, 1862, found by Lowry Ware and provided to me by Jim Gettys.

Unpublished three-page *A Brief Memoir of the Pressly Family in the United States* printed in full in Phillips, *The Good Intent,* pp. 393–97.

"The Writer," probably for the *Associate Reformed Presbyterian,* nd. Found in Samuel Agnew Scrapbooks, McCain Librart, Erskine College.

Pressly, William A. *A Family History*. Typescript, ca. 1980.

Resnick, Benjamin. *The Williams Place: A Scotch-Irish Farmstead in the South Carolina Piedmont.* Columbia: South Carolina Institute of Archaeology and Anthropology, 1988.

Revill, Janie. *A Compilation of the Original Lists of Protestant Immigrants to South Carolina, 1763–1773,* Clearfield: Genealogical Publishing Company,1999.

Roulston, William J. *Researching Scots-Irish Ancestors: The essential Genealogical Guide to Early Modern Ulster, 1600–1800.* Ulster Historical Foundation, 2005.

Rubin, Benjamin. "Planters and Presbyterians: South Carolina from Atlantic Microcosm to the Eve of the American Revolution." *Journal of Backcountry Studies,* vol. 5, no. 2, Fall 2010.

"South Carolina Emigration and Immigration." Family Search. Accessed March 28, 2016.
https://familysearch.org/learn/wiki/en/South_Carolina_Emigration_and_Immigration.

Sloan, Rev H. T. "A Historical Sketch of Cedar Spring and Long Cane Abbeville District, SC," *Due West Telescopic Press,* 1860.

South Carolina Department of Archives and History Online. "Districts and Counties, 1785." Accessed March 28, 2016.
http://www.archivesindex.sc.gov/guide/CountyRecords/1785.htm.

Stephenson, Jean. *Scotch-Irish Migrations to South Carolina, 1772*. Strasburg: Shenandoah Publishing House, Inc., 1971.

Stowe, Steven. *Doctoring in the South: Southern Physicians and Everyday Medicine mid-nineteenth century*. Chapel Hill: University of North Carolina Press, 2004.

Tyson, Jackie, et al. *Rural Commerce in Context: South Carolina Country Stores 1850–1950. Reported prepared by New South Associates*. Stone Mountain, Georgia 2013.

Walter, Edgar. *South Carolina A History*. Columbia: University of South Carolina Press, 1998.

Ware, Lowry. *Abbeville District, South Carolina newspaper notices of land cases and sales, 1836–1872*. Columbia: SCMAR, 1999.

A Place Called Due West The Home of Erskine College, ca. 1997.

Erskine Alumni Record Antebellum Years, 2013.

Due West: South Carolina's Oldest College Town. Due West. SC, 1993.

Slave Holders of Abbeville District, 1790–1860 and largest property holders, 1860. Due West. ca. 1997.

Watson, Margaret J. *Greenwood County Sketches, Old Roads and Early Families*. Greenwood: Attic Press, 1970.

Wells, Jonathan Daniel. *The Origins of the Southern Middle Class 1800–1861*. Chapel Hill: University of North Carolina Press, 2004.

Wells, Jonathan Daniel and Jennifer R. Green. *The Southern Middle Class in the long nineteenth century*. Baton Rouge: *Louisiana State University*, 2011.

"West Yorkshire County." *Wikipedia*. Accessed March 28, 2016.
https://wikimedia.org/wiki/File:West_Yorkshire_County.png.

Young, Willie Pauline, compiled by. *Abstracts of old Ninety Six and Abbeville District Wills and Bonds*. Greenville: Southern Historic Press, 1996.

Index